A MEIR HALF CENTURY

Photographs and news both church and secular from the years
1889 to 1939
covering the Meir and its near neighbours

nicholas jon cartlidge

Published by

CHURNET VALLEY BOOKS

43 Bath Street
Leek
Staffordshire
01538 399033

Copyright Nicholas J Cartlidge and Churnet Valley Books
1996

ISBN 1897949 15 4

Printed in Great Britain by The Ipswich Book Company, Suffolk

This book is respectfully dedicated to
the memory of

JOHN CARTLIDGE

ACKNOWLEDGEMENTS

I should like to record my thanks to the following for their invaluable assistance in the compilation of this book.

Kathleen Smith of the Public Record Office in Stafford for quiet patience with my ignorance of the protocol; Mithra Tompkins of St Mary's House, Lichfield, Staffordshire who was instrumental in unravelling the convoluted terminology of the church and for the map of the parish of Meir circa 1926 along with her many letters. Henry Button, archivist at Christ's College, Cambridge; Judith Bright of the Kinder Library, Auckland and Marjorie McConachie of New Plymouth, New Zealand; Robert Headland of the Scott Polar Research Institute in Cambridge. Thanks to Diana Lay, archivist of the Bass Museum at Burton upon Trent and to Bass Breweries for access to early documents of the King's Arms, Meir and to the staff of the William Salt Library in Stafford, especially Pauline Thomson for her help on my many pleasurable visits; and afterwards, the Saturday lunchtimes with my wife in the Gate House Theatre restaurant across the street. Those occasions will linger long in my memory.

Many photographs reproduced here are previously unseen; the Lovatt, Olive Hill, Arthur Bennett and Priestley collections. A special vote of thanks must go to Arthur Bennett who by a single action, recorded for all time, views and sights from afternoons long ago which will amaze today's generation. Thank you Tony and Joy Priestley for their collective guidance and wisdom and to Elton Prints who trade in Leek market and who supplied some of my early photographs. My sincere thanks to Margaret Beard for her trust in me, for consent to use pictures from the Lovatt Collection housed at the Hanley Reference Library and to Miss Winifred Lovatt: It seems entirely proper for her father's photograph to appear in the book and receive the recognition he so richly deserves.

I am also indebted to John Abberley of the Sentinel; David Whitehouse with whom a conversation was the stimulus for the source of the maps; Philippa Cartlidge for the photograph of Rev Edward F Woodward from among her memorabilia; Reg Bishop for reminiscences and memoirs of early days at Meir aerodrome; Tommy and Maureen Cliffe of Multicraft Supplies, Weston Road, Meir; Michael Lodge, Yorkshireman and Optometrist, and Rev Gordon Whitty for access to the Holy Trinity church registers. Also to my friend and colleague Malcolm Wright, with whom I discussed much of this during our lunchtime walks.

A large measure of gratitude should also be given to my colleagues at the University of Keele, notably in the Library Special Collections Department; to Martin Phillips for his invaluable guidance; to Sheila Walton, curator of the Air Photo Library for permission to use the aerial view of Meir; to Michael Edge for his unswerving help and good humour; and not forgetting Irene Pryce, Andrew Lawrence, Brian Peach and Gerald Burgess.

Mal Beech has skilfully resurrected crumpled and sometimes fusty photographs, which have lain undisturbed until now, in old brown envelopes and cardboard boxes. Her effort has given the reader illustrations which are worth a thousand of my words.

I acknowledge permission given to me by Penguin Books to use a portion of "Three Men in a Boat" by Jerome K Jerome; by England, Their England for the historical background of E.Albert Egerton VC and by Diana Condell of the Imperial War Museum, London. I also give acknowledgement to the Havergal Brian Society and Wilf Chadwick for the picture of the master, reproduced by Messrs Williamson's of Longton with the flyleaf inscription to Mr Bertram Walker in 1892, and to his daughters Agnes and Monica Walker for the photographs of St Gregory's RC church, Longton; to the Stoke-on-Trent City Council who gave their assistance with detailed work on council housing and to Gloria D'Elia, a correspondent of many years who is a long way away but whose encouragement was much appreciated.

The editor of the North Staffs Advertiser deserves my heartfelt thanks for permission to use material from over 50 years of the Staffordshire Advertiser. I discovered two things pouring through these aged publications; one was that today's newspapers generally have devolved to a tabloid format which has the tendency of trivialising the noble art of journalism and secondly, I really need reading glasses!

A book such as this is not written without considerable disruption of home, family and social life. I therefore willingly record the patience, infuriatingly helpful comments and numerous suggestions from my wife, José Anne, who has been my staunchest champion during my darkest days.

n j c,
Meir,
Stoke on Trent,
Staffordshire
June 1995

Meir Road — Normacot

A view taken at the western edge of Meir, showing the agricultural nature of the village towards the end of the nineteenth century, the horse and rider and the two befrocked children redolent of the true nature of life in Meir at that time. The houses in the distance stand in what is now Uttoxeter Road; these, and the terraced housing between the two children on the left still remain, 90 years later. The building on the extreme left, level with the gas lamp, has gone and it now the site of a garage. Alexandra School now stands on the right, behind the trees, which have since been felled. Although labelled Normacot, the term Longton was often applied to all of Meir, its boundaries changing several times over the years. This road, still called the Meir Road in 1995, is the A5035.

Foreword

This book is a nostalgic account covering fifty years of Meir seen through the events of its churches and other more temporal institutions. Many of the prominent men and women, clergy and officials who shaped the local scene are encountered here: John Aynsley, Henry Hill, William Webberley and Vincent Riley to mention just a few.

To give a more balanced view, I have brought in some of Meir's neighbours and their news as the narrative in places is somewhat threadbare. This record of Meir is an exposure of life at the time, caught forever like an insect in amber.

Events from the formative and innocent years are recalled from St Peter's Caverswall, SS Mary & Chad, Sandford Hill; Holy Evangelists, Normacot; Church of the Resurrection, Dresden; St John's and St James' churches, Longton; Meir & Normacot Methodist churches and St Gregory's and St Augustine's RC churches in Longton and Meir; along with their fetes, bazaars and gatherings, joyful and sorrowful.

Then there is the saga of Meir Aerodrome and the dithering that lost the city an important business opportunity. The book stretches to the beginning of the Second World War, with the appearance of the army and RAF at the aerodrome and on the streets.

Thankfully, the church, through its high standard of scholarship, has ensured records of its good offices are never far away. While this has nearly always been the case, on several occasions the trail has been a tortuous one and despite great care some of the minutiae do not bear close scrutiny.

Tracts in italic type are the actual English of the period and may appear stilted to our late 20th century ears. For all its awkwardness, it has been left unaltered. Throughout this account Meir is referred to variously as 'The Mear', 'The Meir'', and 'Meir'. The first dates from the middle of the 19th century, the second from the late 19th and early 20th centuries, whilst the last version is now in common usage. Many may recall the landmarks, features, characters and customs that have disappeared or fallen from favour. Only they will be able to pass judgement as to whether we are the poorer for their loss.

Caverswall Village

Caverswall village seen in this charming view about the turn of the century remains almost unchanged by the passage of time. The tree, centre right, was felled and replaced in the 1930's. The curved garden wall, extreme right, peters out but the road carries on past St Filumena's RC Church, Caverswall Castle and St Peter's C of E church which are on the right, out of view.

Priestley collection

CHAPTER 1
1889-91
'Begin at the beginning' the King said, gravely, 'and go on till you come to the end: then stop!'
Lewis Carroll: Alice's Adventures in Wonderland

Of those who lived in Meir between 1889 and 1939, a few may remember the changes that took it from an isolated rural village at peace, to a bustling modern town at the time when this country found itself struggling for its very existence at the onset of the Second World War. The days of haymaking, harvesting and rural tranquillity, quickly faded as the new Meir grew apace. Numerous examples from Meir's early days still remained half a century later in 1939, in word, photograph and memory; reminders of what had been and pointers to what was ahead.

Lying on the southern edge of Arnold Bennett's 'Five Towns' of the Potteries, with Caverswall its spiritual centre, these 'Potteries' greatly affected its adolescence and development into maturity. With Normacot, Dresden, Sandford Hill and Weston Coyney only a cockstride away and tethered at the western edge by Meir Lane to Longton, - 'dirty Longton, filthy Longton', where many from Meir found employment - it was, from the outset, a naive and unprepossessing place. But Meir's spelling; surely that's a paradox! *'i' before 'e' except after 'c'. How many times have I told you?*

Meir had undergone a long transformation starting from the 15th century and in 1422 it is recorded by the account of Henry Bigges Reeve, *'a twelvepence toll for the passage of Mere'* while in more recent times, *'There is a Roman Road running from Meir to Blythe Bridge and beyond, going between Chesterton and Rocester to Little Chester near Derby, which provides a safe way across the marshy lands of 'the Mere' to the fording place at Blythe'*

But let us return to the halcyon days in the embers of Victoria's reign, to the lanes with the chattering of skylarks and smell of May blossom, to a time before this rural Eden had all gone. The inheritance of many of Meir's buildings in a variety of styles, perhaps best described as 'pleasantly unmemorable', is not a rich one; the casual observer being left with the impression of them having been sketched on the back of a menu during the course of a disagreeable lunch!

In amongst this North Staffordshire townscape, there have been some real gems indeed, but even by 1939, many had vanished forever. Such is Meir's condition; in a changing world, it reflects that change. It seldom appeared on civilian maps and in truth, it must be said, one could have driven straight through the town and never noticed its passing. - *'It's a one horse town-and I've just seen the horse!'*

But some people liked it that way while others would not even give it the time of day. And during this half century, world events more or less passed it by - more or less.....

In 1889 this rural backwater was about its business, a cluster of cottages, a few farms, and a school. In the midst of this rustic charm two public houses, the King's Arms and the Saracen's Head, stared each other out from either side of a crossroads which bissected the village into two asymmetric parts. These were places to drown one's sorrows and inevitably, in some cases they were the catalyst of social unrest and hardship for the families whose breadwinner would drink away the money for their next meal. Most of the dwellings were poor and humble; the people who lived in them, were mainly God-fearing and with what could be called a tenuous hold on life. There were big houses of course; the Meir House occurs many times in this account, but the smattering of expensive residences of professional men, some in Weston Road, were very much the exception.

From 1840 to 1892, the outlook for many depressingly changed very little. But throughout the next 50 years, there were improvements through social changes, better nutrition, and sanitation. Does the passage of the years mellow the fading memory and cloud a reasoned judgement? After all, how many recall long summers from a distant childhood when all the days were sunny from dawn to dusk?

One of the nearby villages, Caverswall, the scion of Meir, dates from Norman times; that is well documented, but its history does not fall within the bounds of this

These photographs, originally in colour, taken by the author in 1993, show headstones in St Peter's churchyard Caverswall, Staffordshire. They illustrate:
The use of the name of Meir Lane dates from at least 1855.
That in 1858 people from the Meir were buried at Caverswall.
That Meir was once called the Mear (1828).

book. However, certain notables and incidents cannot be overlooked for it is from Caverswall that the nucleus of Meir derives a long time ago. Caverswall presents its best face early in the day; to appreciate its way of life at the end of the 19th century, only a bench in the square is needed from which to quietly watch the world go by. Whilst cooing pigeons swoop and soar by the castle, the stocks where miscreants paid the price for their misdemeanours are still in evidence beneath the tree and amongst all this is the Red House which rubs shoulders with the churches of St Filumena and St Peter like bookmarks at the end of the lane. In 1889 Caverswall, and its Anglican church of St Peter's were umbilically linked to the Meir since there was no church at the Meir at that time. The faithful made the two mile walk from the Meir down country lanes to worship and carry on a liturgy which had been performed on the same site for over 800 years. Many were baptised there and married there. Many were buried there.

Caverswall parish was fortunate to secure the services of a priest who would be at the helm during what would be, it transpired, the formative years for the church in the Meir; a church which would become known as Holy Trinity. His vitality was to underscore this expansion. It is not to overstate the fact to say that his influence was to change the whole outlook of those who lived in the Meir in the decades ahead:

> *The Rev J G Addenbrooke of St Luke's Church, Wolverhampton has accepted the offer of the Hon E S Parker-Jervis of the living of Caverswall.*

With no local church, Meir Board Schools were used for Divine worship. Built in 1876, they were situated in Meir Lane, later Uttoxeter Road, just beyond where Meir Methodist Church now stands. William Frederick F Pickles was the master and his wife Julia, the mistress. In 1894, it was enlarged to accommodate 400 children. The self-same buildings which during the week reverberated to 'times tables' and the swish of the cane, were filled with the faithful on Sundays:

> *The Harvest Festival was held on Sunday 12th October 1890. At morning service, the Rev T H Masters preached the sermon and in the afternoon, the Rev J Beckett, vicar of Dilhorn(e) occupying the pulpit and in the evening the vicar of the parish, the Reverend J G Addenbrooke, preached to a crowded congregation. The ROOM was tastefully decorated and a large quantity of bread and vegetables were given to the poor. The anthem 'and God said let the earth' by Caleb Simper was well rendered by the mission choir. The offertories amounted to £8 7s.*

The number of children at this day school is a good yardstick of the Meir's size; 232 were on the register in 1887; 212 in 1888 and 236 in 1889. Average attendance was remarkably consistent at 172, 167 and 173 over the same years. The efforts of a dedicated teaching staff were reflected in the passes during those years - 88%, 82% and 88%. And the school was flourishing financially as well as academically; the income rose from £267 17s 9d for 1887, to £251 1s 8d the year after and £371 14s 6d for 1889. Total receipts on the average attendance for the same period were £1 11s 4¼d per head, viz, from grants, 16s 4½d; from fees, 14s 1¾d and from sales and rents, 1s 5d. The total costs on the average attendance were £1 16s 5½d; the deficiency, made up from the rates, was 4s 6¼d per head.

In the late nineteenth century, the established churches locally did much social work for the many disadvantaged of the district and this is well documented in Longton. They gave warm clothing and fed the unfortunate when their luck was out, especially during the festive season: Heaven knows there were plenty of them! Not for many, at Christmas, tables piled high with every conceivable delicacy. In the main they were grateful to have a hot cooked meal while the children for a treat, had an apple!

> *On Christmas Day, 600 poor children were entertained to a feast of roast beef and plum pudding in the Town Hall (Longton Town Hall). This was the eighth occasion on which a similar treat has been provided for those children whose poverty entreats compassionate consideration at this time.*
>
> *27th December 1890*

In a way these children could count themselves fortunate: Longton in the middle of the nineteenth century had the worst infant mortality rate in the whole of England and Wales with one child in three dying in infancy! The reality was stark indeed; appalling housing coupled with non-existent public health. Some perhaps driven to despair, could bear it no longer and died by their own hand:

> *......concerning James Davis, aged 50, who resided at Sandford Hill. He was employed at the Beaconsfield Pottery, Anchor Road and on Monday morning was found hanging from a rope suspended in the sliphouse. The deceased had been in low spirits for some time it is said, to some trouble he would not disclose.*

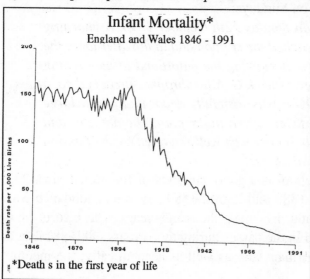

Infant Mortality*
England and Wales 1846 - 1991

*Death s in the first year of life

The remarkable decline of infant mortality during the fifty years covered in this book is highlighted by this graph. Effective medicines, better sanitation and nursing care all added to this general result. Whereas there were about 160 deaths per thousand live births in the 1890s this had been reduced to a little under 50 just before the second World War. Meir would have played some part in that success locally with the new housing that sprang up in the 1920s and 1930s.

Life was wretched in many ways. There was little money, work was long, tiring, poorly paid and dangerous. Just having regular meals was in itself sometimes a luxury. Many went hungry and lived from hand to mouth in a twilight world. But one thing above all that many had was a Christian upbringing, faith and spiritual involvement. Church and everyday life were inseparable and the demands made on the church were varied and extensive - something that would certainly diminish in the years ahead.

It is understandable therefore that with shared premises in the Meir, there was a need for a church of their own. The congregation set about this daunting task with alacrity, to build a shrine as a permanent statement of their Christian faith. In the summer of 1890, Rev Addenbrooke had seen the need for a church in the Meir and in due course collected enough names for a petition to be presented to the Bishop of Lichfield. The case was obviously meritorious for shortly afterwards, his Grace acceded to the entreaties and a decision to build was made.

But what would it cost and more importantly, where would be the most suitable site? As was the case with dozens of projects of the day, the benefactor was the fourth Duke of Sutherland. He gave a piece of land for the church, off Meir Lane which being at the top of a steep hill, commanded a fine view. The Duke also defrayed the cost of many other church buildings in the area including the new north wing of the Church of the Holy Evangelists in Normacot, which no doubt brought a smile to the face of the incumbent of the time, the Rev J R Hutchinson.

The erection of any church was enormously expensive but especially for the small community in the Meir, and without financial help from one or two wealthy individuals, their dream might have foundered. As might be expected, there was Sir Smith Child; the Smith Child family already having given their name to a ward at Longton Cottage Hospital. But one family in particular was to play a key role in this aspect; the name of Bowers of Caverswall Castle is a thread that runs right through the fabric of all the early history of the Meir church; indeed Mrs Bowers name was inscribed on one of the foundation stones visible on the church many years later. Yet amid all the euphoria, money was still needed from the congregation to help reduce the deficit, and fundraising events were popular. Not for the first or the last time, it was the ladies who were the driving force behind this effort: The ladies of the parish, where would we be without them?

On Tuesday and Wednesday of next week (5th & 6th May 1890), a bazaar is to be held in the Town Hall in aid of the building fund of the new church at the Meir. The hall will be arranged to represent an 'Olde Englishe Countrie Fayre' and it promises to be a very pretty scene. The bazaar will be opened at noon by Mrs Hincks of Tettenhall after which a luncheon will be held.

And after the bazaar had closed, sometime later, there was the perennial problem of where to put the 'bargains' which remained unsold!

> *Ye Olde Englishe Countrie Fayre: This bazaar, in aid of the funds of the new church at the Meir, was brought to a close on Saturday 9th May when the services of Mr T H Griffiths was secured to sell by public auction the articles remaining from the previous days' sales. The bazaar has been a most successful one, the amount realised being £447.*

Just as a cost comparison of what that amount would buy at the time, a terraced house in the area would have gone 'under the hammer' for about £250 at auction, if your bid was accepted by the auctioneer, T H Griffiths.

Considering the endemic poverty, and notwithstanding the stupendous effort, it was a classic illustration of what people working together can achieve. Contracts were exchanged in autumn 1890 and the wheels were set in motion. Throughout that winter, the church took shape, until in spring of 1891, the immediate task was fulfilled. The Bishop of Lichfield, William Dalrymple, granted a licence for the performance of divine service in the said 'chapel', dated Monday 20th May 1891 and with it he prefaced an eventful week for the Meir.

The great day arrived! On the Thursday, a goodly proportion of Meir's faithful turned out for the Dedication, although how they all managed to be away from their places of work at that time in the afternoon is something of a mystery:

> *The opening and dedication of the new church at the Meir, was performed by the Right Reverend, the Bishop of Shrewsbury. The consecration was to have been performed by the Lord Bishop of the Diocese, but the sacred rite had to be deferred as a consequence of certain formalities to the handing over of the building to the ecclesiastical commissioners not being completed in time. At present there is only a temporary chancel but when the church is completed it will accommodate about 400 people. It will then consist of a chancel, nave, north and south transepts, vestry and an organ chamber. The estimated total cost is about £2000. One of the largest contributors is Sir Smith Child, Bart who, with his accustomed generosity and zeal for the promotion of Christian and benevolent work, gave a donation of £500. The church, which is in the Early English Style, is constructed of red brick and stone facings[1]. At present there is seating for about 260 people.The plans were prepared by Messrs Scriveners[2] and Sons of Hanley and the contract executed by Messrs Inskip of Longton.*
>
> *The opening ceremony was performed at four o'clock, the Bishop and clergy assembling at the Meir House, the residence of Mr W Webberley. A procession was formed and proceeded to the church headed by the surpliced choir who sang a processional hymn, No 166 Ancient and Modern "All people who on earth do dwell". The clergy who followed wearing the surplice and hood, were the Bishop of Shrewsbury, the Rural Dean (the Rev H C Turner), the rector of Longton (the Rev G F Tamplin), the Reverends J G Addenbrooke (vicar of Caverswall) W I*

Smith (vicar of St John's, Longton) and S Salt, (vicar of Dresden), J Finch-Smith, T Becket (Dilhorn), & T P Forth (Forsbrook). Before a crowded congregation opening prayers were recited by the Bishop and the lessons read by the Rev G F Tamplin and the Rev H C Turner and the subsequent prayers taken by the Rev J G Addenbrooke and the Rev T H Masters.

An able sermon was preached by the Bishop from II Chronicles vi.18, "But will God in very deed dwell with men on earth?" After alluding to Solomon's prayer in the consecration of the temple, he said the circumstances under which they met were very similar to those related in the Old Testament story. They had that day opened a new church which was so far complete that there was no reason why it should not become at once a house of prayer and a place of meeting between God and people who dwelt around.

The fact that the Bishop of Lichfield was not present to perform the high and sacred rite of consecration was assuredly a cause for disappointment and regret, but it was as a consequence of the delay and exclusion of certain legal formalities that the act of consecration was not at present permissable.

At the conclusion of the service, a tea took place in a large marquee erected in the grounds and subsequently an entertainment of wax-works with live models was given by Mr R Clive of Kidsgrove. The offertory at the dedication service, which was in aid of the building fund amounted to £27 16 10½d.

So there it was: After the Maids of Honour and the local Madame Tussaud's, a brand new church which would stand the test of time longer than many others in the community. But that was not the end of the celebrations:

The services were continued yesterday, Friday 22nd May 1891, the special preacher, announced at evensong, being the Venerable Archdeacon of Stafford. Special services will also be held on Sunday and during the week, the preacher on Monday 25th May 1891 being the Venerable Archdeacon of Stoke.

The dedication service connected with the new church at the Meir continued on Sunday and during the week. The preachers were as follows:

Sunday morning 24th May the Rev W I Smith, vicar of St John's: afternoon the Rev E H Spink, curate in charge of St Jude's, Stoke: evensong, the Rev J G Addenbrooke (vicar of Caverswall).

Monday, the Venerable Archdeacon of Stoke; Tuesday, the Rev H C Turner Rural Dean, vicar of Fenton; Wednesday, the Rev G F Tamplin, rector of Longton and Thursday, the Rev E S Carlos, the vicar of Cheadle. The total offertories which were in aid of the chancel fund amounted to £37 9s 1d

30th May 1891

In spite of this, even with the mortar on Holy Trinity hardly dry and at what must have been their finest hour, the Rev John Gordon Addenbrooke already had other ideas turning over in his head!

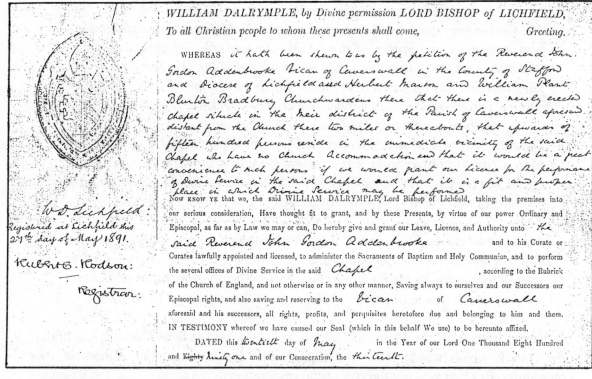

WILLIAM DALRYMPLE, by Divine permission LORD BISHOP of LICHFIELD,
To all Christian people to whom these presents shall come,   *Greeting.*

WHEREAS *it hath been shewn to us by the petition of the Reverend John Gordon Addenbrooke Vicar of Caverswall in the County of Stafford and Diocese of Lichfield and Herbert Marson and William Plant Blurton Bradbury Churchwardens there that there is a newly erected Chapel situate in the Meir district of the Parish of Caverswall aforesaid distant from the Church there two miles or thereabouts, that upwards of fifteen hundred persons reside in the immediate vicinity of the said Chapel who have no Church Accommodation and that it would be a great convenience to such persons if we would grant our Licence for the performance of Divine Service in the said Chapel and that it is a fit and proper place in which Divine Service may be performed* Now KNOW YE that we, the said WILLIAM DALRYMPLE, Lord Bishop of Lichfield, taking the premises into our serious consideration, Have thought fit to grant, and by these Presents, by virtue of our power Ordinary and Episcopal, as far as by Law we may or can, Do hereby give and grant our Leave, Licence, and Authority unto *the said Reverend John Gordon Addenbrooke* and to his Curate or Curates lawfully appointed and licensed, to administer the Sacraments of Baptism and Holy Communion, and to perform the several offices of Divine Service in the said *Chapel*, according to the Rubrick of the Church of England, and not otherwise or in any other manner, Saving always to ourselves and our Successors our Episcopal rights, and also saving and reserving to the *Vicar* of *Caverswall* aforesaid and his successors, all rights, profits, and perquisites heretofore due and belonging to him and them. IN TESTIMONY whereof we have caused our Seal (which in this behalf We use) to be hereunto affixed. DATED this *twentieth* day of *May* in the Year of our Lord One Thousand Eight Hundred and ~~Eighty~~ *ninety one* and of our Consecration, the *thirteenth*.

W. D. Lichfield:
Registered at Lichfield this 27th day of May 1891.
Hubert O. Hodson:
Registrar:

The document seeking permission for the formation of a church at the Meir, Longton, Staffordshire, is from the archives of the diocese. The new church remained part of the parish of Caverswall.

By kind permission of the Lichfield Diocese.

Notes.
1. Contrast these with the Church of the Holy Evangelists, Normacot, which is built of sandstone and has weathered more extensively.
2. Architects of Fenton Town Hall, built in 1887 which cost £ 10,000

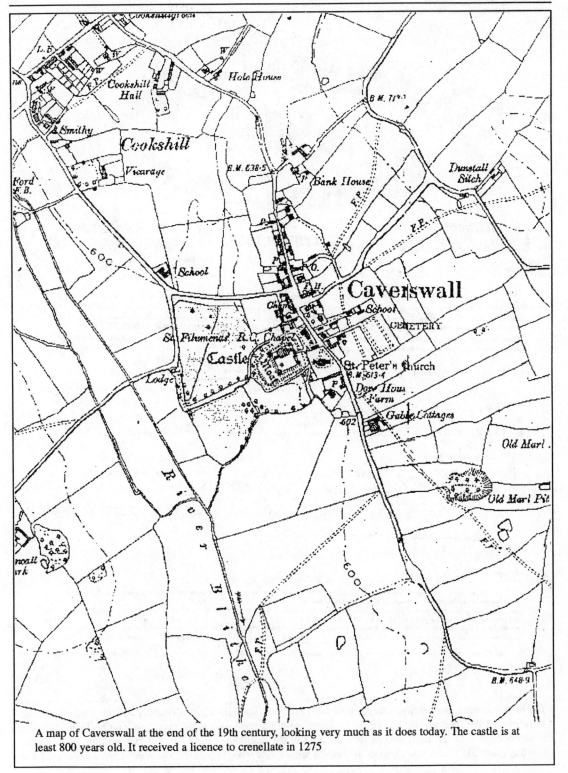

A map of Caverswall at the end of the 19th century, looking very much as it does today. The castle is at least 800 years old. It received a licence to crenellate in 1275

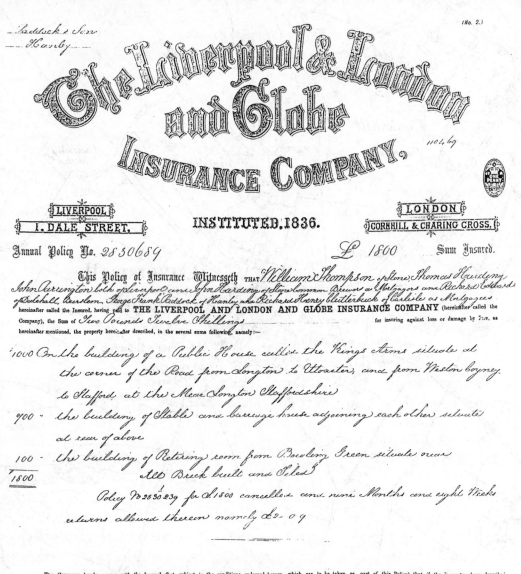

The insurance agreement between the London and Liverpool Globe Insurance Company and the Kings Arms, the *Mear* dated 1883. The inn was owned by a consortium of business men at the time; and later by John Joule and Sons of Stone. The inn itself was insured for £1000; the outbildings for £700 and the 'retiring room' to the bowling green (on which John Aynsley sent down many a fine wood) for £100. The annual premium was £2 12s

CHAPTER 2

1891

What is life an emty (sic) bubble,
Floating on a sea of trouble,
What is life a dream of sorrow,
A little day without tomorrow.

Epitaph in Caverswall Churchyard to
Charles Brassington of Catcut Lodge
Died 9th January 1850

As Holy Trinity in the Meir during the latter part of the nineteenth century, was an 'off-shoot' of St Peter's at Caverswall, it is no surprise to learn that it was from Caverswall that the church obtained its curates and it appears that it was not just the weather that was infinitely variable; stipends or annual salaries reflected the fortunes of the diocese.

Date	Name	Stipend
18 November 1844	Charles John Sale MA	£100
29th May 1870	Walter Brown Corfield	£ 80
31st October 1874	Bennett Blakeway	£130
23rd December 1889	Thomas Heywood Masters MA	£130
24th February 1890	Thomas Bradberry MA	£150
26th September 1892	Hugh Nanney Smith BA	£130
15th March 1894	John Edward Carey	£160
23rd September 1894	Edwin David Bush	£120
19th September 1897	James Grosvenor Halford	£120
24th February 1898	Charles Addenbrooke MA	£160

Three of these who officiated at Holy Trinity are of special interest. The first, Rev David Edwin Bush, an organ scholar at St David's College Lampeter, moved to the Lichfield Division becoming a deacon at Caverswall in the autumn of 1894. Hugh Nanney Smith, a Cambridge man, was awarded his BA in 1891, made a deacon in 1892 and a priest a year later. He was a curate in Caverswall from 1892-1894, when he left for the diocese of York and the parish of Walkley. The third and most interesting was the Rev Thomas Heywood Masters MA. It was he who gave inspiration and stimulus to a 'mere' local man and helped transform him into one of England's most prolific composers of the 20th century.

At diocesan level, the year was notable for the fact that Lichfield had a new Bishop, the Rev Canon Legge - working out his ancestry would have been simpler if calculators had been around at the time:

The new Bishop of Lichfield is the Rev Canon Legge and is a son of the fourth

WILLIAM DALRYMPLE, by Divine Permission Bishop of LICHFIELD, to our beloved in CHRIST *Thomas Heywood Masters, Clerk, B. A.*

Greeting;

We do by these Presents give and grant unto you our Licence and Authority to perform the Office of Stipendiary Curate in the *Parish Church of Caverswall* in the County of *Stafford* ___ within our Diocese and Jurisdiction in preaching the Word of God if thereto licensed by us in reading the Common Prayers and performing all other Ecclesiastical Duties belonging to the said Office according to the Form prescribed in the Book of Common Prayer, made and published by Authority of Parliament, and the Canons and Constitutions in that behalf lawfully established and promulged, and not otherwise or in any other manner: and we do by these Presents assign unto you the yearly Stipend of *One hundred and thirty pounds* ___ to be paid Quarterly for serving the said Cure. And we require you to reside in the Parish of *Caverswall aforesaid* ___

In Witness whereof We have caused our Seal which we use in this case to be hereto affixed: Dated the *twenty third* *day of* *December* ___ *in the year of our Lord One Thousand Eight Hundred and Eighty* *nine* *and in the* *twelfth* *year of our Consecration.*

Signed)
W. D. Lichfield

The licence of Thomas Heywood Masters, curate in charge of Holy Trinity, the Meir, who was the first cleric at the church after its opening in 1891. His stipend or salary was a mere one hundred and thirty pounds a year! From these humble beginnings he went on to be appointed Chaplain to King George V.

AUGUSTUS, by Divine Permission, Bishop of LICHFIELD, to our beloved in CHRIST *Charles Addenbrooke, Clerk, M. A.*

Greeting;

We do by these Presents give and grant unto you our Licence and Authority to perform the Office of Stipendiary Curate in the *Parish Church of Caverswall* in the County of *Stafford* ___ within our Diocese and Jurisdiction in preaching the Word of God if thereto licensed by us in reading the Common Prayers and performing all other Ecclesiastical Duties belonging to the said Office according to the Form prescribed in the Book of Common Prayer, made and published by Authority of Parliament, and the Canons and Constitutions in that behalf lawfully established and promulged, and not otherwise or in any other manner: and we do by these Presents assign unto you the yearly Stipend of *One Hundred and Sixty Pounds* ___ to be paid Quarterly for serving the said Cure. And we require you to reside in the Parish of *Caverswall aforesaid* ___

In Witness whereof We have caused our Seal which we use in this case to be hereto affixed: Dated the *Twenty fourth* *day of* *February* ___ *in the year of our Lord One Thousand Eight Hundred and Ninety* *eight* *and in the* *seventh* *year of our Consecration.*

(Signed)
Augustus Lichfield :

Depicted here is the curate's licence from Caverswall of the man whose brother was the vicar of Caverswall, Rev John Gordon Addenbrooke. Charles Addenbrooke was curate in charge on the Meir in the late 19th century and following his departure his wandering and ministrations led him to the other side of the world where, in New Zealand, he died in the 1940s.

By kind permission of Public Record Office

Earl of Dartmouth by his second wife, Frances, who is second daughter of the 5th viscount Barrington. Canon Legge is half-brother of the present Earl of Dartmouth who is Lord Lieutenant of the county. Canon Legge is 52 years old and was educated at Eton, Christ's College, Oxford. He obtained his BA in 1861 and MA in 1864

Rev T H Masters was fundraising in late September 1891 for a new mission room at St Pauls, Edensor and a bazaar was arranged in the Town Hall:

Rev T H Masters attended a Michaelmas fair and bazaar to raise money for a new mission room for St Paul's, Edensor at Longton Town Hall. £250 has already been promised but between £140-£150 more is needed.

October 3rd 1891

A bazaar typically consisted, as on the above occasion, of the following including the actual names of those who took part:

Fruit and Vegetables	*Mrs Prince & Mrs Greaves.*
Groceries and provisions	*Mrs Finch-Smith & Mrs Turner.*
Drapery & Fancy good	*Mrs Boughey & Mrs Newton.*
China and earthenware	*Messrs J Goodwin, Garner&Hampton*
Meat and Vegetable	*The vicar (Rev Finch-Smith)*
Pictures and Toys	*Misses Finch-Smith (daughters of the vicar)*
Refreshments	*Messrs Boughey and Chew*
Tea and Coffee	*Mrs Ash & Mrs Colclough.*

There was also an art gallery in the hall run by Miss Adderley as well as a dramatic re-enactment by a Mr R C Clive of Kidsgrove.

For the Victorians, 'church' was far more than putting on good clothes, trotting along to a service and belting out a few hymns once or twice a week. Their ethos involved them deeply in the many problems faced by their fellow countrymen. The insidious scourge of alcoholism and its social consequences were one example. In Longton with dozens of alehouses, one on almost every street corner, the well-being of many local families was frequently compromised. And as if this was not bad enough, a move was made by the landlords to extend drinking time. The church, vigorously opposed this lengthening of the licensing hours and formed a vigilante committee to restrict the number of public houses. At its head was the Rector of Longton, the Rev G F Tamplin. A meeting was held on the 5th June 1891.

Another positive side to the church's work was in the schools, and particularly through the annual treat, something children looked forward to with eager anticipation for weeks. Not for them exotic watering holes abroad, but near Midsummer 1891:

The teachers and scholars attending St James' Church School, Longton[1] and Mount Pleasant Mission School had their annual treat and visited Sandon. Two special trains left Longton at 8.50 am and 2.05 pm for the

21

convenience of the excursionists who on arriving at Sandon made their way to the park to which they were admitted by the kindness of the Earl of Harrowby. Pork pies and milk were provided at noon and the children indulged in various amusements to their hearts' content - the return trains leaving Sandon at 8.30 pm and 9.00pm.

But not all was sweetness and light. In the autumn of that year, a robbery was to take place in the Meir which had ecclesiastical implications and where time, it seems, was of the essence. From the story which appeared in the local newspapers, it is surely but a short step to imagine the involvement of two famous men of the time in the mystery which occurred in the Meir in September 1891. Dr John H Watson and his friend and colleague Sherlock Holmes, were to stroll through the pages of English detective fiction to immortality. Their creator, Sir Arthur Conan Doyle made several attempts to rid himself of Holmes, provoking a national protest, but the sleuths were to haunt him throughout his life, appearing for the final time in Shoscombe Old Place in 1928, just two years before his own demise at the age of 71. What would Holmes and Watson have made of our particular problem in the Meir? Perhaps:

It had been sometime since my friend, Mr Sherlock Holmes, had looked up from examining a slide under his microscope at the end of rooms we shared at 221b Baker Street. When he did so, he sprang to his feet and smiled with singular satisfaction.
"You know Watson, I believe we've got him this time"
"Who have we got Holmes?" I enquired, looking up from my paper.
"Barrington, Watson; Alfred Barrington. You remember Barrington? The cigar ash we found at the scene of that singular murder in Shoreditch. It's identical to that found at his lodgings just off the Kennington Road. Note the peculiar ash it leaves Watson - it's from the wrapper. You remember the monograph I wrote? Of course you do. Without doubt," he said, walking across to the fire, "it's the final piece of the case that'll stretch his miserable neck once and for all."
My eyes fell back towards my newspaper. There was a short silence. Walking from the fire he sank back into his favourite chair. With one case solved, his great brain was once more in a state of idleness, something he detested. Taking a handful of tobacco from the Persian slipper, he selected a pipe from the rack. Clouds of smoke filled the air as he stared absent-mindedly into the flames.
I turned to the front page of my copy of the Advertiser a medical colleague in Staffordshire had sent me. Just then, an item on the printed page caught my attention.
"That's curious, Holmes." I said, not diverting my eyes from the printed page.
"Oh, what is it old fellow?" he murmured, looking up.
"Robbery in the Meir, in North Staffordshire. It seems a clergyman was away on

holiday and a break-in was effected through a very small rear window at the house and a timepiece stolen. Whatever next? I know.........," I paused and laughed, "What about the Curious Case of the Curate's Chronometer? Sounds a good title don't you think!"
"I trust it'll be a trifle easier to solve, Watson, than it is to say." Holmes replied dryly, a chuckle in his voice.
"Well," I went on, "it seems a young fellow, curate of the Holy Trinity church, the Meir, Longton, name of Masters, Thomas Heywood; clever too, Rugby blue; well, seems he was away on business and had his house in Weston Road, the Meir forcibly entered on Tuesday 8th September. Great Heavens Holmes; there's a valuable watch missing!"
"Really Watson. It's only a petty house breaking! It's of no consequence to us." Holmes said, rising from his chair and poking the fire. Suddenly it had become quite cold.
"But, Holmes" I went on, "the back window they got through was so small, no man could have possibly got in. Don't you think that's odd? You don't think it could be one of those.......well, those Andaman Island natives? You remember the case? It has all the hallmarks."
"What on earth makes you think that? There isn't anything to remotely suggest it was anything other than petty housebreaking. I really must caution you against jumping to conclusions, Watson. It's obviously the work of a child!"
I laid the paper on my lap and looked at him. "What on earth makes you say that?"
He chuckled. "Because it says a boy named Albert Trickett, who lives in Uttoxeter Road with his mother, offered Master's watch in pledge and then couldn't give a satisfactory answer as to how he came into possession of it. The hearing of the case has been adjourned for a fortnight as the Rev Masters is away. It's all there for the trained eye - in the Stop Press actually," he said with a twinkle in his eye.
"Really Holmes," I sighed aghast, "As simple as that?"
"Indeed it is my dear fellow. Now come along and be a good chap. Look out our Bradshaw for a train to Reigate, where there's something more taxing than, the Case of the Curate's Chronometer to occupy our minds. Really Watson!"
The fate of the real Albert Trickett was never disclosed, for which perhaps we should give thanks!

The Meir at this time was an agricultural community and the celebration of the harvest naturally assumed a greater significance in the calendar than would be true in later years. The first service in the new Holy Trinity church was doubly important for the villagers:

> *The Harvest thanksgiving services were held on the 8th inst. and Sunday 11th.*
> *The new church was tastefully decorated. On the 8th, the vicar of Dresden*
> *(Rev S Salt) was the preacher. On Sunday morning, the vicar of the parish (of*
> *Caverswall) J.G.Addenbrooke officiated. On Sunday afternoon the Rev A.B*

> *Standford assistant curate of Holy Trinity, Hartshill addressed the schoolchildren and in the evening the Rev W I Smith preached to a crowded congregation a practical and earnest sermon taking his text from St Mark iv. 28. - 'The full corn in the ear.' The offertories amounted to £10 18s.*

Many people at this time used their leisure time learning to play a musical instrument. Some were good and doubtless others were undeniably awful, and a few were very gifted. One such man, then only fifteen, fell into the latter category. Born on the 29th of January 1876 in Ricardo Street Dresden, he was to become one of this country's most prolific composers of this century. He was Havergal Brian.

Although still a chorister, he became deputy organist at St James' Church in Uttoxeter Road, Longton at the age of 12. Because the principal organist there tried to dissuade Brian from practising, it was left to him to seek guidance and help from the organist at St Gregory's Roman Catholic Church in Longton. Sadly this beautiful Pugin-designed church was demolished in 1969 and along with it, the organ on which Havergal Brian played.

While at St Gregory's, Brian was taught by the resident organist, Bertram Walker[2], who encouraged and cajoled him at every verse end. Brian thought highly of his mentor judging from the inscription he wrote on the fly leaf of a book (shown with photo), given to his tutor as a present. With the organist at St James Church resorting to juvenile escapades such as 'losing the key' to the organ, it motivated Brian to seek a position elsewhere and an advertisement for organist at Holy Trinity the Meir attracted his attention: It is difficult to assess whether it was the thought of unlimited access to the organ or the salary, the princely sum of £12 a year, which made up his mind. The thought of Havergal Brian scanning the 'Classified Advertisements' for an outlet for his talents, however humble and poorly paid, seems faintly ludicrous now, but everyone has to start somewhere!

> *Brian applied for the post of organist at Holy Trinity the Meir and greatly to his relief succeeded in obtaining it. The church was small and recently built.'*

Wisely using his salary to extend his technique and with the guidance of the organist of Stoke Parish Church, Theophilus Hemmings, his progress was rapid. By happy coincidence, the curate in charge at the Meir, the Rev T H Masters was also a keen musician and on his insistence, Brian was introduced to works by Chopin and Schumann and the piano works of Grieg. He also encouraged Brian to study musical papers with a view to extending his horizons further.

Rev Masters was a Cambridge graduate - admitted to Christ's College in January 1886 - and well placed to help by coaching Brian for an organ scholarship at St John's College, Cambridge. Despite this, Brian's father demured and insisted 'young William' should 'have a trade in his fingers'. For some time afterwards, his musical ambitions had to play second fiddle to a day job, as an apprentice joiner with a jobbing master, and he was eventually kitted out with smoothing plane, cross-cut saw, tenon saws, chisels and tri-square from the ironmonger's shop. But his days there were numbered from the beginning, and even in this workaday environment his effervescent musicality found an unusual outlet. A workmate, who being a fair player himself, spotted Brian's talent, encouraged him, and young Havergal the joiner would plane his 11" deal boards, cut them off at 5'6" and 'iron' them at each end ready for use for carrying precious pottery ware in the pot banks. Then using a T-square, he would rule the musical stave lines upon these pine boards and write down the organ marches he had composed.

Brian was immersed in music and he played the organ at Holy Trinity from 1891 until 1894, leaving then to take up a vacancy at Old Rode Church in Cheshire 20 miles away. But he did, on rare and special occasions, return to his old stamping grounds in the years ahead.

His career prospered during the first decade of the 20th century, when Brian numbered amongst his friends Sir Edward Elgar, who admired his eloquent and accomplished choral work. It was to be Brian's setting of Shakespeare's sonnet *'How shall I compare thee to a Summer's day?'* that brought him much deserved acknowledgment in the Three Choirs Festival at Worcester. But his 'magnum opus' was the gargantuan Gothic Symphony No 1; a piece he dedicated to fellow composer Richard Strauss and which, unfairly, thereafter depicted Brian as a *'composer of unperformable works'*. It was to be many years before he heard it played in full in London. As the last note died away, and cheered onto the platform like a celebrity, he later confessed to his bewilderment at such accolade.

Later in life he struck a rich vein, just as his star was setting[3], and he wrote over twenty symphonies whilst living at Shoreham-by-Sea, Sussex, which rekindled much interest in his work. Following a fall at his home, he died on 28th November 1972, two months short of his 97th birthday.

25

And so, as the parishioners of the Meir approached their first Christmas, there must have been the sense of a job well done as the church was decorated for the festival. It was well done as far as it went, but the new year was to bring more surprises.

All buildings evolve throughout their lives: Holy Trinity was no exception and in the years that followed numerous changes were effected, some beneficial, whilst others showed more effort than ability in design. The new Meir church was not the finished design; the most noticeable omission was the elusive north and south transepts and of course, the chancel, which was the next goal for Rev John Addenbrooke. The architect's original drawings of the church, with its elegant scripted measurements and copper plate lettering, are surely treasures in their own right.

Notes.
1. This school in Webberley Lane, Longton was completely refurbished and renovated with financial assistance from the European Union in 1993 and is, without doubt, one of Longton's finest buildings.
2. His daughters, Monica and Agnes, are still living in Longton in 1995.
3. In April 1940 Brian was awarded £140 in recognition of his services to music.

The church of St Peters, Caverswall, with the chimneys and roofs of Caverswall Castle in the background. At this time William Bowers, who died in August 1911, was the Squire of Caverswall.
Lovatt collection

The Church of the Holy Evangelists, Normacot. This sandstone church, financed partly by the Duke of Sutherland and designed by Sir Gilbert Scott, was built by William Evans and cost £1760. It was consecrated in July 1847. On many occasions the incumbent from here visited Holy Trinity Church, the Meir.
Author's collection

This is the chancel and part of the nave of St Gregory's Roman Catholic Church , Longton, Stoke on Trent, which which was demolished in 1969 as a result of mining subsidence. Here the young Havergal Brian received his tuition on the organ from Bertram Walker. The church was designed by Augustus Welby Pugin, a convert to the Roman Catholic faith, who was also responsible for the magnificent St Giles RC church in Cheadle, Staffordshire (and the Houses of Parliament). Father John Stringfellow, whose grave is in Longton cemetery, was the incumbent here for many years.   *Agnes & Monica Walker*

Holy Trinity Church, standing high up off the road on the land given by the fourth Duke of Sutherland.

The chancel added in 1894 is at the right end. The final cost of the whole church was £2800. All the trees seen here are to be cut down for the A50 'improvements'.

Author's Collection

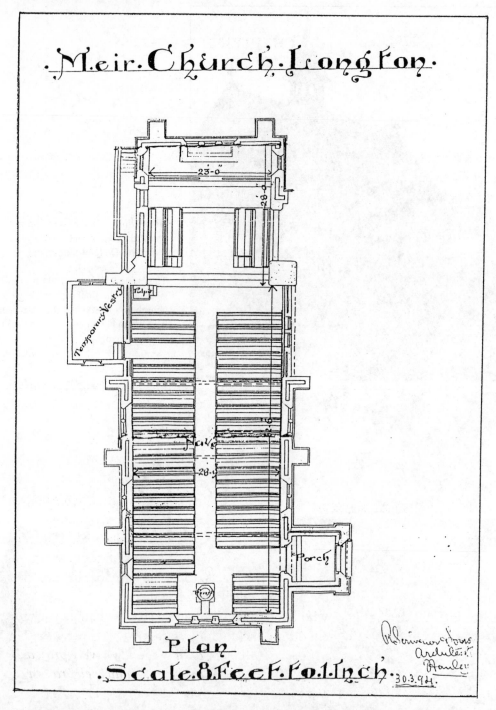

Taken from the original drawings made in March 1894, this is the plan for the later additions to the Holy Trinity Church, the Meir. They were made by Messrs Sciveners of Hanley.

CHAPTER 3
1892-3
'I show you doubt, to prove that faith exists.'
Robert Browning

There was a pride, nay an affection for the individual towns in the area which sadly was to disappear somewhat in later years. For the inhabitants of Longton and the Meir the dawning of the New Year 1892 saw the arrival from the printers of a much awaited calendar of events. The prominence given to politicians (national and local) shows that public duty and service was held in high esteem:

Messrs. Hughes and Harber of Stafford Street have published their annual Borough almanac. A new feature of this work is a frontispiece with very faithfully executed vignettes of Mr G Leveson-Gower MP and of James Heath, the Conservative, Mr L K H Shoobridge, the Gladstonian candidate for the north-west division of the county and of Mr Sampson Waters of Barlaston Hall, the Unionist candidate for Stoke-on-Trent. The almanac is sold at the nominal price of 2d.

Not to be outdone a rival almanac featuring a local and highly respected dignitary vied for the voter's allegiance:

Mr W H Wright of High Street has published a useful 'Illustrated Almanac' which includes a considerable amount of local information and a portrait of the Mayor (Alderman B. Prowse).

In Longton town there was to be no lingering in bed from now on during those cold winter mornings since the re-instatement of some much missed 'friends':

The peal of eight bells in St John's church, which through want of repair have remained silent for nearly three years, have been restored and re-hung.

The church of St John in Longton was the third oldest church (built in the 18th century) in what is now referred to as the Potteries. Unfortunately, like a considerable amount of our architectural legacy, it was to be demolished in later years, having become redundant when hundreds left the area through slum clearance.

But in 1892, the children who lived in and around its shadow had their dreams of the festive season to sustain them during the coming year:

On Christmas Day, the poor and destitute children of the town were provided with a substantial dinner at the Town Hall. This was the ninth celebration of the feast and about 500 little ones were permitted to share the happiness which everyone desires at Christmas. Roast beef and plum pudding were provided. On leaving, each child received an orange, an apple and a copy of a pictorial paper

They would probably receive no other presents.

The Meir, just up the road from Longton, was also caring for those living on the margins of society. The Holy Trinity church were always innovative when it came to homely entertainment and even the weather forecast for the 4th January 1892; *'Light breezes chiefly north-westerly; some snow at first but afterwards fair'* could not keep them at home:

> *On Monday evening a concert was given in the Meir Board Schools, the vicar of Caverswall (the Rev J G Addenbrooke) presiding and there was a large attendance. Among those who assisted were the Rev Thomas H Masters and Mrs Masters, the Misses Storey, Barlow, Middleton, Jones and Pothecary and Mrs Martin, Bevington and F Forth. Tableaux representing 'Pygmalion and Galatea', 'A Gipsy Scene', 'After tea in Japan', 'Florence Nightingale' and 'Bluebeard and his Seven Wives' were cleverly performed.*

At another regular church event two weeks later, the enthusiastic congregation turned up in force to see how their children had 'gone on':

> *The annual distribution of prizes to the children attending the Holy Trinity Church School, The Meir, took place on Monday evening at Meir Board Schools. The vicar of Caverswall, the Rev J G Addenbrooke presided, being supported by the Rev T H Masters and there was about 250 scholars present, besides a large number of their parents and friends. The prizes were distributed by Mrs Stephen Mear in the absence, through illness, of Mrs J G Aynsley.*
>
> *An interesting entertainment was then given - songs being contributed by Miss Pothecary, the Rev J L Murray and Mrs H Bevington. Pianoforte duets were given by the Misses Barlow and Middleton and several recitations given by the scholars. During the evening the vicar gave an address alluding with satisfaction to the prosperous state of the Sunday Schools. To the children especially, he gave much good advice.*
>
> *At the end of the evening each child received a parcel of warm clothing, the results of much hard work willingly given by the many friends interested in the new church at the Meir. It is intended that clothing shall be distributed annually as Christmas gifts.*

There was obviously a real demand for this clothing since Rev T H Masters decided to make it an annual event and this underlines the notion that most of the people in the Meir at that time were poor but definitely honest!

The clergy held a special place in many communities at that time, not least for their educational abilities and leadership qualities and their individual passing from the world was a source of great sorrow to their parishioners. January saw the death of two in the area; the Rev J R Hutchinson, the vicar of Normacot, on 2nd January 1892, and the Rev G R Ramshaw of the United Free Church, High Street, Longton who *'died suddenly on Monday morning (11th January) at his residence in Uttoxeter Road, the cause of death being heart disease. He was 59 years of age.'*

There were many idiosyncratic Victorian delights at the end of the 19th century and one of the more notable was the Pleasant Sunday Afternoon Society (PSA) whose very name conjures up befrocked children enjoying the fresh air and countryside of some seldom visited beauty spot. Pleasures were simple; the bell ringers from Keele church going down the road for an outing to Betley, for example! They did not expect very much but was it a poorer society for that and did people set greater store on personal values than fifty years later? It certainly seemed to act as a counterbalance to the worst shortcomings of a society that sometimes gave the impression of being on the verge of becoming unglued at the seams; suicides were frighteningly common and reflected the despair of many:

> *On Thursday morning, Hannah Myatt aged 37, the wife of Joseph Myatt, labourer of Red Bank, Dresden committed suicide by cutting her throat.*
>
> *6th February 1892*

Even the Mayor, Alderman Browse, seems to have had enough of it all when referring to the prevalence of *'swearing and betting in the streets'*, although, being a politician, he left it at that.

After all the successes of the past few months at Holy Trinity church, it was inevitable there would be a hitch, albeit temporary:

> *The bazaar arranged to be held in the Town Hall (Longton) this week on behalf of the Holy Trinity Church, The Meir, has been postponed until Michaelmas.*
>
> *21st May 1892*

It must have seemed a setback at the time as they wanted to increase the chancel fund to get its building under way without delay. And then in October, they lost one of their patrons from whose house the Bishop of Shrewsbury had walked 18 months before for the Dedication.

> *We regret to announce the death of Mr William Webberley JP, which occurred at his residence, The Meir House. He also took an active part in the erection of the new church at the Meir contributing liberally to the funds.*
>
> *22nd October 1892*

Undaunted, and at their second Christmas in the church, the parishioners pressed on with yet another sale on the 27th and 28th December 1892 and hoped for a new year start to building their chancel:

On Tuesday and Wednesday a sale of work was held in the Meir Board Schools on behalf of the building fund of the Holy Trinity Church. The sale consisted of a quantity of useful and fancy articles left over from the Michaelmas fair and about 350 warm winter garments which were disposed at cost price to the mothers of the Sunday school children. The sale was opened by Mrs W E Bowers of Caverswall Castle who was supported by the vicar of Caverswall (the Rev J G Addenbrooke) the curate in charge of the Meir church (the Rev Thomas Heywood Masters MA) Mr Henry Hill JP and others. The vicar, in opening the proceedings, explained that the May Fair on behalf of the church building fund resulted in a clear profit of £ 368 8s 5d and the Michaelmas Fair (the postponed May Bazaar) a profit of £174 10s. They now required about £150 to complete the building of the chancel. The trustees thought if they could raise £50 of that sum, they might commence the work in the Spring and it was with that object that the sale was held. Mrs Bowers had laid the foundation stone of the chancel in the figurative sense and had collected from the ladies of the county a sum of £76 and Mr Bowers had given £20!

She said she had much pleasure in declaring the sale open. She was very pleased to do what she could in assisting to complete the church and she hoped the sale would be successful. On the motion of Mr Hill a vote of thanks was passed to Mrs Bowers for her kindness. A concert was given each evening; amongst those taking part being Mrs. Boulton, Miss Godfrey, Miss Boulton, Miss Blair, Messrs A & E Brooke, Aynsley, Bevington, Heath, Leach & Ridgway. The accompaniments were played by Mr F. Millington.

31st December 1892.

In the space of three months, the gallant clergy and their willing congregation had raised well over three quarters of the new chancel's cost, an astonishing feat many today would envy. Having the effervescent Mrs W E Bowers of Caverswall Castle on board must have been a great help; she seemed to make a career out of wringing huge sums of money from people for charity. What would Holy Trinity have done without her?

There was also Henry Hill JP, who also gave his name to a large and important charity, the interest from which assisted poor people in the parish. Some years later, Havergal Brian played the organ in Holy Trinity Church when this generous instigator of the bursary died.

A curious clutch of stories in the new year of 1893 illustrated the spectrum of life at the time, from tragedy to success. It was not uncommon for inquests into sudden deaths to be held at public houses and the demon drink itself was often named as the cause of death. A paradox indeed. Lives regularly slipped away with consummate ease:

On Thursday morning (2nd March 1893) Mr John Booth held an adjourned inquest at the Newtown Hotel touching the death of William Ernest Warner of 27, Alfred Street, Fenton, who was found in an unconscious state in Ludwall Road, Normacot on the 21st ult. and who died upon removal to the Cottage Hospital. Death had resulted from a fracture to the skull and a clot of blood on the brain.

But the church did its best to steer people to better things. One indication of this was always the Service of Confirmation and two Bishops paid the area a visit for this reason in March:

On Tuesday afternoon, the Bishop of Shrewsbury performed the sacred rite of confirmation at Normacot Church, 71 candidates being presented by the vicar the Rev E C Hipkins.

On Wednesday evening the Bishop of Lichfield held a similar service at St John's parish church, 100 candidates being presented by the rector (the Rev W I Smith) and the assistant clergy.

Such was the strength of the church in this small area, it was possible to muster over 170 souls for confirmation!

And then there were various 'treat' funds which showed the strength of the community spirit - and that that spirit was not all 70% proof!

At a meeting of the Old Folks' Treat committee a substantial balance was at hand by the treasurer Mr J Gadsby and it was agreed that a cheque for £10 was to be forwarded to the governors of the Cottage Hospital.

While at Caverswall, attached to the church, there was a vigorous debating group, where the secretary reported, *"discussions on Cremation and on Association Rules versus Rugby!"* were enjoyed. In April the Caverswall Young Men's Club wound up their busy schedule in this way:

The winter session of the club was brought to a close on the 13th inst. The proceedings were commenced with supper which was much enjoyed. A vote of thanks was passed to the ladies for their presence and their kind attention to the wants of the members. The president and treasurer (the Rev J G Addenbrooke) read his report followed by the secretary's (Mr Harry H Sargant). The club is in a most flourishing condition. It is entirely unsectarian and self supporting.

Caverswall was not alone in having its clubs. The Meir had one too, although theirs was a little more athletic - but only a little more so:

After having been closed for some years, the Meir Bowling Club was formerly re-opened with a tea at the King's Arms Hotel on Thursday night . Mr John G

> *Aynsley has been elected President, Mr T Jacks, Captain, and Mr J H Keeble Hon Sec.*

And with the coming of Easter, it was open season for tea parties. At St John's, Longton they did not do things by halves:

> *On Monday evening (3rd April 1893) the annual Easter Tea Party in connection with the parish church of St John's took place in the town hall (Longton). Around 450 were present to tea and the first part of the entertainment was of a musical character. Glees were given by the choir, Mr Forrester and Miss H. Barker; part-songs and duets were also rendered by Misses Birks and Houldsworth, Barker and Forrester. Mr Brookfield gave a violin solo, 'Cavatina' (Raff) and the entertainment was concluded with the comedy 'The Area Belle', the characters being taken by Messrs. Byatt, G Goodwin and A Trickett, Mrs Ratcliffe and Miss G Cooper. The proceeds were in aid of the churchwarden's funds.*

By now, with funds growing daily, the Holy Trinity congregation had got the bit firmly betwixt their teeth and threw caution to the wind. They decided to proceed with the new chancel without anymore delay:

> *The congregation of the new church of the Holy Trinity, the Meir have decided to proceed with the erection of the chancel, the ceremony of cutting the first sod was performed on Monday (26th June) in the presence of the vicar of Caverswall (the Rev G Addenbrooke), the curate in charge (the Rev T H Masters) and members of the Building Commissioners and a number of parishioners. The act of turning the first sod was performed by Mr E Cartwright who has taken a deep and practical interest in the erection of the new church. The architects are Messrs Scriveners & Sons, Hanley and the builders Messrs. Tompkinson & Bettelley, Longton and it is hoped that the work will be completed by the end of October. The sum of £250 is still required to complete and furnish the chancel.* 1st July 1893

There were no cars at the time and long distance travel was almost non-existent for the vast majority. The news that all that was about to change was greeted with pleasure and great expectation. Horizons were about to be broadened beyond the tinkling of tea cups at the local garden party:

> *In view of the rapid growth of the Meir district, representations were recently made to the North Staffs Railway Company with the object of inducing them to provide a station for the accommodation of the inhabitants of that district and it is satisfactory to note that the company have definitely decided to accede to*

their request. The station is to be situated near to the bridge beyond the Normacot tunnel and near to the water works. Most of the land in the neighbourhood is being laid out in building plots and a still further development of the district is to be hoped for. The company will endeavour to have the new station completed and opened by Wakes Week.

The tunnel and track bed dated from the 1840s: so it had only taken fifty years for the village to get its own station and staging post to the outside world at large!

With the warmer weather, people living in the towns and villages had chance to escape to the local parks, especially Queen's Park, Longton (which is actually in Dresden). Dozens of amusements were on display at the Whitsuntide Fetes and to these people flocked in droves:

At the Queen's Park, Longton on Whit Monday and Tuesday the public are to be well amused. There will be a grand military assault-at-arms and the band of the 1st Lifeguards will play here for the first time. A Japanese wire-walker, female trapeze performers, a 'strong-woman' and the Quaglieni trio of clowns and acrobats are among the artists engaged. A novel feature is a dressed doll competition. There will be fireworks and illuminations at night and the large lake will be brilliantly illuminated.

Throughout early 1893, the congregation at Holy Trinity church were slowly moving towards the completion of their much needed chancel and on a Thursday in August, the great day finally dawned:

The commissioners having decided to proceed with the erection of the chancel of Holy Trinity church, The Meir, the foundation stone was laid on Thursday afternoon (16th August 1893) by Mrs W E Bowers of Caverswall Castle, a lady who had taken a particular interest in the new and handsome church. The church, which was erected at a cost of over £2000 on land given by the late Duke of Sutherland, was opened for public worship in May 1891 and there still has to be added to complete the edifice, a chancel, organ chamber, vestry and north and south transepts. At present it is proposed to proceed with the erection of the chancel only and for this, a sum of over £700 is required. Most of this money has already been subscribed, viz £415 10s 8d which including a balance on the church building fund and proceeds of sales of work amounts to £276 7s 8d; £76 from Mrs Bowers Ladies Fund, £50 from the Incorporated Building Society, £30 from the Diocesan Church Extension Society, £20 from Mrs J G Aynsley, £20 from Mr Bowers and other donations. The chancel will be constructed in the early decorated style in conformity with the nave and will be 28 feet in length and 23 feet in width, the height from the floor to the ridge being 42 feet. On the south side there will be an arch so as to admit the erection of the organ chamber and on the north side a doorway for communication for the vestry. The east window will have three lights and the floor and a portion of the inside walls will be paved with Minton's tiles. The chancel is to be completed by the end of October

The ceremony of laying the stone was preceded by a short evensong, the choir singing as a processional, "Onward Christian Soldiers". The service was conducted by the Bishop of Shrewsbury and amongst the clergy who took part were the Reverends J G Addenbrooke (vicar of Caverswall) T. H. Masters (curate in charge of the Meir), E S Carlos (Rural dean); JW Beckett, J Beech, W I Smith, E C Hipkins, W B Hunter, S W Hutchinson, W Blackett and T C Bradbury. The Bishop, in the course of a short address, said he had been happily associated with the church at the Meir from its commencement and he was glad the time had arrived when there was a prospect of completing the church by the addition of what was the most sacred part of any church. The rest of the office was said by the stone by the Bishop and the stone was laid by Mrs Bowers who was presented with the silver trowel suitably inscribed. The vicar announced the patron of the church (the Hon E S Parker-Jervis) had

subscribed £150 and sent a further donation of £25 and he thanked Mrs Bowers for the kind and practical interest which she had manifested in the church, mentioning the fact that the fund she had collected was really the nucleus of the chancel fund. While the offertory was being made, the hymn "Christ is our corner stone" was sung; "At the name of Jesus" being used as recessional hymn. Messrs. Scriveners and Sons are the architects and Messrs. Tompkinson & Bettelley[1] are the contractors.

The foundation stone of the chancel at Holy Trinity Church, the Meir, laid in 1893 by the first Mrs W E Bowers. What the weather of almost a century has failed to do, the vandal has accomplished with ease.
Author's collection

A triumph indeed for the vicar of Caverswall. This ebullient cleric, through his enthusiasm and vitality, had succeeded in furnishing the Meir with what would become one of its most enduring institutions. But what of this man's origins and what of his future? John Gordon Addenbrooke[2] (his father was also John), began his ministry in Derbyshire and was at several parishes before holding his present position.

Curate of Holy Trinity, Chesterfield	*1879-1880*
Curate of Holy Trinity, Burton on Trent	*1880-1882*
Vicar of St Luke, Wolverhampton	*1882-1889*

Vicar of Caverswall, Staffs	*1889-1902*
Rural Dean of Cheadle, Staffs	*1901-1902*
Vicar of St Mark's, Tutbury	*1902-1908*
Vicar of St Wenn, Bodmin, Cornwall	*1908-1915*
Curate of Tiverton on Avon, Bath	*1915-1922*

His brother Charles[3] also followed the calling and spent five years at Holy Trinity. He was fifteen years younger than John. A deacon in 1888, a priest at Lichfield in 1890; between 1898 to 1903 he was a curate in the Meir and the Addenbrooke brothers must have been in weekly contact at Caverswall and Meir during the course of their ecclesiastical duties:

Curate of Dawley Magna, Salop	*1888-1891*
Curate of St George's Edgbaston, B'ham	*1891-1898*
Curate in charge, Holy Trinity, the Meir,	*1898-1903*
Vicar of St Chad's Smethwick	*1903-1906.*

Then, almost as a postscript to 1893, a year which had seen giant leaps forward for the local churches, what might have been a tragedy was averted at the Longton Church, St.Paul's, Edensor:

A fire was discovered at 3pm on Sunday 10th December by the vicar. Captain Cartlidge and the fire brigade were turned out to attend. Little damage was done.

Notes.
1. The builders secured another contract in 1893; 'by building a large infants' classroom, lavatories and cloakroom at St James School, Webberley Lane, Longton at a cost of £900.'
2. He died July 3rd 1922 at his home at 80 Bloomfield Avenue, Bath, at the age of 72.
3 Charles Addenbrooke died in the early 1940s in New Zealand.

Probably the earliest photograph of the Meir, taken over 100 years ago. It is the opening of Meir station in 1893. The photographer is looking towards Blythe Bridge; the signal box is beyond the right hand platform in front of the roadbridge and Meir Board Schools is at the top right hand side. The photograph was probably taken using the daguerreotype process where the image was first captured using a silver halide coated copper plate. The picture was developed with the aid of mercury vapour, itself generated by warming the liquid metal with a spirit lamp - a practice which would quite definitely be prohibited today. It is a fascinating record of a proud occasion marking the beginning, for many, of contact with the world outside. *Author's collection*

One of the roads joining Meir to Normacot was Meir Road. This photograph is at the western end of Meir, which is behind the photographer J A Lovatt, with Normacot running into the distance.The block of 2 storey brick houses facing the camera are still there 90 years later; note the Police sign above the door of the house at the left of this trio. The cottage seen centre middleground is probably one of the oldest buildings in the whole area. On the same side, Normacot Church School is also visible farther down after the terraced houses but before the gable ends of two houses. The point where the cart has stopped, on the left, is where Star & Garter Road entered Meir Road in later years. Further down on the left and out of shot is Normacot church lying on a bend in the road. *Lovatt collection*

The staff of Longton Cottage Hospital in 1907. It was founded by the rector of Longton, the Rev Adam Clarke. The foundation stone ceremony on 27th June 1889 was followed by the opening, by his widow, on 25th September 1890. Matron (Miss S.E.Barton) and her staff are seated outside the entrance to the nurses quarters. Many from the Meir were treated at this hospital providing as it did a local service. There were no interminable jaunts up to the North Staffs Infirmary for patients and relatives then!   *Lovatt collection*

Principal nursing staff at the hospital in 1912 were Joseph William Dawes MB, LL Burton FRCS (Eng), T H Richmond MB ChB and Alfred Parkes LRCP (Edin). Presumably the doctor in the photograph is one of these.

A pony and trap with three people aboard clatters along Stone Road (now Lightwood Road), surrounded by the craggy splendour of Shooter's Hills, Lightwood. Only a mile from the Meir and a popular picnic spot, this was a picturesque locality until the road was widened. However, 80 years later it is still on the edge of rolling countryside with the Common at Rough Close nearby.

Lovatt collection

CHAPTER 4
1894-5
'Earth's crammed with Heaven,
And every common bush afire with God'
Elizabeth Barrett Browning 1806-1881

The need for a railway station at the Meir in 1893 illustrates the bald fact that the population of this tiny village and Staffordshire was increasing at an alarming rate. In January 1894, figures from the census of 1891 were published. During the 10 years from 1881 to 1891 the population of the county had increased by 9.6%, whilst in the previous decade 1871-1881, it had gone up by 14.6%. It had almost doubled from 608,000 in 1851 to 1,083,408 in 1891, and from only 294,000 in 1811. In eighty years, there had been virtually a 400% increase in the population of the county, placing incredible pressures on housing as well as public health. The time was rapidly approaching when it would be necessary for some of the Meir's rolling acres to be used to house new families from places like Longton, where disease and malnutrition were rife[1].

In February 1894, Holy Trinity had a new man at the helm:

On Tuesday evening (6th February) a social gathering was held in the Meir Board Schools, the principal object of which was to welcome the recently appointed curate-in-charge of Holy Trinity, the Meir and his wife (the Rev J E & Mrs.Carey). About 130 were present to tea and afterwards the chair was taken by the vicar (the Rev J Gordon Addenbrooke) who introduced and welcomed Rev & Mrs Carey. Amongst those who assisted with entertainments were Mr H Bevington, Mrs Barnett, Mrs Tivey, Miss Barlow, Mr H Heath, Mr J M Philips, Miss Philips, Miss Middleton, Miss Barlow, Mr T Barker and Mr Swift.

That grand old man, septuagenarian and philanthropist John Aynsley was still taking it upon himself to help level the bumpy playing fields of Life by distributing 1000 four pound loaves to the poor of the town. And further: *'We understand Alderman Aynsley contemplates giving away a large quantity of potatoes in a few days.'*

But food was not the only gift bestowed on the locals in 1894. The children of Longton were the recipients of some unusual generosity in March and it is highly probable that some of those who accepted this hospitality were also from the Meir:

Through the instrumentality of the Deputy Town Clerk (Mr W L Cope) over 2000 poor children were presented with free tickets to Mr Ohmy's Circus. The building was packed and the youngsters expressed their delight by boisterously applauding the performers. Cheers were given for Mr Cope and the gentleman who had assisted him and on leaving each child received a bun and an orange.

At the beginning of Lent, the usual celebrations took place in Longton which, it must be said, placed more emphasis on the temporal than the secular:

The customary Bell and Orange Fair took place on Shrove Tuesday. It had been removed from the Market Place and was celebrated in the covered market on a piece of land off Edensor Road. All schools were closed for a half day along with several of the Potteries! Unfortunately two nasty accidents were reported from the swing boats against which better protection is needed on showgrounds.

And as Easter approached, so too did the season's more genteel functions:

......several tea parties were held. There was one at St James' where 400 hundred were present; a large number were also present at St John's and in Queen's Park Longton, there was a concert given by the Longton Town Military Band. In Dresden (Queen's Park) the fair was to raise funds for St Luke's (later in Carlisle Street, Florence). The amount raised was later disclosed to be £42 5s 8d: At St Paul's Edensor one hundred and fifty sat down.......

Much of this revenue was raised to offset the capital cost of construction of more fine buildings that were to be bequeathed us. The hard grind and endeavour of our forebears in constructing such places is too easily forgotten in the haste to knock them down and put up something new. But now, for those in the Meir, the waiting was over. Remarkably in so short a period, they had amassed £450; it was time to get out the china and sherry glasses once more:

CONSECRATION OF THE MEIR CHURCH

A new chancel having just been added to the new church of the Holy Trinity at the Meir at a cost of £700, the ceremony of the consecration of the church was performed on Monday (16th May) by the Bishop of Lichfield. The foundation stone of the new chancel was laid in August last by Mrs W E Bowers of Caverswall Castle.

In construction, the chancel follows closely the character of the nave having brick facings on the outside walls and stone dressings to the windows and angles. Inside, the dressings to the windows and walls are also of stone and the lower portion is faced with tiles. The chancel is fitted with a large three-light window in the east wall and single-light windows in the north and south walls.

Provision is also made for the addition in the future of an organ chamber and vestry. Towards the cost of the chancel the sum of £250 is still required.

The service of consecration was the first of a special series extending into May and there was a large congregation. Amongst the clergy present were the Reverends J G Addenbrooke (vicar of Caverswall), J E Carey (curate in charge), H V Smith, W I Smith, T P Forth, D H Briggs and the Hon S G W Maitland. The usual office for the consecration was used, the Registrar (Mr W. Hodson) reading the deed of consecration which was signed by the Bishop of Lichfield who ordered it to be enrolled and preserved in the registry of the diocese. In the course of his address, the Bishop reminded the parishioners present of the deep responsibility which rested upon them and urged them to take an active part in the work of the church. A celebration of the Holy Communion followed. The organ has been presented to the church by Mrs Stephen Mear and the credence table has been purchased from the Lenten savings of the teachers and children of the Sunday School.   21st May 1894

Afterwards, the Rev J G Addenbrooke hurried back to Caverswall to take another of his numerous and varied duties. The Young Men's Club was rewarding one of its members with a special token of their admiration for his literary expertise:

Mr John Hawkins carried off the secretary's prize (a day ticket to the seaside) for his paper, "A day in a coal pit."

And later that month, all the Young Men's club went to the seaside on a day trip:

The second seaside outing of the club took place, Liverpool being the place selected for the trip. The party, accompanied by the president, the Rev J G Addenbrooke MA, vice-president Mr T A Hand, and secretary Mr Harry Sargant left Normacot at 6.40am approx. arriving in Liverpool at about 9.45 am. The return journey was a comfortable but a tedious one, a long wait occurring at Crewe and it was about half past twelve when the party arrived home.

If many things were to change over the next fifty years, then the length of time taken for a train journey via Crewe was not one of them. It seems to have been always punctuated by a long wait on platform five, for reasons nobody seems able to explain!

At the Meir, the Bowling Club held a meeting at the King's Arms Hotel on Thursday 10th May:

when about fifty members had a sit-down meal. Several toasts were proposed and the evening was spent in a convivial manner.

Another pastime avidly pursued in this quiet era before the advent of the motor car and lorry, was cycling, and there were numerous local clubs and societies, and to satisfy the competitive streak, events were staged to sort out the men from the boys. In 1894:

On Wednesday, a 20 mile scratch cycling race took place on the Stoke Athletic

Ground. In a field of 10 starters the winner was Mr H Brookfield in 1 hour 8 minutes 34 seconds.

The well used gavel of T H Griffiths was swinging well in May with two property auctions: at the first he succeeded in selling four dwelling houses, Nos 102-108 Russell Street, Dresden for £700; whilst at the second, he failed to find a buyer for Mr W Adderley's house, The Beeches, *'situate in Spratslade'* (now in Trentham Road, Dresden) and it was withdrawn at £1000.

Meanwhile, the Fire Brigade, under the commendable Captain Cartlidge, was called out on at least two occasions during the year to fires in and around the Meir and Longton. In both cases they were successful and returned triumphant. The first was a fire at the factory of H Aynsley in Commerce Street, Longton at which, *'Superintendent Evans & several constables were present to direct operations,'* while at the second in July, the gallant fire crews were all involved. It was obviously a far more serious incident. Messrs H & R Inskip, the builders of the nave of Holy Trinity Church, the Meir, owned several acres of ground at the back of Stone Road and School Lane, Longton and suffered a very severe fire[2]:

> *The damage ran to £7000 which was all insured and at one point, it appeared that St James' School was in danger of being burned down by a change in the wind direction.*

It was quite customary for the town to show its appreciation and esteem for such 'services rendered' and in the week before Christmas, at a special presentation, Mr Cartlidge Superintendent of the Fire Brigade, received a handsome silver-plated helmet while his deputy was presented with a framed photograph of himself.

At Holy Trinity, the Meir, clergy were on the move once more and the congregation as always were quick to show their appreciation to the departing cleric. This time it was the Rev Hugh Smith who had been at Caverswall for two years:

> *On his departure he was presented with a handsome gold watch, chain and cross attached. The presentation was made on behalf of the parishioners by the vicar (the Rev J G Addenbrooke). The subscriptions numbered about 120 and the Rev Smith was also the recipient of gifts from individual friends.*

Christmas came and the schools closed down for the holiday. At the Meir school, the 303 children on the rolls gleefully left chalk and slate behind and looked forward to Christmas eve. The income for the school had been rising steadily and by 1894 had reached £392 and with expenses of £386, the average cost was 19s 11d to teach each pupil[3]. By contrast, at Dresden school there were 800 pupils, a pointer to the comparative size of the Meir and Dresden at this time, just a mile or so apart.

At the beginning of 1895, the plight of many in the area had altered little and it is comforting to note that charity was still about in broad measure:

> *During the severe weather of the past week or two, 30 tons of coal have been distributed to 43 poor families and widows residing in Blythe Bridge and Forsbrook*
> 20th January 1895

It was so desperate in Longton during February that grave concern was expressed about the welfare of many of the children living there. Something had to be done!

> *A meeting was held at the Court House on Monday for the purpose of forming a committee to raise funds to provide free breakfasts during the severe weather for poor children in the elementary schools in the town.*
> 9th February 1895

But the bad weather persisted through the long winter, causing the Duke of Sutherland to intervene with generous assistance to those in dire need:

> *The continuance of the severe frost through another week has considerably added to the distress amongst the poor, and the difficulty of the situation is being added to by the scarcity of water on the factories through the freezing of the water pipes. Beef, bread and coal has been distributed through the generosity of the Duke of Sutherland.*

And in early March:

> *645 lbs of beef, 232 loaves of bread and 6 tons of coal were given away. This with the previous two distributions takes up the total amount of relief by the Duke to 2410 lbs of beef, 960 loaves and 51 tons of coal.*

Many hung on as best they could. By the 23rd March 1895, the inventory of his kindness was astronomic:

> *The relief given by the Duke of Sutherland now amounts to 6570 lbs of beef, 2543 loaves and 115 tons of coal.*

But through all this misery for some, the social events continued:

PICKWICK CLUB DANCE

> *The first annual ball in connection with the Pickwick Club was held on the 8th inst. at the Dresden Church Schools and was successful with about 80 ladies and gentlemen being present. The catering was in the hands of Miss Thomas of the Union Hotel[4] and the music supplied by Mr Brough's band.*

And:

STRANGE DINNER PARTY

> *30 felons were treated to a meal by Supt. Bakewell who referred to them as "the submerged tenth".*

The fire brigade were also en fête:

Captain Coleman proposed the health of the superintendent and members of the
Longton Brigade and praised their efficiency and in reply Captain Cartlidge
said that with the amount of practice his brigade had during the year, they could
hardly be anything but efficient!

Only a month later, these firefighters, doubtless remembering Captain Cartlidge's pithy
invective, attended a fire at J H Middleton's factory with their 'steamer' and in
December they were tackling a conflagration at Alderman Leak's Pottery, which they
doubtless raced to in double-quick time.

As the summer unfolded, the Duke of Sutherland and his wife turned their attention to
pleasant social 'chores', with a garden party at Trentham on 27th June 1895:

In aid of funds for the Meir church. Unfortunately, the weather was very
stormy in the afternoon but the evening being fine, a goodly number of visitors
were attracted to the beautiful gardens.

The weather it appears, never changes!

In Longton, the Rev W I Smith was somewhat undecided where his future lay. On 30th
March, he might have gone after eight years at St John's, but he turned down the
possible move and decided to stay put. By June, he was wavering about going to
Australia and then he received the offer of a diocesan job in one of the largest dioceses
in England, which he also turned down. By November though, his mind was made up;
he placed his resignation with the Bishop of Lichfield, the patron of the living:

The Rev W I Smith has accepted the incumbency of St James, Australia. The new
vicar is to be the Rev George Oliver, the vicar of St George at Darlaston for the
past ten years at an annual salary of £500.

It would be a long walk back for his oatcakes on a Sunday morning!

Two unconnected events took place at Holy Trinity in 1895. The first was the departure
of an old friend. Churches depended heavily on the patronage of wealthy benefactors
and one such, in the case of Holy Trinity, was Henry Hill. Born in 1816 and a Justice
of the Peace, he died on Thursday 28th March 1895:

The funeral procession left the deceased's residence, Beech House[5], the
Meir shortly before 2 o'clock and was met by the choir of the Holy Trinity
church, the Meir; the deceased being a prominent member of the
congregation.

The service was conducted by the vicar of Dresden (Rev S Salt) and the
curate-in-charge the Meir Church, (Rev J E Carey). As the procession
entered the church Mr W Brian, organist at Meir church (Havergal Brian,
who according to Reginald Nettel[6] had left the Meir church in 1894) *played*

Chopin's "March Funébre" and at the close the "Dead March" in "Saul".
Also present although not officiating was the Rev J G Addenbrooke (vicar
of Caverswall).

Through the generosity of Henry Hill, the poor and needy of the parish were to benefit for many years from the perpetual legacy he bequeathed out of his concern for his fellow men.

The second Holy Trinity event of 1895 gave a glimpse of better things to come for the inhabitants of the Meir. With its wide open spaces, it seemed inevitable that an unhurried and civilised sport beginning to be enjoyed by many at the time, would not be long in coming to the parish:

'OPENING OF A GOLF COURSE

The Waterloo Golf Course which is directly behind the Meir church and within three and seven minutes walk respectively of the Meir and Normacot Stations was opened for play on Thursday afternoon. This course is one of 9 holes; in good condition and from the configuration of the ground, it is claimed it is superior for beginners to any in North Staffordshire. A very pleasant game was enjoyed by the members, who at present number between 20 and 30. A considerable addition to the membership is looked for now that the game is at the height of its popularity.   5th October 1895

Early in May, T H Griffiths, the auctioneer, was again busy. In Longton, in amongst the crushed velvet and the wilton carpet of the Crown and Anchor Hotel, he was finely observed by the local tipplers; at the afternoon sale, since one of the lots was none other than the Saracen's Head public house in the Meir: *"The bidding began at £600 and rose (slowly) to £1400 when it was withdrawn from the sale."*

While on another occasion, later in the month: *"a brickyard and premises in the occupancy of H & R Inskip* (the builders of part of Holy Trinity church) *were withdrawn at £1250"!*

Once in awhile, events occur that make even the most cynical stop to ask, why? How sad when the life of a child ends and that too, on a return trip from Sunday school! No tearaways these children, just wandering home to afternoon tea in a quiet road in Longton:

Annie Grace Ball, aged 8 years crossing the Millfield crossing was hit by the 3.10pm Normacot train whilst trying to save her brother whilst they were returning from Sunday school.

One person, in particular, was deeply moved by the story and took more than just a passing interest in the tragedy. Famous at the time as the editor of a journal, and for years afterwards as an author, he is perhaps best remembered through one of his most famous books. It begins:

> *There were four of us - George and William Samuel Harris and myself, and Montmorency. We were sitting in my room smoking and talking about how bad we were - bad from a medical point of view I mean, of course. We were all feeling seedy, and we were getting quite nervous about it.*

Many will recognise the opening passage of 'Three Men in a Boat'; its Staffordshire born author responded during the following weeks to the tragic story which had appeared in all the papers;

> *Jerome K Jerome, the editor of a journal called 'PLUCK' has forwarded through Superintendent Bakewell a donation of 2 guineas to Thomas Ball of Railway Terrace, East Vale, whose little girl, Annie Grace Ball was killed at the Millfield Gate Crossing on April 7th bravely attempting to save her younger brother who ran across the railway in front of an approaching train.*

It was something straight from the pages of Victorian melodrama!

Notes.
1. In Longton in 1896 the death rate for children was below average before the outbreak of diphtheria. Afterwards it was twice as high and in 1897/8 had risen to ten times the average. The spread of the disease was thought to be due to children living in poor housing and, unable to be isolated, being sent back to school wrongly diagnosed. Woodhouse School, Sandford Hill, was identified as the source. The Sunday Schools were closed from October 1897 until January 1898.
2. This did not prevent them from tendering for the enlargement of the infants' schools at Hulme and Werrington later that year.
3. A state of affairs we seem to be heading for ten decades later!
4. In 1995, situated in Uttoxeter Road, Longton, below the Gladstone Pottery Museum.
5. His residence was in Weston Road, Meir.
6. See *'Havergal Brian: The Man and His Music'* Dobson 1976

A train speeds through East Vale, Longton to Derby, passing on its way, Normacot and Meir stations up the line. The Terrace Inn depicted below is on the far right behind the bridge. Here in Railway Terrace, lying just on the other side of the tracks, Annie Grace Ball lived with her family and it was on this section of the line she forfeited her life attempting the gallant rescue of her brother. *Lovatt collection*

The grim reality of inner Longton in Paragon Road, East Vale lying alongside the Derby to Crewe railway line, which crosses the bridge from right from left, caught to perfection by the lens of J A Lovatt circa 1910. With the Terrace Inn to the right, in the murk is the tower of St James' Church in Uttoxeter Road, with numerous examples of the oft-rememberd bottle ovens peppering the landscape. The air was often so thick when these were "fired", the only occasion it was possible to see more than a few hundred yards came during the local Wakes holidays in August. As a result people lived in a twilight world of poor housing and non-existent sanitation: little wonder that life expectancy was so low. *Lovatt collection*

Taken at the end of the nineteenth century, the photographer was standing in what in 1996 is called Sandon Road (A 520) and has pointed his camera across Meir crossroads to Weston Road. The building in the middle ground with its grey walls and blinds drawn at the upper windows is the original King's Arms public house, which was acquired by John Joule & Sons of Stone on 30th December 1899. Near right is the Saracens Head public house. On the left, just behind the telegraph pole, is the Toll cottage, demolished around 1930. The A50 enters on the left (from Longton) where the three figures and a dog are standing, and crosses on its way to Blythe Bridge (right) between the two public houses.

Author's collection

CHAPTER 5
1896-1900
'True happiness consists not in the multitude of friends,
But in the worth and choice'
Benjamin Jonson 1573-1637

The bright new year, for the congregation of St John's in Longton, was tempered by a twinge of uncertainty. What would their parish priest, Rev W I Smith do? They would not resent his leaving, but would indeed be sorry to see such a respected and revered friend leave for the Antipodes to continue his ministry. But the decision was finally made:

The parochial branches of the Lichfield Diocesan Church of England Temperance Society in the Stoke archdeaconry have presented the Rev W I Smith with the society's gold badge and an illuminated address on his leaving for Australia.

The Rev W I Smith left Longton on Wednesday morning having previously officiated at an early celebration of Holy Communion at which there were over 200 communicants. The Rev W I Smith, former rector of St John's, sailed for Australia by the ORIENT line today.

But even without the Rev Smith, progress really was in the air in Longton. The Duke of Sutherland was enthusiastically involved with a project that would leave the town with one of its finest buildings, although the proposed original site was not the one it finally occupied.

Site of the New Free Library: The site will be the vacant land on the Stone Road at the junction of Rosslyn Road and Cromartie Street. The new library (Sutherland Institute) is to cost £8,000!

But:

As it was found the first site between Rosslyn Road and Cromartie Street first offered by the Duke for the purposes of a Free Library and Technical School would in some ways be unsuitable, His Grace, upon learning this, at once wrote offering an adjoining site. This lies between Stone Road and Cliveden Place and Rosslyn Road and contains 3700 square yards, or nearly double the area of the other plot.

It is interesting to recall that until the new library was built, the better-off townspeople of Longton and Meir allowed those who wished to read into their own homes; a noble gesture that must have led to some unforeseen circumstances.

Ask anyone who lives on Sandford Hill what they think of the place and you will be bowled over by their loyalty, but in the last few years of the 19th century it was not exactly Eldorado. What they needed above all else was discussed in early January 1896:

> *A meeting was held on Monday evening to consider what steps should be taken towards building a permanent church to take the place of a temporary structure at Sandford Hill (an offshoot of St John's) which was damaged by a recent storm. It is estimated that the amount required will be about £5000 exclusive of site. Subscriptions will be received by the Rev T L Murray.*

The collecting tins were out on many a street corner once more.

Mercifully, the previous biting winter of 1895 was not repeated; quite the reverse. For any gentleman naturalist out and about in early 1896, with their net and killing jar at the ready, the sight of a summer visitor must have been a red letter day:

> *During the mild spell at the end of last week, 2 butterflies were caught at Normacot. They were of the tortoiseshell species (Vanessa urticae), the handsome insect with rich mottlings of black and chestnut brown - which is only less plentiful in the summer than the common white butterfly.*   25th January 1896

In the Meir, one indication of its expansion was the interest shown in land coming on the market - the first of what would be an insatiable appetite for its rolling pastures, which during the next fifty years would become greatly depleted:

> *For Sale: Three freehold fields or closures of meadow and pasture land situate on the NE side of Meir lane in the occupation of Mr J Hodkinson. The bidding rose from £1000 to £1750 at which price the property was purchased.*
>
> April 4th 1896

Local newspaper reporters were often assigned, as part of their training, and much to their dismay, to attend the deliberations of the local councils. At nearby Weston Coyney, the chairman, finding himself in the midst of a furious row, appeared to handle the meeting with great aplomb:

> *A monthly meeting of the Caverswall Parish Council was held at Weston Coyney on Monday evening, Mr J Marson presiding. There was a scene of disorder at the commencement of the meeting. Mr R Jones complained that at the end of the last meeting, Mr J Hughes called him a fool and as a parting shot on leaving the room, the Council, a lot of blackguards and he appealed to the chairman to call on Mr Hughes to withdraw these offensive remarks. The chairman said what passed between Mr Jones and Mr Hughes was a private matter and that he would have nothing to do with it. Mr Jones retorted that he would stop the minutes being read till this matter was cleared up and addressing the chairman said, 'If you don't give me courtesy, you are not worthy of the position you occupy. You want taking where your parents took you when you were a lad and*

putting under the pump to cool your energy. You are insulting the urban members in occupying the seat as you do!'

On an appeal by Mr J Shaw & Mr W Forrester, Mr Hughes withdrew the remark and the withdrawal was accepted by Mr Jones. A wordy and ill-tempered discussion ensued, the accuracy of the minutes being challenged. In the business proper of the Board there was absolutely no point of public interest, the members dispersing within 5 minutes of the passing of the records of the previous meeting.

Elsewhere, local worthies directed their energies more usefully to the plight of the infirm in the hospital with donations of gifts:

At the Cottage Hospital monthly meeting of directors, the following people gave the following gifts: Rhubarb from Lady Manningham-Buller: Mr Prince-firewood: Mr Emony - old linen: Miss Nixon - coal & sticks: Mrs Southerton-cucumbers & jellies.

But in the Meir it was summer; birds were singing in the green leaved trees along Meir Lane by the church and the annual round of fun for the children was just starting:

On Monday the children of the Sunday School in connection with the Holy Trinity Church, which is a chapel of ease to the mother church of Caverswall, had their annual treat at Shooter's Hills by the kindness of Mr A B Bailey. The Werrington Brass Band supplied the music. Before dispersing they all gave cheers for the Rev J E & Mrs Carey, Mr Bailey and all those who had contributed to their entertainment.. 4th July 1896

The year had its usual sadness and tragedy as well. Rev J G Addenbrooke officiated in February at the funeral of Mrs Goddard, widow of the late Samuel Palmer Goddard MD; whilst, for what now seem petty offences, a young girl's life slipped away, weighed down with guilt:

Minnie Swetmore aged 14 years drowned herself in Rough Close Pool; she had been in trouble for taking a neighbour's watch and a trifling debt for cakes at a shop.

And:

Yesterday a man was found in the Meir Tunnel about 200 yards from the Normacot entrance. His head was shockingly injured and his right arm was severed from his body. He proves to be Emmanual Shaw, for several years he was the manager of the Upper Bull's Head, Cheadle for Messrs J Joule and Sons of Stone Brewery. His body was removed to the Cottage hospital. At the inquest a week later, the verdict, 'Suicide, while of unsound mind' was brought in.

Life often seems to reward the do-gooder unfairly. At St Gregory's R C Church,

Longton, a piece of pure gallantry by the parish priest led to his 'downfall':

Father Stringfellow in allowing a lady to pass on to the platform slipped from his seat and sustained leg injuries that required surgery.

But some local clerics did better:

Dresden Parish Church held 5 services on the same day for which the collection amounted to nearly two thousand eight hundred coins of value £58 12s 2 d

5th July 1896

And as the final curtain of the year came down, some worked hard for their gains:

A grand 'rainbow' bazaar which will be opened in the Town Hall by the Duchess of Sutherland is in aid of the new mission church at Sandford Hill. This splendid effort was being made by Rev T L Murray.

Christmas at Holy Trinity meant the usual celebrations, enhanced by an amusement simple in its style but loved by everyone. For the folk of the Meir, a walk to Longton and a visit to the theatre was a treat anticipated for weeks:

The Queen's Theatre: 'Cinderella' was performed and produced by Messrs. Hardie and Van Leer Company. The "Theatrograph", an exhibition of annotated pictures is a great attraction.

January 1897

But unfortunately the weather was in character:

Gales and driving snow swept across the kingdom today. Heavy snows fell in many places and the wind being below freezing point, streets and roads were soon icebound

And by the 30th of the month little had changed:

The wintry weather which had set in on the 15th January continued during the week and the temperature was low.

The Prince and Cinderella were replaced by a feline favourite in early February.

The pantomime at the Queen's Theatre was 'Sir Richard Whittington and his Cat' which is produced by Messrs. George B Philips and Company.

Early in the year, a builder connected with Holy Trinity had fallen on hard times:

The matter of H Inskip: the debtor came up for his adjourned examination at Stoke Bankruptcy courts yesterday before Mr Marshall, the registrar. The debtor was formerly connected with a firm of builders at Longton.

In Longton, the plans to build the new library inched forward:

Plans of the Sutherland Institute went on view on Wed. & Thursday. 22 sets of plans were sent in and adjudicated by Mr Gilbert Scott. The premiums of £75 and £25 have both been awarded to Messrs. Wood & Hutchins of Tunstall - three assessors considering their designs more commensurate with the estimate of £8000. He however criticised the entrance and that the laboratory faced south .

And a local printer was given a regal accolade:

Arthur J Harber, of the firm Hughes and Harber's[1], art printers Longton, has had the very real honour of being appointed printer by Royal Warrant to his Royal Highness, the Prince of Wales.

With Queen Victoria's Diamond Jubilee approaching, various bodies were formed throughout the country, to plan their celebrations for the momentous occasion. The Meir was not to be outdone:

At a meeting of the committee formed to make arrangements for the celebration of the Jubilee - Mr Heath presiding - it was decided to provide tea to all the children less than 15 years, to the older people older than 55 years and to all widows residing at the Meir.

Fortunately the parties missed August, when the heavens opened:

Violent thunder storms plagued the Potteries; there was the greatest fall in 25 years.

But the clouds rolled away, and for those in Sandford Hill there was some good news:

Though money is still required, it is hoped that the building of St Chad's Mission Church at Sandford Hill will begin in a short time. The Rev T L Murray, who is in charge of the Mission has returned to duty after a long holiday and was welcomed at a social gathering at St John's School room.

Not everyone would be so pleased about Rev T L Murray's return though:

There were objections to a licence to John Joule & Sons of a public house close to the site of the new mission of St Chad's on Sandford Hill.

The outbreak of a major epidemic of diphtheria in Longton made life even harder than usual for many. Longton still had the highest infant mortality in the administrative County with a death rate of 229 per 1000 live births. These appalling statistics were blamed in a local paper at the time on unfeeling mothers and incredibly not the insanitary conditions!

In Victorian times, a benefit commonly bestowed by a person of financial standing was called 'a dole', whereby a specified sum of money was invested and the interest on it provided a few needy souls with help during desperate times. One such was the gift of Mr William Webberley of Meir House opposite Holy Trinity church:

The distribution of Mr William Webberley's dole was performed on St Thomas' day by the rector of St James' parish. The distribution took place in the vestry after a short service to widows not in receipt of alms: 15 half sovereigns and 30 5 shillings were distributed; £15 7s 6d in all.

At a time when the annual salary of a clerk to the school board was £210, if each major recipient had ten shillings and sixpence, the gift was certainly of real benefit.

The year 1898 started with a mild spell; very mild if compared with that of early 1897:

> *The thermometer maintains a level more suitable to a period much nearer Mid-summer and building operations have gone on uninterruptedly since Christmas, the men working in their shirt sleeves in the open air.* February 20th 1898.

There always seems to be a church somewhere in need of funds for repairs or restoration! Likewise, there is always a pool of fantastic fundraising ladies who knit, sew, bake, make chutney and turn their hands to a thousand things domestic for ecclesiastical purposes. They put their talents to good use during February:

> *A grand bazaar to help with the restoration of the Old Church* (St John's) *was held in the Town Hall; the proceeds amounted to £656 and after expenses the fund will be £600 up.*

While in April, there was a sale of work on Stone Road for the new church of St Mary & Chad, the *'foundation stone of which was laid last week'*, while in Longton, building would soon be under way as the construction of the library began:

> *Messrs Tompkinson and Bettelley of Longton got the tender for the Sutherland Institute. the amount of the contract was £8247².*

Never before had brothers been together as clergymen in the parish of Caverswall; with the departure of the incumbent at the Meir, this was about to change:

> *The Reverend Charles Addenbrooke has been appointed to the curacy of Holy Trinity, the Meir vacant through the resignation of the Rev J E Carey.*

The parish took John Addenbrooke's eccentric brother to their hearts and he was the driving force for many ambitious projects, not only connected with church activities. Charles launched classes in the Meir which enabled many to learn to read and write; a precursor of Dr Tawney and his colleagues.

The world was changing fast, and in the Meir there was further evidence of innovation. Let there be light!

> *With the adoption of the Lighting Act and fixing of 10 lamps - 2 in Station Road, 1 in the Avenue and 7 in Meir Lane - it will lead to a better atmosphere for those living in the Meir. The Gas Manager had given an estimate the cost of laying down the 10 lamps would be £37 10s 0d and the annual expenditure would be £16 for the gas and £9 for the lighters. This would be equal to a 3d rate for the first year and afterwards a 3 ½ d rate. There was an objection to only partial lighting by several present.* June 18th 1898

One suspects that the '£9 for the lighters' referred to the cost of paying someone to turn on the gas and light the lamp and the reverse, every day of the year - 730 times - quite a bargain.

By the end of July it was decided that St James' Church Longton, closed since the 24th July for renovation, could be used for weddings. Presumably falling plaster and masonry would miss the wedding parties, but not the regulars! It was reopened in October when the schoolboys from the church school won the swimming trophy. The cost of repairs left St James' with a hefty bill for £828. A familiar course of action was called for - a bazaar:

> *The deficit on the balance held by the church was considerable and so a bazaar was planned for January 1900.*

Suddenly, the whole area was awash with sand and mortar again. While St James was being spruced up, building was progressing at the Sutherland Institute in Longton and at St Mary & Chad's, Sandford Hill.

> *The consecration of St Mary & Chad will be performed by the Bishop of Lichfield on the following Wednesday. Following the ceremony there will be a public luncheon at St Chad's Hall at which Colonel Hughes CD CMG will preside.*
>
> November 1898

And as a direct result of the consecration, the parish of Caverswall made an adjustment to its area. It was announced:

> *In October, the vicar consented to surrender Adderley Green to the parish of SS Mary & Chad and to receive in exchange, a block from Forrester Street to the railway bridge, Wharf Street, Longton.*

The last year of the nineteenth century began spectacularly. Brass bands, dignitaries, champagne and vast crowds turned out to cheer a triumph of British engineering -'*The launch of the Oceanic of the White Star line at a cost of £600,000 and of 28,000 tons displacement.*' She was the stable mate of the ill-fated Titanic in which Hanley born Captain Edward John Smith and 1500 other souls would slip beneath the icy waters of the North Atlantic in April 1912.

During November, a drowning accident, involving an eight year old boy, made the newspapers. Thomas Barker's death touched even the hardest of hearts in the Meir:

> *On Monday evening at a concert held at the Meir Board Schools, in aid of the Sunday School Building Fund, - Mr T B Cull presiding, certificates of the Royal Humane Society were presented to Charles Henry Barker and John Harvey respectively. Barker's certificate was "In Memoriam" of his son, Thomas aged 8 years who lost his life nobly endeavouring to save that of his younger brother, Willie who had fallen into a pond at the Meir. The other was in recognition of distinguished bravery in gallantly rescuing William Barker. The presentation was made by Mrs Alfred Mear. The Rev Charles Addenbrooke spoke on the work of*

the Royal Humane Society and took occasion to mention the efforts being made to free Meir church from debt. They had, he said, a generous offer from Mr Cartwright, one of the trustees of £67.10s - being half the debt - if they would make up their share, of which some £15 or £16 had yet to be subscribed. Mr Cartwright had further promised to make his donation up to £100 in 2 years. This, he added, should encourage others to assist in the project.   28th January 1899

In February 1899, on Sandford Hill, the church now received the authority of the printed word:

The Church of Saint Mary & Chad: The London Gazette of yesterday (Friday) night states that the Queen has ratified the scheme of the Ecclesiastical Commissioners for the assignment of a consolidated chapelry to the church of SS Mary & Chad, Longton in the new parish of St John the Baptist, Lane End, Longton , the same to be named the consolidated chapelry to the church of SS Mary & Chad, Longton.

The prodigious amount of money raised by the various local churches was vastly disproportionate to the wages of those who attended. Huge financial debts were amassed but in nearly all cases they were quickly whittled down.

Across the road from SS Mary and Chad's Church, Sandford Hill, a new headmaster had arrived:

Mr Horton has been appointed as Headmaster of the Woodhouse Schools in succession to Mr Gadsby at a guaranteed salary of £200 per year!

While a nearby colleague at Queensbury Schools in Normacot, Mr H E Baxter, would toil all year for £85 as a woodwork instructor. This was not a great deal when compared with the cost of a popular bicycle of the time, 10 guineas for a Rudge Whitworth "Standard"; or you could splash out on a "Special" for 15 guineas - which would take almost a fifth of the above teacher's annual wage.

With the increasing number of worshippers in the Meir, it was not unexpected news to learn that another church was to be erected. And once more, it was the gallant Duke who generously released a piece of land, now at the junction of the A5035 and A50 at the western end of the town:

The Duke of Sutherland has promised a site for the Meir Methodist New Connexion Chapel in Meir Road. The site is opposite the present iron chapel.

11th March 1899

Many of the parishioners of SS Mary & Chad had pencilled in July as the month in which their new church would be ready for occupation. What a fine building it was[3]:

The Rev T L Murray was on Saturday inducted by the Bishop of Lichfield as the

*first vicar of the newly formed parish of Saint Mary & Chad, Sandford Hill which
is to meet the spiritual needs of a rapidly extending part of the Borough of
Longton, that has been carved out of the parish of St John's. The net value of the
'living' is only £92 a year.*   10th June 1899

With a salary of only £7 a year more than the poor woodwork master at Queensbury, it
was obviously not a position in which the incumbent could live the high life.

High summer came and with it the sound of wood on willow throughout the land; the
redoubtable W G Grace was performing the feats that would ensure him a permanent
place in the hearts of the cricketing faithful and 'Wisden':

*Dr W G Grace has taken 5 wickets for 23 runs out of 24 overs, 14 maidens in
the match M.C.C. & Ground versus Staffordshire.   Well played sir!*

But the very fine weather had led to a drought which had serious consequences for
other sportsmen. One man's meat was another man's poison.

*The drought affected the bowls match when Stone played Longton at the
Dunrobin Hotel last week.*

Things really were getting serious when the local bowls match was threatened!

It was at this time that a new form of transport was being promised to the residents of
Meir:

*The extension of the tramways to Meir and Blythe Bridge were looked forward
to with great interest.*

If the price of a bicycle was too much for most then the coming of the trams to this rural
community stuck on top of a hill at the Meir would have been of more than just a
passing interest. Very few regularly ventured out of the district and then it was only on
special occasions, often associated with the churches, to visit exciting places like
Sandon and Betley!

Yet once in a while, a trip to far away Liverpool, like the one from Normacot
church, was contemplated avidly; but it was the exception. Now, the time was not long
off when they would ride not walk, and with the dawn of mass public transportation,
little did they realise that perhaps the seeds of their own destruction had been sown.

September, as always at Holy Trinity, brought the glorious round of thanksgiving *'for
all these gifts around us'*, when almost all the produce would have been homegrown;
the advent of tinned ravioli adorning church window sills was still a long way off!

*The harvest festival was held on Sunday (24th Sept 1899) and the church was
crowded at each service. In the morning the sermon was preached by the Rev A
Paice, the vicar of Hartshill, and at the evensong, the Rev A E Brise-Owen,
rector of Stone occupied the pulpit. The anthems were "O Lord how manifold"*

> & *"Ye shall dwell". The church was tastefully decorated. The offerings which will be devoted to the new Sunday Schools Building Fund realised upwards of £40.*

Hardly had one lot of mortar dried before they were planning ahead again. Although undoubtedly suffering from fundraising fatigue by now, the gallant congregation had their sights set on a further goal. Just before Christmas 1899, another milestone was reached:

> *On Thursday afternoon, Miss Child of Stallington Hall laid the foundation stone of the new organ chamber at Holy Trinity church, the Meir which was estimated to have cost £205. The congregation have acquired the old organ of St John's church, Longton at the very moderate price of £20 and it is proposed to expend an additional £30 in erecting, repairs and tuning. A short service was held in the church, the clergy present being the Venerable archdeacon of Stoke, the Revs J G Addenbrooke (vicar of Caverswall) C Addenbrooke (curate in charge) W B Hunter and J Holford.*
>
> *At the site, Mr Heath, having presented Mrs Child with a silver and ivory trowel in the name of the congregation, the stone was laid. The archdeacon, in an address, said they had done well in choosing that the stone should be laid by Mrs Child, who represented a family full of honour and good working in the district & whose name was famous not only in Staffordshire but almost throughout England. She was also the daughter of one who took a very leading part in the promotion of church music in his generation. A collection in aid of the organ fund was placed on the stone and thus concluded the proceedings.*

This of course would have left St John's, Longton without an organ and they obviously had a replacement quickly lined up. By the end of the same month it had been plumbed in; its greater cost a measure of the difference in the size of the congregation between the Meir & Longton:

> *The new organ at St John's was used for the first time at evensong on Christmas Eve, the organist Mr J H Bamber officiating. The organ has cost £400. It is of pneumatic action and has three manuals and thirty four stops. Mellow and powerful in tone, it cannot fail to enhance the services of praise at this church. The organ is to be dedicated on the 11th proximo and the Rev T H Spinney FCO will give a recital on this occasion. The old organ has been sold to Holy Trinity, the Meir, where an organ chamber is being built for its reception.*   30th December 1899

Living in the rural community of the Meir, it would have been difficult to realise that this country was involved in a bloody war in South Africa; many men fought and died there. Aid was given willingly for the troops. To assist with War Relief, local people staged events to help *'our boys fighting the Boers'*; *Mr & Mrs A Bailey held a successful concert at Rough Close on behalf of the War Relief Fund.* Misses Gertie and

May Averill of Bourne House, Blythe Bridge, gave £50 to the fighting fund. One campaign at home to which everyone could contribute was launched by a clever piece of advertising:

Vinolia Soap: Vinolia War Fund
4,000 guineas have already been forwarded - one halfpenny is sent on every tablet sold, to soldiers' families, widows and orphans

With 240 pence to the pound and 21 shillings to the guinea, the donation and the sales were obviously enormous.

Local men, fighting with 'Brabant's Horse' in South Africa, would soon be joined by more. One of these, PC W Bird, stationed at Longton, *having been called out to rejoin his regiment, the 1st South Staffs, was presented with a gift of £2 4s which was added to the guinea from the Longton "send-off" Fund.*

He would not be alone, for as the patriotic constable went south, the mobilisation gathered momentum:

On Wednesday, upwards of 50 men belonging to the 4th Battalion (Militia) North Staffs Regiment (late 3rd Staffordshire Militia) left Longton for Stoke, where they joined other contingents from the Potteries towns and were conveyed by special trains to Lichfield. The Militiamen were cheered as they steamed out of the station at Stoke.   20th January 1900

Sadly, for some, the gesture, however noble, was too late:

The death is announced of Robert Wooldridge of the 67 Battery, Royal Field Artillery who died from disease at Ladysmith on the 8th February 1900; the deceased was the son of Mr Joseph Wooldridge of Foley, Longton.

The benevolence some firms showed towards their workers was reassuring in such uncertain times. With the lengthening days, an event which was becoming increasingly common took place - the works outing. Messrs Tompkinson & Bettelley (who constructed the chancel of Holy Trinity Church and the Sutherland Institute, Longton), took their staff away for the day:

The annual outing took place on Saturday to London. The party, numbering 300, went the Midland route via Derby. They were accompanied by Mr H Tompkinson and Mrs Tompkinson, Mr W & Miss Bettelley, Mr W Brain and Mr J G Andus, who was Hon Sec for the trip.The weather was fine and greatly enjoyed. Many of the visitors stayed in London for the weekend. The day excursionists started on the return journey at 12.20 am and arrived home at 5.00am.   23rd June 1900

A journey which was not that much slower than today!

The Rev T C and Mrs Bradberry left the parish of Caverswall in early August and at a touching presentation, their efforts were rewarded when they were presented with the usual *'handsome marble clock and a tea service'* from Hulme, whilst from Werrington came, *'a set of robes and a travelling basket.'*

The guiding hand of Mrs W E Bowers was at work in September again when a trained nurse was appointed for the parish of Holy Trinity:

And in December, the Duchess of Sutherland was to involve herself in yet more fundraising for the deserving and disadvantaged in the area:

Meir New Schools and Institute: the Duchess of Sutherland has kindly arranged to provide a dramatic performance and concert at Stoke on the 12th and 13th proximo: half the proceeds to go to the new schools and working men's institute at the Meir, and the other half to go to the pottery cripples guild.

Notes.
1. Later in the year they were to move into new premises in Market Street.
2. By comparison the Dunrobin Hotel on the Stone Road, out of Longton (now the A5005) owned by Messrs John Joule & Sons cost between £7000 and £8000; the bowling green there was opened on Wednesday 25th June 1898.
3. Through mining subsidence, eighty years later, the church closed for safety reasons. After having the roof line lowered it was returned to service.

The Sutherland Institute in Longton was built mainly to serve as a library between 1897 and 1899. The builders were Messrs Tompkinson and Bettelley of Longton.

St James' Church, Longton. Built in 1832-34 for the rapidly growing population of the burgeoning Longton, it is a large and imposing building.

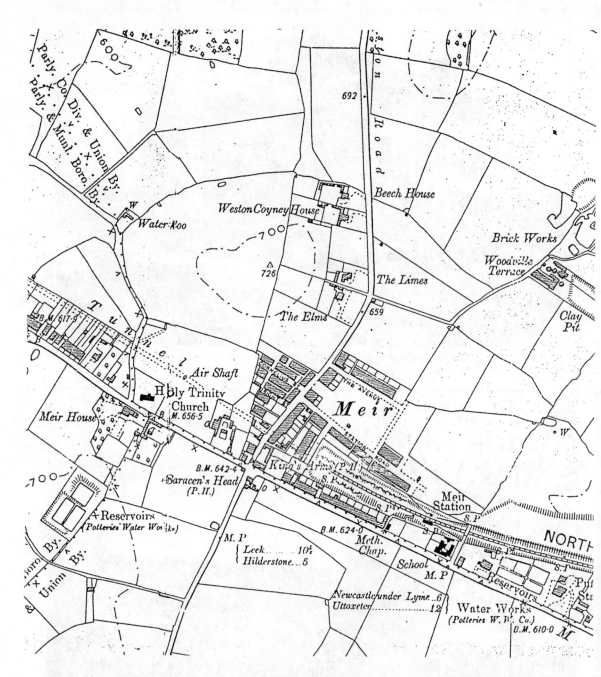

Map of 1901 showing many of the recents developments in the Meir including Holy Trinity and the railway station. Compare this with maps of 1925 and 1935 on pages 145/146 and 187 - 189 respectively. They illustrate the rapid expansion of Meir over 40 years.

In 1901, Woodville Terrace, a superb example of Victorian building erected in 1886, still stands in splendid isolation and people walked from Meir via this to Caverswal which is just off picture to the upper right.

CHAPTER 6
1901-1905
'What's lost upon the roundabouts, we pulls up on the swings'

Patrick Chalmers 1872-1942

For those caught up in the Boer War[1] in South Africa, the New Year 1901, meant the beginning of a period of uncertainty for them and their families. In spite of this, many local men still had no hesitation in 'joining the colours.' In a chivalrous age, it was the honourable thing to do:

PC Glennie stationed at Longton for 2½ years has gone to South Africa to be a trooper[2] with General Baden-Powell's police. January 15th 1901

It was not just death by bullet or shell that lay in wait for the troops, but also disease and primitive battlefield medical treatment. Surgical and anaesthetic techniques were still in their infancy. But even here at home, nothing could be guaranteed:

An accident occurred at Longton Cottage Hospital as a result of a chloroform anaesthetic ....

The death of Queen Victoria united the country in grief when she passed away in January at Osborne House on the Isle of Wight. As a mark of respect the '*occupants of Longton lowered the blinds in their houses.*'

March 1901 saw the irrepressible Mrs W E Bowers rallying her troops for an 'offensive' on the home front.

In the neighbouring district of the Meir, (Caverswall Parish) arrangements are in progress for a sale of work in the grounds of Caverswall Castle in June by invitation of Mr & Mrs Bowers. The proceeds will be for the Meir Sunday School and Institute Building Fund.

While just before Easter at a newly completed church in the area, they held the first of many confirmations to be held there in coming years:

The Bishop of Lichfield, held a confirmation service at SS Mary & Chad's, Sandford Hill. There were 120 candidates: 42 from SS Mary & Chad's, 40 from St John's & 38 from St. James.

And in a distant corner of the Empire, a local 'old boy' showed no matter how many miles lay between him and Longton, he still had his old parish in his thoughts:

The Rev W I Smith, the former rector of St John's was in New Zealand as a Labour Commissioner appointed by the New South Wales Government to study social conditions in the colony. He is going to send £5 for a new church window.

6th April 1901

It was none too soon, for in early August, news that St John's was to be refurbished by Messrs Battison & Bridgett was disclosed - *'services were to be held in the schools'*

The scene in Caverswall on the 18th July of that year must have been a sight to behold. Months of meticulous planning by the ladies deployed by Mrs Bowers had been well spent in an effort to raise funds for the proposed new Institute.

A garden party and sale of work took place on Thursday in the grounds of Caverswall castle by the kind permission of Mr & Mrs Bowers, the object being to assist a fund which has been inaugurated for the purposes of erecting a building to be used in connexion with Holy Trinity Church, the Meir as a Sunday School & Men's Institute as well as for holding Bible classes, concerts and various meetings. In view of the large and increasing population of the Meir, such a building has been found essential to the proper carrying on of church work and a fund has been opened to provide the necessary means. It is estimated at the building will cost about £1300 towards which £600 has already been raised.

The picturesque and pleasantly situated castle with its beautiful grounds made an ideal spot for a garden party affording as it did, pleasant shelter from the hot rays of the sun. A marquee had been erected in the shelter of the trees just below the castle and in this, stalls had been arranged and with Miss Ethel Aynsley as Hon Sec with other ladies having brought together a large assortment of goods. The stalls and stallholders were as follows;

> *No.1: Mrs Bowers and friends.*
>
> *No.2: Meir Congregational Stall; Mrs S Mear, Mrs J G Aynsley, Mrs Ashwell, Mrs Barlow,*
> *Mrs A.Cooper, Mrs Middleton & Mrs Radford.*
>
> *No.3: Mrs Burton & Friends, Mrs Hollinson, Mrs Inskip, Mrs Deakin, Miss Eve and members*
> *of the G.F.S (Girls' Friendly Society)*
>
> *No.4: Crockery Stall, Mrs E. Barker, Mrs Chapman, Mrs F H Heath, Mrs W.J.Taylor*
> *& Mrs Wooldridge:*
>
> *No.5 Fruit Stall: Mr & Mrs James Bradbury;*
>
> *No.6:Flower Stall: Mr & Mrs James Ward;*
>
> *No.7: Children's Corner; the Misses Nancy & Gwynne Bowers & friends.*
>
> *No.8: Strawberry & Cream tent:Mrs Lucas and Miss Heath, Mrs Stevenson and Miss Taylor.*

The opening ceremony was performed by Mrs Jas. Heath and amongst those also present were the Rev J G Addenbrooke (vicar of Caverswall) & Mrs Addenbrooke, J G Halford, and Mrs & Miss Meakin. The Reverend J G Addenbrooke in introducing Mrs Heath said they wished to give her a hearty reception. The Meir people had worked excellently in maintaining their church and all that belonged to the church's organisations in the parish and Mrs Heath was doing excellent work in coming down from London that day to open the sale. They very much regretted that Mr Jas. Heath MP was prevented from attending owing to illness.

Mrs Heath, who was heartily received, said she must first of all express her regret that her husband would not be there that day. Unfortunately he had not been at all well lately and the doctors advised him to go abroad, but, he hoped first to finish his parliamentary duties for the session. Mr Heath was always interested in church work and he was sure the building that they proposed to erect would be a great benefit in every way and a most effective way of carrying on church work. She thought that very often some of the best church work was done outside the church itself & certainly this new institution ought to be of great benefit religiously and socially for the whole parish. It always gave her great pleasure to come to North Staffordshire to meet her many friends and she had great pleasure in declaring the sale open amidst such lovely surroundings as had been placed at their disposal by Mr & Mrs Bowers. (Applause)

The Rev C Addenbrooke, in proposing a vote of thanks to Mrs Heath, expressed their sincere thanks for her kindness in helping them with their sale and also signified their appreciation of the kindness of Mr & Mrs Bowers on throwing the grounds open on that occasion. Mr Bowers seconded the vote of thanks which was carried with acclamation. During the day the band of the 1st V B North Staffs Regiment played a selection of music, courts were open for tennis and various amusements were provided, dancing taking place in the evening.

Although the Meir probably had its fair share of lovers of the turf (and still has), the very notion of horse races actually taking place now seems incredible:

There was a very good attendance at the Meir when the Galloway races and sports were held for the first time at the Meir. Among the runners were Bob, Handsome Boy, Lady Tempest, Jim, Fishboy and Surprise.

It would have cost a king's ransom to buy a racehorse in those far off days but failing that you might buy a cart horse for £50 or a Welsh pony for a mere £6 - and start a milk round!

As the year drew to a close, worshippers at Holy Trinity must have been gratified with the results of their labours. In just 11 years, they had raised about £4500 and put up the main church, the new chancel, and the organ chamber. A truly impressive feat for an area that was not overtly prosperous.

The decade, roughly 1900 to 1910, was a watershed between the cessation of the Boer War and the build-up to the Great War. Victoria had gone and a new spirit was abroad in the realm. At the dawn of this Edwardian age, nothing typified the spirit of adventure and heroism more than a small expedition that left England in the summer. Sailing from Cowes amidst great cheering, it steamed southwards for five months. Engaged primarily in scientific exploration, it captured the imagination of the world and there were high hopes of success and advancement.

By November 1901 the ship had been refuelled, taken on fresh provisions and slipped out of Port Chalmers, New Zealand, amidst more celebrations, to traverse the largely uncharted southern ocean - for their destination was Antarctica. For Commander Robert Falcon Scott, the captain of the Discovery it would be three years before they would set foot on English soil again.

Back home, a scheme which had flowered from the germ of an idea by the Bishop for church funds was making slow progress. The Million Shilling Fund (it seemed a mite exaggerated at times) had been instigated a few months before and in the parish of Caverswall they had reached almost 12 guineas!

In another similar, though not exactly rival collection on behalf of the Soldiers and Sailors Families Association, the total had almost reached £36. It was obvious where public sympathy lay and a very public-spirited £227 was raised by a special War Fund Ball, later in the year. Some people just could not do enough for those *'in harm's way'* fighting the foe.

The coronation of King Edward had to be postponed through appendicitis. However the plates of cucumber sandwiches were not entirely wasted, since it signalled the start of another ambitious venture by those at Holy Trinity church:

New Parish Institute at the Meir : The laying of the foundation stones of a Sunday School, Men's Institute and parish room for educational and parochial purposes in connexion with Holy Trinity church, the Meir, took place on Thursday afternoon (15th May 1902). The scheme has been in hand for a number of years having received its first impetus from a legacy bequeathed by the late Mr Henry Hill. The sum has gradually grown by the aid of parochial concerts and while generous help was given by the Caverswall garden party, which realised £240 and the Duchess of Sutherland's entertainment at Stoke in December 1900 when from the proceeds of the splendid performance given on at occasion, the Institute fund participated to the extent of £100. The site has been given by the Duke of Sutherland and is on a plot of land that is contiguous to the church. The opening part of the ceremony took place in the church, the office being that for the laying of foundation stones of a parish building.

The prayers were said by the Rev Charles Addenbrooke, curate in charge and the Venerable Archdeacon Lane gave a brief address. The clergy, choir and congregation having proceeded to the site, the stones were laid as follows:

South west corner stone by Mr W R Parker-Jervis of Meaford Hall (patron of Caverswall); the Henry Hill Memorial Stone in the central bay by Miss Ethel Aynsley (representing Mr John Aynsley of Blythe Bridge); South east corner stone by Mrs J Warren of Belleview, Shrewsbury (formerly of the Meir); The Institute Library Corner Stone by Mrs Stephen Mear of Weston Coyney House.

The builder's contract is for £1,200 and the furnishing will bring the cost up to £1,600; to make up which a further sum of £450 is required. Towards this, subscriptions have been received as follows: the Rev J G Addenbrooke (vicar of Caverswall) £21: Mr W E Bowers £50: the Mayor of Longton, Alderman Bennion £10: Mr Parker-Jones, Mrs James Warren, Mr John Aynsley, Mr J G Aynsley & Mr Stephen Mear £25 each; the Rev Charles Addenbrooke, Mr W Gordon & Mr JH Barlow, £10 each and many other sums . Among those present were the Rev JG Addenbrooke, Rev H.E Beech, Mrs Parker-Jervis, Mrs Brand, Mrs J G Aynsley, Messrs Stephen Mear and Mr J H Barlow (churchwardens) , J F Wardle, F H Heath & W J Taylor (former churchwardens) J Hall, H Ashwell, A Hewitt and W Skelson and many other parishioners and former parishioners. The architect is Mr Thomas Tindall and the contractor Mr Bagnall of Fenton.

A week later, it was recounted that Mr J W Philips of Heybridge has endowed £20 to the above fund as a late contribution. Even weeks later, still it came flooding in:

The offertory at the recent stone-laying together with donations given as promised on the occasion amounted to £154. 4s. Mr J G Aynsley, in addition to his contribution of £25 has kindly promised a donation towards furnishing the building later on. Mr J Capel-Philips of Heath House has sent £10 towards the scheme on condition that nine others should give an equal sum.

It should be added that the Duke of Sutherland generously extended the boundary some forty feet to the north for the purposes of the site, and at the same time gave a valuable strip of land to the east of the church, eighty feet in width fas a site for the parsonage house to be built a some future time.   7th June 1902

Arthur James Balfour became Prime Minster in July, while on a humbler plane, that far-flung cleric, Rev W I Smith had returned from Australia where he was priest at St John's, Sydney, just to talk to the Mothers' Union at St John's, Longton! Perhaps that was where his heart was, as bad as it was in Longton; or was it to get away from the cricket? *'At stumps, Australia were all out for thirty six. V. Trumper scoring 18.'*

It was high summer in England, and far away peace had been signed in the Boer War. The whims of politicians for the moment had ceased to cut a swathe through the youth of two nations. It was a time for celebration abroad and at home. The Coronation of Edward VII finally[4] took place, although it was shortened[5] in deference to His Majesty's wishes. At sleepy Caverswall there were tangible mementoes of the royal

71

occasion:

> *In connection with the Coronation celebration, three commemorative trees were planted in the ancient churchyard at Caverswall - a yew tree by the vicar* (the Rev J G Addenbrooke) *and a variegated sycamore each by Messrs Bowers and Bradbury (churchwardens).*
>
> 13th September 1902

Advent and Christmas beckoned again; a time of love and goodwill but sadly there was no relief from the privations endured by some. Two charities in the area continued to help mitigate the distress:

> *The Henry Hill charity for the benefit of the aged poor was distributed at the Court House on Monday (the birthday of the donor). Each year, the annual interest on £1000 less legacy duty is divided in the proportion of 5 shillings to each person, on this occasion there were 198 recipients, the oldest of whom is 98. The Mayor made the distribution.*

> *The charity left by the late Mr W Webberley for the relief of the poor widows in St James's parish was distributed on St Thomas's day. There were 50 recipients among whom £15 was distributed.*

Admittedly it was a small amount but, for a few perhaps the difference between life and death. It was hard being poor in the reign of Edward VII: a period that saw a great contrast between the haves and the have-nots. The very evident crushing poverty moved members of the local clergy to initiate a scheme for the denizens of Longton and one assumes, also the Meir:

> **Distress in the Borough:** *Not since the hard winter of 1895 has there been anything like the amount of distress in the town which exists at the present time. On the suggestion of the Rev G Oliver it was resolved to ask the churches to give a collection or portion of their collection towards the fund. The Rev S Salt said he had calculated there were 500 needy families in the town and that out of 600 children in the Dresden schools, 1 in 6 came from a home in which the breadwinner was out of work.*

John Aynsley, the grand old man of Longton, once more weighed in with 1000 loaves and 1000 half-pounds of cheese. By the end of February 7750 loaves had been distributed at a cost of £122 18s 9d and there were free breakfasts for children attending elementary schools at the cost of £116 11s 9d for the month.

On Sandford Hill, the church showed the way: '*a soup kitchen was opened at St Mary & St Chad's church*',
and in Longton:

> *On Tuesday and Thursday, over 200 have as much as they can eat with bread while in St James' parish there was about 150 families with 'father doing no work'.*

Given those circumstances, it was all the more extraordinary that the following ever got off the drawing board in January 1903:

It is proposed to build a Wesleyan chapel at the Meir and it was agreed that plans were to be prepared.

At Caverswall, the parishioners were witnessing the end of an era, for having seen through all the complexities of the building of Holy Trinity Church, its chancel, the organ chamber and the Institute, the redoubtable J G Addenbrooke bowed out and bade a fond farewell to them and the quiet, leafy lanes of Caverswall and Meir. Into his shoes, in March 1903, stepped the equally capable Rev M A Fowler M A, who lost no time in getting out and about:

The new vicar, (Rev MA Fowler) has been visiting East Vale and Werrington and a strong link has already been formed between him and the mission churches at these places. The vicar gave a lantern lecture at the Industrial school on the occasion of the distribution of the Sunday school prizes. He was introduced by Mr Horth and met with a very cordial reception.

Later in the summer, he preached at the 139th anniversary of the dedication of St John's, Longton, at the evening service.

In April, most of Meir turned out for yet another important local church affair and grand ceremony:

The new Sunday School, Men's Institute and parish room for Holy Trinity church, the Meir were formally opened on Thursday (2nd April 1903). The Institute scheme received its first impetus from a legacy of £225 bequeathed by the late Mr Henry Hill. The sum was gradually increased by the aid of parochial concerts etc., while generous help was given by the garden party at Caverswall which realised £240 and the Duchess of Sutherland's entertainment at Stoke Theatre on that occasion, the institute fund participated to the extent of £100. The site was a gift from the Duke of Sutherland that is contiguous to the church. The foundation stones were laid in May last year by Mr W R Parker-Jervis, patron of the mother church of Caverswall, Miss Ethel Aynsley (representing Mr John Aynsley), Mrs J Warren (formerly of the Meir) and MrStephen Mear.

The opening ceremonies[6] were performed on Thursday by Lady Manningham-Buller and the Mayor of Longton (Alderman G Bennion). In the course of the proceedings, the Rev Charles Addenbrooke, curate-in charge, stated that the building had involved an outlay of £1600, towards which £1280 had been raised. During the proceedings, further donations of 5 guineas were announced from Lady Manningham-Buller and the Mayor. The building has been erected by Mr Bagnall of Fenton from designs by Mr Thomas Tindall, architect of Longton.

After all this hurly-burly it must have been something of an anticlimax for the incumbent to return to more mundane duties:

> *Holy Trinity vestry meeting was held on Tuesday evening (21st April 1903) at the parish Institute, the Rev Charles A Addenbrooke presiding. Mr Stephen Mear and Mr J H Barlow were re-elected and thanked for their past services.*

But in a few months the parish of Caverswall was to bid farewell to the remaining Addenbrooke:

> *The Bishop of the Diocese has preferred the Rev Charles Addenbrooke, curate-in-charge of the Meir to the living of St Chad's, a new parish in the Borough of Smethwick. The foundation stone of the new church of St Chad was laid a few years ago by the Earl of Dartmouth with masonic rites.*

And so in October of that year came the affectionate farewell;

> *The Rev Charles Addenbrooke preferred to St Chad's Smethwick has been presented with two large photographs of himself, one to take with him and the other to hang in the Institute at the Meir, plus a smokers' complete outfit. The presentation was made by Mr W Bowers, Mr Stephen Mear presiding.*

In between these events, a new stained glass window was unveiled in St Peter's, Caverswall by the eminent Mr W Parker-Jervis who was probably only a little less well known to the population of the area than a man who was visiting nearby Stafford at the time:

> *Colonel W F Cody (Buffalo Bill) and his Wild West Show will appear at a one day show on 10 thJune 1903 in Stafford. Prices of admission: 1s. 2s. 3s. 4s. with a box seat at 5s and 7/6d.*

For many the prices must have been entirely out of reach!

The summer of 1903 was, putting it mildly, disappointing. Despite the weather, the perpetual givers of the area were helping those much worse off than themselves, through the coffers of an account specifically devised for this purpose:

> *On Saturday upwards of 400 poor children were entertained in the park through the medium of "Pearson's Fresh Air Fund", about £16 being allocated to Longton. Each child had a meat pie and a buttered scone and a lunch cake. As they left each child received a bath bun and an orange.*

Pearson's Fresh Air Fund[7] was one of many charities for the poor. Its very name conjures up a temporary escape from congested terraced streets and the gloom of industrial England.

At this time and only of course for those thankfully in work, it was reassuring when the church introduced a scheme which would underwrite them and their families against financial hardship if they fell ill. With no government assistance, the consequences of no regular work were dire. It had fallen to the clergy to give what many only a few decades ahead, would look upon as an unalienable right:

A Sick and Dividend Club is being started in connection with St Chad's parish, Sandford Hill. It will be open to all who pass the committee between the ages of 16 & 50. The subscription will be 4d a week and sick pay 5 shillings. A levy of 6d will be made from all in case of death and £2 paid to the nearest relative of the deceased. The dividend will be paid out just before the Wakes.[8]

Those pursuing certain occupations though were automatically insured. Corporal Merry was just such a case; a local fireman and a former serviceman who was killed in the course of his duty, leaving a widow and three children. She was awarded £100. This must have been a Godsend, with no earnings, there was a very real danger of women having to go out to work. This in itself created further social problems which did not escape the resolute scrutiny of one of Sandford Hill's more outspoken clerics in October 1903:

The Rev T L Murray, at an entertainment, mentioned mothers going out to work, which had resulted in young children being left to their own devices, resulting in injuries.

Another New Year saw the charities in great demand again; the 'Henry Hill' giving 132 people 5 shillings each, while John Aynsley's (who celebrated his 80th birthday in December) Gift to the Poor, disbursed the annual interest on £500 to 80 people giving them 5s each.

Although there are many paintings and photographs of the time showing people and their dress, perhaps a more complete illustration is sometimes revealed through narratives of the day:

POLICE REPORT - MISSING PERSON

Frances Eliza Barker aged 18 years, 5 feet tall, stout build, fresh face, sandy brown hair, <u>black mottled blouse, black stockings and laced boots</u> has been missing since the day before Christmas.

As today, the consequences of a young girl missing for a week were sufficient for the police to be 'concerned for her safety'. In October 1898, six years before, Sarah Elizabeth Berresford aged 26 years had been murdered in Meir Hay Fields and on May 21st 1904, Miss Barker was listed as 'still missing.'

The parish of Holy Trinity, the Meir anticipated a new curate in charge in early 1904, a replacement for the much admired Rev Charles Addenbrooke. And musical changes were sought:

An order has been given for a new organ and a very great improvement to the

> *musical portion to the service is looked for through its instrumentality. The Rev Edwin Wheeldon has taken up the duties of curate-in-charge at the Meir, in succession to the Rev Charles Addenbrooke and Mr J W Tait has been appointed evangelist for the East Vale Mission in succession to the Rev J G Halford.*

And at Sandford Hill there were also comings and goings:

> *The Rev F R Briggs, assistant priest of St Mary & Chad, is about to leave the parish after 5 years and the Rev L G Brown succeeds him.*

Earlier in the year, a memorial window, portraying the Annunciation, was blessed. It was to a former curate Rev V Y C Griffith BA, who was killed in an accident. He had been in the parish of SS Mary & Chad for six years.

At a garden fête later in the year, it was announced there was good news; the dramatic reduction of the massive deficit on the building of the church of SS Mary & Chad was nothing short of astonishing. The Rev T L Murray stated that it had, in five years, been cut from £4400 to £1700.

By October SS Mary & Chad's added another two windows to the lady chapel; a gift from the Misses Haines of Adderley Green as a memorial to the late Mrs Haines. All that was left now was the window in the east chapel and *'it was earnestly hoped this would be fulfilled by a voluntary effort on behalf of the congregation.'*

A decision taken in 1903 to build a chapel in the Meir, took a positive step forward with the laying of the foundation stone;

> *The stone laying ceremony took place at the Wesleyan chapel in the Meir, on Thursday and the total estimated cost is £2360. The designs are by Mr T P Hulse and the builders Messrs Tompkinson and Bettelley.*

The same builders would tender for and win the contract to build the Police Station in Longton six months later. The estimated cost was £7000. Mr W H Cheadle the county surveyor and Mr A R Wood of Tunstall were the architects and fourteen firms from as far away as Blackpool and Wolverhampton had tendered.

With a shortage of large public buildings in the Meir, there would be numerous occasions when the Institute was used for purposes for which the parishioners could never have imagined. In July there had been a fatal gun accident involving Mr Harry Ashwell, a partner in British Anchor Pottery and the inquest took place in the Holy Trinity Church Institute! The coroner, Mr C B Cull, brought in a verdict of 'accidental death' - the victim had shot himself with his own shotgun.

As the leaves turned gold in the Meir, some warmed to the possibility of a quick 9 holes. Life was definitely on an upward swing:

MEIR GOLF CLUB

A new club house was opened on Saturday (30th October 1904), Miss Edwards taking the principal part in the opening and presenting the club with a cheque to meet expenses. Among those present were Mr W A Adderley, the Rev the Hon L F Tyrwhitt and the Rev E & Mrs Wheeldon etc. After the opening ceremony, watched with great interest, an exhibition game between W Ulton (Trentham) and J Collins (Pipe Gate) took place.

Situated as it was, just behind the Holy Trinity church, it must have given those at prayer one or two anxious moments when the Club's less able members teed off!

Christmas in the Meir and Longton again and the familiar poverty reflected at the Christmas party in the Town Hall, when twelve hundred and fifty mites attended, ate a slap up meal and left with God's blessing. The changing of the new year from the old meant little: It would be just as hard scratching a living next year, the breakfasts were most welcome though thank you, just the same:

Free breakfasts for 100 poor children on New Year's morning consisted of buttered bread with some warm tea - plus a bun.

The clergy no doubt helped in no small measure to allay people's worries and fears; and the Rev Sam Salt, at the Church of the Resurrection in Dresden, rolled on and on. He had already received a marble clock in late 1889 from Captain Edwards-Heathcote to mark the *'quarter century'* and as recognition of the gratitude for his ministry, the old boy was made a present of £50, but on the strict understanding *'that he had a holiday to recuperate'*. He was in his 73rd year and feeling the strain!

Religion, it seemed, was everywhere in the Meir and an integral part of everyday life. The new Wesleyan church was opened on the 13th April 1905 and was still one of the Meir's more pleasing buildings 50 years later. Another change took place at the Holy Trinity:

The Rev E Wheeldon on leaving the Meir church on his preferment as rector of Biddulph Moor was on Tuesday evening (11th July 1905), presented by his former parishioners with a purse of twenty sovereigns. The Rev H M Fowler, the vicar of Caverswall presided and the presentation was made on behalf of the subscribers by Mr Stephen Mear.

It was to be a season of farewells:

At a meeting at the Church Institute, the Meir on the 15th inst, Mr S P Brander, who for several years has been choirmaster at Holy Trinity church and has now been appointed headmaster of the church schools at Goldenhill, was presented with a handsome clock as a mark of the appreciation of his work in the church.

A new choirmaster would have to be found. But then we read:

Mr Hassell, organist at the Meir church sustained a serious accident on Sunday evening (24th November) while he was taking a thermal bath for a cold, the heating apparatus exploded and he was badly scalded. On Christmas Day it was so bad, it was deemed advisable to remove him to the cottage hospital where he was in a serious condition.

A blow for the choirmaster, the church and its music.

Notes.

1. There was, patriotism apart, great concern expressed in Britain and abroad over the treatment of 75000 Boers, mostly women and children, held in camps after the destruction of their farms by British troops. Mr St John Broderick, Secretary for War, told the House of Commons that the High Commissioner, Sir Alfred Milner, was giving his personal attention to the improvement of their conditions.

2. There were 240000 men under the command of Lord Kitchener, of which one third were mounted troops at that time.

4. The Coronation was delayed as the King had an operation for the removal of his appendix. The ceremony was eventually performed on 9th August 1902.

5. The Coronation service had no sermon and the King did not carry the heavy sword of state. The monarchs walk to the four points of the compass to make a declaration was also dropped. He made them beside his chair. At the end of the service, it was the Archbishop of Canterbury who needed medical attention as he felt faint.

6. A brass tablet commemorating this event is to be found in the corridor joining the new church hall with the church.

7. There was also a Primrose Guild and Watercress Society and the Pleasant Sunday Afternoon Society plus various 'doles' to assist the impoverished.

8. Wakes Week was usually in August.

SS Mary & Chad Church, Sandford Hill.

Longton Cottage Hospital

After descending Meir Road, passing Normacot Church and Longton Cottage Hospital towards Dresden, this scene comes into view. Called Belgrave Road there are as yet no houses above the row of Victorian terraced homes on the right. In the middle distance the spire of the Church of the Resurrection, Dresden, about a mile from Holy Trinity Church, is visible. The Rev. Sam Salt was the parish priest there for over forty years.

Lovatt collection

This is Market Street, Longton, a mile or so from Meir, where many would have bought items unavailable in what was still a village. The beautiful building on the right is the much lamented, Heathcote Arms, with its stone facings and bow window, which was ultimately replaced by an amusement arcade. Two adjacent buildings have survived into the 1990s but are in a sorry state of repair. The facade bearing the legend, 'Salter & Salter' was demolished in 1994 for the extended and renamed Bennett Precinct.

Hill Collection

Taken in the 1920s with its tree lined streets, this charming study by Ernest Warrillow shows Uttoxeter Road Normacot just below its junction with Meir Road. Served by trams until the late 1920s, horse transportation is also evident in this view. Every house on the left and many on the right beyond the tram have been demolished putting paid to what was once a thriving, proud and long-lived community.   *Warrillow Collection*

CHAPTER 7
1906-1909
'Change is not made without inconvenience, even from worse to better'
Samuel Johnson

The news that the wife of Stephen Mear, a local Justice of the Peace who lived at Weston Coyney House the Meir had passed away at home on Sunday 7th January 1906, was received with sadness by all those at Holy Trinity church with whom she had shared a long association. The demise occurred too of the ubiquitous John Aynsley, four times Mayor of Longton, who had helped the needy so much. Born in the reign of George IV and in his prime through the long years of Victoria, he had died at eighty years of age. Years later he was to be remembered by the naming of a road in Meir which was subsequently altered to Leason Road. Some people had short memories.

In Longton there was another long innings: *'The Rev J.Finch-Smith of St Paul's, Edensor[1], was presented with a gold purse to celebrate 25 years of incumbency.'*

For the working population (amongst whom there was a dearth of gold purses) one way of altering their lot in life was via the ballot box. The Labour Party returned a healthy majority in Stoke on Trent in the General Election:

Mr J Ward (Labour)	7660
Mr D H Coghill (Unionist)	4228
Labour majority	3372

Reversing the result of 1900, when the Unionists polled 4932 and Labour 4732 - a slim majority of 200. There is no record if either of the losing parties used the time honoured excuse of the weather:

There were severe thunderstorms on the 7th May which flooded Longton and especially the Crown & Anchor to a depth of 4 feet as well as the cellars in the Eagle pub and the 'Gents' in the Town Hall.

Those drinkers who claimed the local brew was watered down (or something less polite) could now make the accusation truthfully. Amazingly, the Meir and Blythe Bridge taverns escaped it all and had literally only a *'sprinkling'*.

Meir church had no vicarage at at time, but the clergy visiting the Meir from Caverswall did have the use of a house at 81 Weston Road, the Meir as a residence. They must have felt a twinge of pique on hearing that St James Church, Longton was to be endowed with a new dwelling. The site, on land opposite to Old Longton High School, was in Trentham Road, Longton. At a cost of £1700, it was a replacement for their previous dilapidated vicarage, set alight during the Chartist Riots of 1842. This time they would be sure to keep up the premiums on the fire insurance.

One member of the clergy who did not really need a vicarage, since he was almost never at home, was the Rev T L Murray whose meanderings amongst fellow clerics were varied and far ranging. Noted for his breaks from the parish, no doubt deserved, his voyages seemed endless. But he had without doubt gone just that little bit too far in the midsummer of 1906:

The Rev T L Murray, vicar of St Mary & Chad, Sandford Hill was arrested in San
Lorenzo by Italian police on suspicion of being an Austrian spy.

Mercifully detained for only a short while, he was allowed to carry on with his holiday, no doubt contemplating that had he stayed in East Fenton, this would never have happened.

In Dresden, at the Church of the Resurrection, parishioners voiced misgivings concerning the frailty of their priest, the Rev Sam Salt. So much so, early in 1907, they finally persuaded him after forty years to call it a day. It was inevitable that with his death in April in the same year, the parish of Dresden would turn out in force to pay their final respects to their old friend, priest and counsellor. A successor had to be found and Rev R M Thompson, a former vicar of Holy Trinity, Hanley for over a decade, was chosen from many.

There was a spirit of comradeship amongst that generation, especially in the church and in community activities, which had diminished markedly thirty years on. Especially prominent was the interactive endeavour found in sports and outdoor pursuits. Baden-Powell was a guiding light in this and the following year he visited Hanley to spread the Scouting creed.

Contrary to popular belief, this did not consist solely of tying knots (useful though that might be at times) and making smoky and indescribable meals. Many of the youngsters who joined came from poor city homes where clean air and light were in short supply and the great appeal of the scouts was the prospect of days of fun in the back of beyond with a few pals; and the change did them a power of good. The scouts from St Mary and Chad's, Sandford Hill went to Llanfairfechan in Wales where, *'it benefited the lads and men in health and morally'*. It was not uncommon for a boy to put on 10 lbs in weight in just 10 days due to better nutrition, fresh air and exercise! The effects of deprivation on the human frame at the turn of this century were dramatic.

In February 1907, not to be left out of all this, the Lad's Brigade attached to Holy Trinity church, joined the scouts movement.

Towards the conclusion of a traumatic year for the Longton parishes, St Paul's at Edensor lost its priest, the Rev C Finch-Smith. And just before Christmas they were almost separated from the vicar of St John's (bike clips and all) on whom God was fortunately looking favourably:

The Rev G Oliver was riding his bicycle out of a road at Fenton on Wednesday when he was knocked over by another car from another direction whilst trying to avoid an oncoming car. He was thrown off and sustained a cut to the head and a severe shaking.

In the Meir, goodwill and gestures abounded:

Mr J H Barlow has promised to give a handsome pulpit to the Meir church. the only proviso is that sufficient money be collected for cleaning the church by the Harvest Festival. Holy Trinity, the Meir, is the daughter of the mother parish of Caverswall.

Mr Barlow 's wife was not to be outdone:

Mrs Barlow and Mrs Hewitt of Lightwood have kindly taken over the secretaryship of the Needlework Guild and it is confidently anticipated that those who generously assisted the late Mrs Bowers will continue their gifts to the guild.   11th May 1907

When the influence of alcohol upon the life of working people at the time is considered, the sheer number of public houses in Longton and the Meir must have been a significant factor. The pubs and inns seemed to outnumber everything else. Some were tied to a brewery, while others were 'freehouses', dispensing the ale from little more than front rooms.

Many breweries owned pubs in the Meir and Longton but two that had extensive interests were Messrs Parkers, and John Joule & Sons of Stone. While the former owned 'Garibaldi' in Short Street, the 'Shakespeare' in Gate Street, and the 'Gifford Arms' in the notorious John Street, Joules' owned the 'Saracen's Head' and the 'King's Arms' in the Meir (at that time on opposite sides of the crossroads).

The roll call of public houses, hotels and inns within 'staggering' distance of the Meir is not exhaustive but illustrates the size of the task the church and other bodies had in persuading the population to steer clear of the demon drink. The majority have quietly dried up in the intervening period but many were still plying their trade in spite of everything up to 1939. Various street names and numbers have gone (not to mention district boundaries) but where there is a modern version, that has been included as well.

Albion	64 High St; (Uttoxeter Road)
Alma Inn	171 Normacot Road,
American Inn	97 Normacot Road.
Anchor Inn	54 Anchor Road,
Antelope Inn	219 Normacot Road,
Ashwood	Wood Street.
Bath Inn	1 Bath Street.
Beehive	6 Willow Street.

Bird in Hand	143 Heathcote Road.
Blue Bells of Scotland	3 Caroline Street.
Borough Arms	4 Caroline Street.
Borough Arms	10 Commerce Street.
Brewers Arms	51 Anchor Road.
Bricklayers Arms	37 Marsh Street.
Bridge Inn	12 Heathcote Road.
British Oak	90 High Street.(Uttoxeter Rd)
British Lion	15 Hope Street.
British Volunteer	33 Lower Lockett's Lane.
Bulls Head	16 Chancery Lane.
California Inn	21 California Street.
Carpenters' Arms	91 Wood Street.
Castle Inn	25 High Street. (Uttoxeter Rd)
Cheshire Cheese	66 Edensor Road.
Cheshire Cheese	10 New Street.
Cinderhill Hotel	137 Weston Coyney Road.
Clarendon Inn	40 Stafford (The Strand) Street.
Coach & Horses	90 Stafford (The Strand) Street.
Cock Inn	8 Middlehill Street.
Compasses	22 Market Lane.
Congress	14 Sutherland Road.
Cottage Spring	25 John Street.
Coyney Arms	65 Sutherland Road.
Cricketers' Arms	50 Stafford (The Strand) Street
Crown & Anchor	Church Street.
Crown Inn	21 Commerce Street.
Daisy Bank	Spring Garden Road.
Dog & Partridge	70 High Street. (Uttoxeter Rd)
Dog & Pheasant	70 New Street.
Dresden Inn	35/37 Carlisle Street.
Duke of Cambridge	40 Middle Hill Street.
Duke of Wellington	9 Bagnall Street.
Duke of York	136 High Street. (Uttoxeter Rd)
Duke's Motto	53 Stafford (The Strand) Street.
Dusty Miller	37 Commerce Street.
Dunrobin Hotel	Stone (Lightwood) Road.
Eagle	Stafford (The Strand) Street.
Edensor Hotel	102 Spring Garden Road.
Edensor Terrace	51 Edensor Road.
Flint Millers' Arms	Marsh Street.
Flint Tavern	51 Stafford (The Strand) Street.
Forresters' Arms	41 High Street. (Uttoxeter Rd)
Fountain Inn	66 Ashwood.
Fountain Inn	70 Caroline Street.
Fox & Grapes,	80 Stafford (The Strand) Street.
Furnace Inn	71 Gregory Street.
Gardeners Arms	38 Spring Garden Road.
Gardeners' Rest	30 Trentham Road,
Garibaldi	14 Short Street
Gasworks Tavern	28 Edward Street.
George & Dragon	2 Heathcote Road.
Gifford Arms	24 John Street.
Globe Inn	44 Heathcote Road.
Golden Cup	33 Market Street.
Golden Lion	Market Street.

Halfway House	Anchor Road.
Hare & Hounds	18 Gower Street.
Harp Inn	98 New Street.
Heathcote Arms Hotel	30 Market Street.
Horse & Jockey	72 Heathcote Road.
Jolly Potters	124 Normacot Road.
Kimberley Arms	Gom's Mill Road.
King's Arms	King Street.
King's Arms	Meir Lane (Uttoxeter Rd)
King's Head	32 Ashwood.
Lawn Weavers' Arms	Upper Hill Street .
Leopard Inn	32 Lovatt Street.
Lord John Russell	Russell Street.
Lord John Russell	91 Trentham Road.
Lord Nelson	48 King Street.
Lord Nelson	164 Market Street .
Market Tavern	8 Market Street.
Mason Arms	63 Sutherland Road.
Meynell Arms	94 Edensor Road.
Millfield	198 Sutherland Road.
Mill Street Tavern	18 Edensor Road.
Miners' Arms	273 Anchor Road.
Miners' Arms	37 Goddard Street.
Miners' Rest	74 Caroline Street
Miners' Rest	16 Earl Street.
Morpa Arms	19 Carlisle Street.
Mount Pleasant Inn	181 High Street. (Uttoxeter Rd)
New Inn	38 Church Street.
New Inn	57 High Street. (Uttoxeter Rd)
Newtown Hotel	24 High Street. (Uttoxeter Rd)
Normacot Arms	155 Normacot Road.
Normacot Hotel	292 Normacot Road.
Old House at Home	54 High Street. (Uttoxeter Rd)
Old Millfield Gate	53 Gate Street.
Old Red Gate	10 Russell Street.
Old Roebuck	1 Goddard Street.
Old Roebuck	2 Wood Street.
Park Inn	45 Carlisle Street.
Pheasant Inn	20 Gower Street.
Plough Inn	18 Anchor Road.
Portland	Church Street.
Potters' Arms	4 Marsh Street.
Prince of Wales	172 Anchor Road.
Princess Royal	34 Carlisle Street.
Railway Inn	Railway Terrace.
Red House	145 Heath cote Road.
Red Lion	Church Street.
Red Lion	20 Marsh Street.
Ring of Bells	81 Normacot Road.
Robin Hood	71 Stafford Street. (Lightwood Rd)
Roebuck	Villiers Street.
Roebuck	Caroline Street.
Rose Inn	216 High Street. (Uttoxeter Rd)
Rose & Crown	69 Stafford Street. (Lightwood Rd)
Royal Oak	143 High Street (Uttoxeter Rd)
Royal Studio	15 Commerce Street.

Royal Standard	31 Edensor Road.
Saddle Vaults	11 High Street (Uttoxeter Rd)
Sailor Boy	130 High Street (Uttoxeter Rd)
Saracens Head	16 Commerce Street.
Saracens Head	21 Victoria Street.
Saracens Head	Meir Lane (Uttoxeter Rd)
Saracens Head	Normacot.
Sea Lion	9 John Street.
Sea Lion	43 Normacot Road.
Sea Lion	34 Anchor Terrace
Shakespeare	3 Gate Street
Shakespeare	128 Stafford Street. (Lightwood Rd)
Shamrock	9 Heath cote Road.
Sheridan Arms	6 Chancery Lane.
Shoulder of Mutton	117 Wood Street.
Sir Charles Napier	140 High Street (Uttoxeter Rd)
Sir Robert Peel	50 Church Street.
Sir Robert Peel	58 Peel Street.
Staffordshire Knot	Star & Garter Road.
Staffs Knot Inn	3/5 St Martin's Lane.
Star Inn	161 Heath cote Road.
Star Vaults	189 High Street (Uttoxeter Rd
Sutherland Arms	Sutherland Place.
Sutherland Crescent	188 Normacot Road.
Sutherland Hotel	210 Normacot Road.
Sutherland Inn	67 Sutherland Road.
Swan Hotel	Church Street.
Seven Stars	Lightwood Road. Lightwood
Station Hotel	Uttoxeter Road, Normacot
Talbot Inn	1 Commerce Street.
Tam O'Shanter	260 Normacot Road.
Three Tuns	56 Edensor Road.
Three Cups	87 High Street. (Uttoxeter Rd)
Tiger	92 Wood Street
Travellers' Rest	21 Heath cote Street.
True Blue	81 Cornhill Passage.
Uncle Tom's Cabin	19 Heathcote Road.
Uncle Tom's Cabin	154 Normacot Road.
Unicorn	95 Sutherland Road.
Union Hotel	High Street. (Uttoxeter Rd)
Union Inn	30 Barker Street.
Vauxhall Tavern	28 Normacot Road.
Vine Hotel	High Street. (Uttoxeter Rd)
Volunteer Inn	20 King Street.
Vulcan Inn	24 High Street. (Uttoxeter Rd)
Waterloo Inn	58 Stafford (Strand) Street.
Wheatsheaf	64 Normacot Road.
White Hart	60 High Street. (Uttoxeter Rd)
White Horse	14 Anchor Terrace.
White Lion	5 Church Street.
Willow Tavern	2 Willow Row.
Wood Street Tavern	32 Wood Street.
Woolpack Hotel	17 Commerce Street.

They were all at it; even the mayor of Longton owned a public house. This was the

Crown & Anchor, in what is today King Street, also home to the Longton Horse Repository at which W H Hart often had monthly sales.

The fête and bazaar season was once more upon them; the Meir was doing its share in filling the church coffers (albeit briefly) but this time it was to be quite a test of endurance for the faithful:

> At the Meir church Institute on Wednesday (23rd October 1907) a '2-day bazaar' was opened to clear the debt of £500 from the mission church at Werrington. The Revs H M (Herbert Metcalfe) Fowler, W H Haslett and A A Brooks were present. Mr Bowers gave £ 100 and the total raised was £ 250.

The concept of a two day bazaar is difficult to grasp; it is interesting to speculate whether they carried on until every vestige of produce was sold or until the vendors collapsed exhausted behind their stalls. Variations on this theme were rife and the tireless Rev T L Murray, held a *"Shakespearean Bazaar"* at St Mary & St Chad, Sandford Hill earlier in the year. - "Is this a bargain I see before me?"

As massed choirs sang carols to praise the feast of Christ's birth, there was available a nifty little parcel for the connoisseur from Messrs L B Scott's of Sandford Street, Lichfield. Their half guinea parcel contained:

One bottle of fine old blended Scotch Whisky	*3s 6d*
One bottle guaranteed pure Cognac	*4s 0d*
One bottle brown sherry	*2s 0d*
One bottle old Port	*2s 6d*
Total	*12s 0d*

The discerning would thus save 1s 6d!

And the vicar of Caverswall summed up the general wellbeing in the parish with some pithy yuletide philosophy that was not unlike an 'end of term' report:

> The Rev H M Fowler in his Christmas letter says there have been signs during the past year in each part of the parish of real and substantial progress and a deepening of the reality of the Christian life. The Christmas tree and tea which Mr W E Bowers provided for the children of the day and Sunday schools was held as usual on Christmas Eve. The delight and pleasure of the children was Mr Bowers' reward. At the Meir Mission church it is hoped to organise early in the New Year a branch of the Scripture Reading Union for all who are interested in heathen lands. Much satisfaction is felt at the Meir with a gift of a new pulpit from Mr J H Barlow, churchwarden.

There were few parishes that could boast a more varied list of clergy occupying the position of vicar, than that of Caverswall. From an illuminating article printed in the parish magazine in 1908, a list starting from the 13th century detailed the parish's clergy save for one or two gaps (of 265 years) until the present day:

The earliest records were:

1230   Persona de Kaveriswalle
1284   William de Fenton
1307   Richard de Caverswall
1320   John de Smallys.

There is no further record until Gregory Scarlett in 1585, after whom the names seem to be in complete sequence. 1795 saw the parish with a titled incumbent, Sir George Bowles, while in 1824 we have the familiar name of the Rev Ralph Sneyd (of Sneyd Hall, later to become the University of Keele). The immediate predecessors of the Rev H M Fowler, the vicar at this time, were the Rev F A Goddard (whose son is the present vicar of Christ Church, Stafford) and the Rev J. Gordon Addenbrooke.

Notes.
1. Unhappily this church is no longer standing. All that remains is a disfigured commemorative plaque marking the approximate location of this once popular place of worship.

Longton would have looked like this during much of the time covered by the book .

A crowd gather at a ceremony at Normacot Methodist church in 1910 on the boundary of Normacot and Meir. The women in the foreground are walking in Meir Road; its junction with Uttoxeter Road can clearly be seen on the left. Surprisingly, most of the fine Victorian houses here are still standing: The trees opposite are the site of Meir Residential Estatebuilt in the early 30s; the vast proportion torn down for the 'A50 improvements' in 1994/5.

Warrillow Collection

Queens Park, Longton about 1900. Although children would go or be taken to the park, there was no provision of playing areas for sport or of swings, etc - see 1932 in Chapter 13

CHAPTER 8
1910
'Some work of noble note may yet be done '

Alfred Lord Tennyson 1809-1892

On Sandford Hill, the year dawned with hope when a financial millstone was reduced by a very generous gift. Charity, it appeared did begin 'at home':

A debt of over £2000 was wiped off St Mary & Chad's church by a gratuity given by an anonymous friend of the Rev T L Murray.

No time has been lost in pushing on with the completion of St Chad's church consequent on the generous anonymous gift received for this purpose. The vicar writes in the parish magazine that Messrs Tompkinson & Bettelley of Longton have secured the contract and Mr Hand of Anchor Road has been appointed clerk of the works by the vicar. The contract is under the £3000 mark, so the vicar will not have to worry about architect's fees and clerk of the works.

Around Easter, on 16th April 1910, the Methodists too gave the green light to the builders for their new church, which would be the last in the Meir for some time. At a time when the average wage was under £2 per week, this venture equalled the weekly wages of over 1500 men:

A new United Methodist church in Meir Road, Normacot: Messrs Bennion is the builder and the cost will be £2657 18s 7d but when the lighting and fittings are completed the total cost is estimated at £3000.

For a small village, the rate of expansion was astonishing: Was there ever a time when nothing was either being improved, added to or just plain altered? But there was time for play as well:

Residents at the Meir had the opportunity on the 14th inst of hearing the Newcastle Voice Glee Union which has attained a high standard of excellence under the conductorship of Mr S E Lovatt. the concert was arranged in aid of the church organ fund and there was a crowded audience. Miss Lizzie Williams & Mr S Edwards rendered songs and Mr S Bagnall contributed violin solos. Mr W Drakeford[1] was the accompanist.

But while the Glee Union harmonised in Meir, over in Caverswall, the life of a country cleric had never been so hectic. In a well measured outburst the vicar rang more than a few bells: Writes the Rev H M Fowler in the April magazine:

I don't think we ever had so many as nine weddings on a single day before; we were certainly kept hard at work for the time being.

And then the sting in the tail.

I am glad to think that people have given up the irreverent practice of throwing senseless confetti in church; but I wish they would learn to reverence the churchyard more and abstain from besprinkling the pathways, not to speak of the graves with the wretched stuff. There used to be some symbol in throwing rice over a newly married couple, dangerous as the practice became, for it implied the good wish of riches and plenty, but confetti has neither meaning nor beauty!

The Meir locals turned out, (shoes shining and trousers pressed) to lend an ear to a military man with a bent for economics. Military men were everywhere it seemed in politics at the time (Col A H Heath had been returned as M P in February):

Captain E S Grogan addressed a meeting under the auspices of the Meir branch of the Leek Unionist Association in the Church Institute, Meir on Monday evening. The Meir Boy Scouts and Church Lads' Brigade acted as a guard-of-honour for the captain. Captain Grogan dealt chiefly with the food question: wheat which formerly could be bought for 26s a quarter was now nearer 46s a quarter.

For a farming community these were important questions.

The Edwardian age was often regarded as a period in English history when the country was at its most prosperous, portrayed by strains of Elgar's music and misty photographs of dewy-eyed young women in flowing, white dresses. But in truth, there were great inequalities at the time with no welfare system to help the enormous number of disadvantaged. When King Edward VII died after a short illness in May 1910, it marked the passing of an era. The days of a glorious Empire on which the sun never set were beginning to fade.

For many of the 38 million people in this country, health was a problem, although if the advertising jargon from Quaker Oats was given credence, you could go a long way to remedying this with a bowlful of their breakfast cereal. The general wellbeing of the great majority was far from good. People suffered in silence from ailments easily curable forty years later. Wild and wonderful remedies, many of which have thankfully passed into history, proliferated. You might also be forgiven for thinking that people rattled when they walked, since they swallowed so many pills! Many years would yet pass before the medical world had a major impact on infectious disease and other serious conditions.

The extra curricular activities offered by the churches were heavily patronised by the community and in great demand. From athletic and outdoor pursuits, to cooking and sewing; from horticulture to first aid; the church set out to amplify a persons overall view of life. But strangely very little insight into the local training of applicants for the clergy exists. A rare glimpse of this side of the church's activities was shown by Rev T L Murray in June prior to 'cutting the tape' at a fête. His 'no holds barred' approach left the listener in no room for doubt:

The bazaar at St Chad's was opened by Lady Shakerley. In an address at the opening, the Rev T L Murray said :

'There was a hostel at the vicarage for poor lads desirous of entering the ministry. When these were tested, they were sent to college at a cost of £80 each. It was nothing short of blasphemy to say that God only called to the ministry those men whose fathers could afford to pay a matter of £2000 for their college training. The Holy Spirit did not work like that!'

£250 was raised from the bazaar and a stone for the new portion of SS Mary & Chad's was laid on the 6th July.

150 miles away from Sandford Hill and the Meir in London, a ship was being prepared for what would become one of the most famous and tragic journeys undertaken in this century. Built in Dundee, 747 tons gross weight and 187 feet overall in length, she still reeked of whale oil and blubber when brought to London to be transformed from stem to stern.

The ship's captain, Robert Falcon Scott, was the man upon whose shoulders the venture rested in his obsession to be the first to reach the South Pole; although this was not the only aim of thr expedition; many eminent glaciologists, meteorologists, biologists and other scientists were in Scott's party. On June 1st 1910, the ship moved down river to a tumultuous send off from the steam whistles and sirens of merchantmen tied alongside the Thames. She sailed from here to Cardiff to fill her bunkers with a generous gift of Welsh coal and a donation of £1000.

She set course for the Cape of Good Hope; Scott and his wife Kathleen[2] following in the mail ship Saxon. From Capetown, in South Africa, Scott took command of the Terra Nova relieving Lieutenant E R G R ("Teddy") Evans[3]. Arriving in Melbourne in October they were met by an ominous cable which read: *'Am going south. Amundsen'.*

At the end of October, Scott and his crew reached New Zealand. Provisioned and victualled, they slipped their moorings on November 29th and left Dunedin for the final stage of their 10,000 mile journey south. There to see them off were Kathleen Scott, Mrs Wilson, the wife of Dr Edward Wilson and Mrs Evans: It was to be the last time they would see their husbands alive.

For two days, the Terra Nova sailed into an ever strengthening wind across the largely uncharted Southern Sea until they were caught in the teeth of a force ten gale. It would have been serious for a ship less lightly loaded than theirs, but for the Terra Nova it was to be a trial of strength. Had just one plank faltered, it would have been the end for the 65 men along with their varied animal cargo.

The crew of the Terra Nova was divided into four groups: the Shore Party, the Scientific Staff, the Men, and the Ship's Party. All of the first three groups were to over-winter on the Antarctic continent while the ship, under the captaincy of Lt Henry Pennell[4], was to sail back to New Zealand to escape being frozen in during the Antarctic Winter (April to September)[5].

Personnel of the British Antarctic Expedition 1910

Shore parties:

Robert Falcon Scott,	Captain CVO RN
Edward R G R Evans,	Lieutenant RN
Victor LA Campbell*	Lieutenant RN
Henry R Bowers	Lieutenant RIM
Lawrence EG Oates	Captain 6th Innsk. Dragoons
G. Murray Levick*	Surgeon RN
Edward L Atkinson	Surgeon RN

Scientific Staff:

Edward Adrian Wilson BA MB(Cantab)	Chief of the scientific staff
George C Simpson DSc	Meteorologist
T Griffith Taylor BA BSc BE	Geologist
Edward W Nelson	Biologist
Frank Debenham BA BSc	Geologist
Charles S Wright BA	Physicist
Raymond Priestley*	Geologist
Herbert Ponting FRGS	Camera artist
Cecil H Meares	In charge of dogs
Bernard C Day	Motor engineer
Apsley Cherry-Garrard	Assistant zoologist
Tryggve Gran	Sub Lieut Norwegian Ski expert

Men:

William Lashly	Chief stoker RN
W. W. Archer	Chief steward late RN
Thomas Clissold	Cook, late RN
Edgar Evans	Petty Officer RN
Robert Forde	" "
Thomas Crean	" "
Thomas S Williamson	" "
Patrick Keohane	" "
George P Abbott*	" "
Frank V Browning*	Petty Officer 2nd class RN
Harry Dickason*	Able seaman RN
FJ Hooper	Steward late RN
Anton Omelchenko	Groom
Dimitri Gerof	Dog driver

Ship's party:

Henry L Pennell	Lieut RN
Henry E. de P. Rennick	Lieut RN
Wilfred M Bruce	Lieut RNR
Francis RH Drake	Asst paymaster RN(retd)
	Secretary and met man in ship.
Dennis G Lillie MA	Biologist in ship
James R Dennistoun	In charge of mules in ship
Alfred B Cheetham	RNR Boatswain
William Williams	Chief engine room artificer
	Engineer RN
William A Horton	Engine room artificer
	3rd class; 2nd Engineer RN
Francis E. C. Davies	Leading shipwright RN
Frederick Parsons	Petty Officer RN
William L Heald	Late petty officer RN
Arthur S Bailey	Petty officer 2nd class RN
Albert Balson	Leading Seaman RN
Joseph Leese	Able Seaman RN
John Hugh Mather	Petty Officer RNVR
Robert Oliphant	AB
Thomas F Mcleod	AB
Mortimer McCarthy	AB
William Knowles	AB
Charles Williams	AB
James Skelton	AB
William McDonald	AB
James Paton	AB
Robert Brissenden	Leading stoker RN
Edward A McKenzie	Leading stoker RN
William Burton	Leading stoker RN
Bernard J Stone	Leading stoker RN
Angus McDonald	Fireman
Thomas McGillon	Fireman
Charles Lammas	Fireman
W H Neale	Steward

*Members of the Northern Party

As the seas grew steadily more mountainous - Pennell estimated them to be 35 feet high - Apsley Cherry-Garrard, in a memorable book refers to the the deck planks:

> *Had one gone, we would all have gone, and the great anxiety was not so much the existing water as what was going to happen if the storm continued.*

Then came news from below. The ship was taking on water which the pumps were unable to handle. The crew laboured many hours without complaint, emptying out water with buckets and singing shanties to keep their spirits up. As the water level inched upwards, it eventually reached the boilers, extinguishing the fires. Now the ship was without power and in danger of becoming a waterlogged hulk. Huge waves broke over the side of the ship washing away the lee bulwarks and the ship rolled so much it was fortunate not to have overturned. Cherry-Garrard was to write later: *'God had shown us the weakness of man's hand and it was enough for the best of us.'*

The pumps were of necessity located deep in the ship and difficult to reach. Had it been possible to lift the hatches it was a ten minute job, but with the mountainous seas that was out of the question. There was a way through, but it was very risky. The engineers explained their plan to Scott and having heard it he readily agreed for he had no choice. It involved cutting a hole in a steel bulkhead to gain access to the pumps behind it.

After hours of work, Williams and the carpenter Davies, cut open a way forward and at 11pm, Cherry Garrard, Bowers and Lt Evans crawled through, the latter burrowing his way over the coal to the pump well. Once they had made another hole in the wooden bulkhead they crawled through and set to work. The reason for the pumps failing now became evident; coal dust and oil on the upper deck had formed 'balls' and been washed into the bilges, blocking the pump intakes. Evans, working by the light of Davy lamps, with only his head out of the icy water, continued to remove them as best he could, struggling for hours as the ship rolled and pitched.

By 4 o'clock, the first signs that his exertions were producing an effect appeared as the water level began to recede, slowly at first, then more quickly as the pumps emptied the bilges and the areas below decks. Eventually 25 to 30 buckets of these 'balls' were removed; Evans later remarked it took many days to wash away the smell of the oil from his hair! But his action saved the day - and the ship, the men and the expedition. The boilers were relit and the Terra Nova was under her own power once more; with the main pumps working, the ship was soon under way and drying out.

One member of the crew on board the Terra Nova, who endured that gale in the Southern Ocean in December, was a local man, Joseph Leese, seconded from the Royal Navy for the expedition as a surveyor. He was to set foot on Antarctica with Scott's expedition early in 1911. In the light of his actions and his extraordinary privations, he would in later years receive two very rare commemorative medals at a special ceremony for his part in the quest. He was the only man in Staffordshire to be so honoured by the King.

As the ship returned to normal and sailed into calmer waters, it gave Scott and the men a chance to relash the supplies, make fast the loose deck cargo and dry out their clothing. They had lost ten tons of precious coal overboard, 65 gallons of petrol, two ponies and one dog. But they were very fortunate to be still alive!

They now came to the pack ice and by the end of December they found themselves frozen in. It was a frustrating time but during dinner one evening news that the ice was breaking up was received with relief. On 5th January 1911, they finally landed in McMurdo Sound at what is now known as Cape Evans[6], where they unloaded their supplies. Everyone lent a hand and Captain Scott records the event in one of his diaries:

> *Rennick and Bruce[7] are working gallantly at the discharge of stores on board. Williamson and Leese load the sledges and are getting very clever and expeditious. Evans [seaman] is generally superintending the sledging camp outfit. Forde, Keohane and Abbott are regularly assisting the carpenter, whilst Day, Lashly, Lillie and others give intermittent help.*

Joseph Leese was born in Stoke-on-Trent and later lived at the Holy Trinity Church Institute in the Meir. The whole world knows the story of the success of Scott's expedition in reaching of the South Pole. It was for Scott and his party, a bitter disappointment to realise that they had been beaten by a period of 34 days by Raold Amundsen who using dogs, had attained the goal on 14th December 1911. At this moment of utter desperation, Scott wrote the immortal and fateful words, *"Great God, this is an awful place."*

During their return, Petty Officer Edgar Evans was lost on 17th February and Captain Oates walked out to his death on the 17th March. The three[8] who remained soldiered on and probably died in late March. When their bodies were found by Tryggve Gran's search party in November, they were buried with a simple ceremony[9].

Back in the Meir, at the Church Institute in which A B Joseph Leese was to later live, plans were laid for something that would lighten the gloom of the long winter evenings:

> *Efforts will be made during the coming season to make the Institute as attractive as possible. At the anniversary presided over by the Rev A A Brooks on Thursday evening, it was resolved again to compete in the divisions of the North Staffs Church Institute Billiards League. Mr J Poole congratulated the club on gaining the championship of the second division and obtaining second place in the first division last season.*

Dark winter evenings meant the light of oil lamps or gas light. How the members of the Institute potted the ball under the dim light is a mystery but they did! It was one skill for which many in the Meir would be famed in the years ahead.

At nearby Sandford Hill, the members of St Chad's church stepped back in satisfaction:

> *Considerable improvements are being effected in connection with St Chad's parochial buildings. Electric light is being fitted to the church, vicarage & clubs. An extension of the church is being proceeded with and the hostel is nearly ready for use. The latter will provide study and three rooms for some of the missionary lads.*

In early October, the death at 83, of the painter Holman Hunt was announced, in Kensington, London. The middle east window or light in the Church of the Holy Trinity, the Meir, is a stained glass representation of his famous painting, in memory of a long and faithful servant of the church.

He was one of a group of painters known as the Pre-Raphaelites who sixty years earlier had created the Pre-Raphaelite Brotherhood in opposition to the teachings of the Royal Academy. Their inspiration was derived from a period[10] when the subject matter had been painted as honestly as possible without undue embellishment. The driving force of the group was John Everett Millais (1829-1896), with William Holman Hunt (1827-1910) and Dante Gabriel Rosetti (1828-1882). Success was assured with such talent and determination at their disposal and soon more artists joined the group, including Edward Burne-Jones, Ford Madox-Brown, Arthur Frederick, Augustus Sandys and Arthur Hughes.

In 1854, William Holman Hunt shook the artistic world by exhibiting his canvas 'The Light of the World[11]. In religious *and* artistic circles it was both highly praised and criticised. John Ruskin described it as, *"one of the very noblest works of art produced in this or any other age."* For the next twenty years photographs and engravings of the work achieved a huge circulation. The original painting went to Keble College in Oxford after the death of the owner and the artist showed his displeasure by painting the subject once more, this time twice the size of the original and over fifty years later! Today it hangs in St Paul's Cathedral; the earlier version is still at Keble College.

At its first showing, Holman Hunt was approached by someone anxious to tell him of his omission of the handle to the door outside which Christ stood. But Holman Hunt indicated that the painting was allegorical and the missing handle was intentional, likening the door to the soul - only to be opened from the inside.

Notes.
1. He died on a train at Wall Grange, near Leek, Staffordshire.
2. She had left their son Peter - later Sir Peter Scott of the Slimbridge Wildfowl Trust - in someone else's care.
3. Lieut. Evans (not to be confused with Petty Officer Edgar Evans) had a distinguished naval career and later became Admiral Lord Mountevans.
4. Lieut. Pennell was killed during the First World War on the Queen Mary at the Battle of Jutland.
5. In the 1901-1904 Discovery expedition under Commander Scott (he was promoted on his return) the ship was frozen in and two relief ships were sent from England. These were the *Morning* and what was to become Scott's later ship, the *Terra Nova*.
6. Named after Lieut. "Teddy" Evans by Scott.
7. Bruce was the brother of Scott's wife, Kathleen.
8. Bowers, one of the three, wrote even at the end without malice or bitterness, *"my trust is still in Him and in the abounding Grace of my Lord and Saviour whom you* (his mother) *brought me to trust in."*
9. The body of Captain Oates was never found; a cairn marking the approximate spot was erected in his memory.
10. This period was before the time of the great painter, Raphael; hence the term pre-Raphaelite.
11. Among Holman Hunt's other famous works of art are 'Christ in the Temple'. 'The Lady of Shallot' and 'The Triumph of the Innocents'.

The crew of the Terra Nova.
Back Row left to right:: Stoker McDonald, Seaman McDonald, Horton, Burton, Brissenden (with beard), McGillon, Parsons, McKenzie, Heald, Neale, Anton, Balson, Clissold, Mather, McCarthy, (with hat), Davies.
Seated: Skelton, McCloud, Bailey, Forde, Leese.

This is an enlargement from a photograph of the crew of Captain Robert Falcon Scott's ship Terra Nova, which sailed to the Antarctic on the expedition to reach the South Pole during the years 1910 to 1913. Scott and his four companions, although reaching the Pole in January 1912, died on their return; 3 of them just 11 miles from vital stores. Taken by Herbert Ponting FRGS, the official expedition photographer, (although in the ships list he was referred to as a 'camera artist'), it shows Able Seaman Joseph Leese RN,who was born in Burslem, Stoke on Trent in 1884, in his sea-going clothes seated on the deck of the ship. At the time this was taken he was about 26 years of age. On his return he was decorated by King George V with the King's Medal and Bar for Antarctic Exploration for the terrible ordeal he and the crew of the Terra Nova underwent during its voyages in the vastness of the largely uncharted Southern Ocean. During the 1930's Mr Leese lived at Holy Trinty Church Institute in Meir, Stoke on Trent. His death was announced in the Times on 22nd December 1948 in Brookhouse Road, Meir, Stoke on Trent, aged 64 years.

Scott Polar Research Insitute Ref. No P48/38/563

Probably one of the most widely recognised paintings of all time, the **Light of the World** was originally painted by William Holman Hunt and exhibited in 1854. Of it John Ruskin said,it was *"one of the very noblest works of art produced in this or any other age"* The painting has allegorical connotations: the artists omission of the handle on the door is deliberate, to convey the human involvement in Christian faith. The soul, like the door, has no outside handle and can only be opened from the inside. The east window in the church of the Holy Trinity is a stained glass representation of this work and dedicated in 1925 to the memory of F H Heath.

CHAPTER 9
1911-1912
'If there were dreams to sell, what would you buy?'

Thomas Lovell Beddoes 1803-1849

For Meir, the period 1900 to 1910 saw the beginning of a transformation which would go on for thirty years. Anyone leaving then and returning in the 1930s would be hard put to recognise it. In these Edwardian years, there was still the familiar cluster of buildings around the crossing of the two roads, as well as many farms, but the construction of several large houses and churches would signal the start of the metamorphosis. Meir and Normacot Methodist churches and some of the large houses in Weston Road were built at this time. But it was the farms, not unnaturally, which gave the Meir its rural atmosphere, the extent of which can be gauged from the following:

Farmers:
Bartlam, William, Waterloo Farm, the Meir.
Blackhurst & Bartlam, Cinderhill Farm, Weston Coyney.
Blackmore, William J, Caverswall Park.
Carter, Thomas William, Ivy Lodge.
Clowes, Elizabeth, Little Weston Coyney.
Dayson, Henry——
Goodwin, William, Grove Farm, Weston Coyney.
Green, George, Woodhouse Farm.
Hodgkinson, John, Meir Lane Farm, the Meir.
Hood, William, Meir Farm, Meir Lane.
Hughes. Elizabeth, Park Head Farm.
Marson, William, the Sycamores, Little Weston Coyney.
Oakley, Robert, Lower Park Head Farm, Weston Coyney.
Slack, Thomas & Sons, Bolton Gate Farm, Weston Coyney.
Thorley, Jane, Meir Lane, the Meir.
Wainwright John, Wood Farm, the Meir.

Other locals included Shadrach Leese, the landlord at the old King's Arms and Mr D Walters, the stationmaster, at Meir House, almost opposite Holy Trinity church. The town had a sub-post office run by David Tunnicliffe who wore a second hat as grocer and baker at his shop, 63 Weston Road; while PC Tom Brown endeavoured to keep law and order from the Police Station in Weston Coyney. The clergy from Holy Trinity did not yet have a vicarage and the gazetteer shows:

Brooks, Andrew A. Holy Orders, 81 Weston Road, Meir.

As the year 1911 dawned, the usual round of worldly and spiritual activities began with the return of a familiar figure:

> *Meir Church Scouts and Church Lads Brigade were entertained to their annual supper at the Church Institute on Monday 2nd Jan 1911. Over 100 were present under the presidency of the Rev A A Brooks, the chaplain. An address on the aims of the Church Lads Brigade and Scouts was given by Col F G Goodwin of Silverdale who was heartily thanked for his presence. Drills were gone through by members and a number of songs were given.*

At this time, the vast majority of the inhabitants of the nearby city lived in enduring penury. But the plight of the destitute did not go unnoticed and in Caverswall, the second Mrs W E Bowers had decided that she and the local clergy should try and do what they could. A 'Rescue Shelter' had been formed and in February, they held a meeting at her historic country residence:

> *At the invitation of Mrs W E Bowers, a well attended drawing-room meeting was held at Caverswall Castle on Tuesday afternoon (14th February 1911) to hear addresses on behalf of the Potteries Rescue Shelter. Among those present were the Rev H M & Mrs Fowler, the Rev H G & Mrs Mayne, the Rev G & Mrs Plant, the Rev E W Bridgwood (vicar of Forsbrook), the Rev T L Murray and Holy Trinity's own, the Rev A A & Mrs Brooks.*

A few days earlier, some of these had attended a more sociable gathering in the village, 'with the flannelled fools at the wicket':

> *The annual dinner in connection with Caverswall Cricket Club was held on the 10th inst., the Rev H M Fowler presiding. Mr W E Bowers of Caverswall Castle, who alone has done so much to encourage cricket in the village, was amongst those present and he and Mr W E Jewell distributed the prizes won last season.*

But what about 'the muddied oafs at the goal': Football, after the founding of Stoke City in 1863, had become very popular locally. At a typical charity football match played in Queen's Park Longton in Feb 1911, the tireless postmen showed their true metal against 'the boys in blue'. The result after 90 minutes: POLICE 1 POSTMEN 4.

If overcrowding in the cities was a recognised problem, then it must have come as a surprise that it had also become a problem in the village - for the deceased! At Caverswall, tentative steps were taken to remedy an embarrassing predicament:

> *A scheme is on foot for the extension of the Caverswall churchyard. The present graveyard has been in existence for more than 50 years and a suitable piece of land adjoining has been secured. The Rev H M Fowler says, "It will enable part of the burial service to be read in the old church*

in which for 700 years and possibly a great deal longer, the words of comfort have been used over the bodies of our forefathers".

And in April the vicar explained the fiscal implications:

The vicar of Caverswall, the Rev H M Fowler explained a scheme to extend Caverswall churchyard by voluntary effort to avoid having a cemetery rate. He suggested the £350 needed could be raised by cottagers with rentals of £5 to £8, who would each pay 2/6d; with the larger ratepayers giving more in proportion, the amount could be easily raised.

In 1911, seeing one motor car must have been a novelty and two, extraordinary, especially when those two cars met at the same place and at the same time - head on!

A collision occurred at the crossroads at the Meir yesterday and one witness estimated the speed of the cars as being 30 mph. The drivers were Eli Rennison Hudson, a professional flautist, and William Chamberlain, proprietor and manager of the Saracen's Head Hotel, Hanley.

One notable absentee at the accident would have been a local bobby, Sergeant Dowler, who had retired in February after six years in charge of the Meir district.

Meir parish was now growing rapidly; just how quickly was revealed at a favourite ceremony in March:

The annual distribution of prizes took place on the 23rd ult., the Rev A A Brooks, curate-in-charge presiding and the awards being handed by Mrs James Barlow. The chairman said there was a gratifying increase in the numbers of their books. During the year 90 scholars had qualified for prizes as against 60 in 1909. Mrs Barlow presented two extra prizes for the best boy and girl in the school; they went to Tom Parkes and Agnes Marsh,

1st April 1911

In the middle of this year came the Coronation. On the 22nd June 1911, in a seven hour service, King George V was crowned at Westminster Abbey, transformed for the occasion with blue carpets, red tulips, white lilies and blue delphiniums. In the congregation were many reminders that King George was still head of the largest empire in the world. For many it was a chance to drink the health of the new king and light blazing bonfires

In Caverswall and the Meir the celebrations were tempered in the autumn by the untimely loss of a long and valued champion. In the Caverswall parish magazine, the vicar, the Rev Harold M. Fowler has a generous tribute to the late Mr W E Bowers of Caverswall Castle:

His churchwardenship was in a mere honourary position but his interest in

all that concerned the church was always deep and sincere. As I look back at the time I have been at Caverswall, I cannot think how the work could have been carried out without his generous and unostentatious help. If there was one thing above another which marked the character of Mr Bowers, it was his devotion to what he felt was right. I am quite sure no consideration whatever would have caused him to deviate one hair's bread from the path of duty.

Be thou faithful unto death and I will give thee a crown of life' Revelation ch. 2 v10

The opening of a bazaar was the cue to give credit to a well-respected and much-travelled clergyman:

The Rev T L Murray who has just completed 21 years work in Longton has been largely responsible for raising £18000 on behalf of the church. During the past 14 years there have been provided in the comparatively new parish, a parish church, a vicarage, a mens' and boys' club, girls' club, small missionary hostel and an endowment of £186 a year. He referred to the ladies mission house on which there is an overdraft of £240 and to the lads who were being trained for the ministry.

The opening ceremony was performed by Lady Farrar of Idle Rocks. The bazaar[2] was very prettily arranged, a maritime scheme of decoration having been adopted with considerable effect. Around the room were arranged sailing ships from the decks of which goods were sold whilst a tall lighthouse arose at one end of the room.

Reverend Murray had come to the Potteries as a deacon and took charge of Sandford Hill which then was a missionary district attached to St John's parish, Longton. He is no longer a deacon but vicar of a separate parish. The tin church he inherited has been replaced by one of the most beautiful churches[3] in the Potteries. In close proximity are to be found institutes, vicarage, mission house & clergyhouse. The congregation, which at one time was non existent, has grown until there are over 500 communicants and 800 on the Sunday school books.

It was said it was scarcely safe for a lady to go up Anchor Road years ago: I have heard the description of a horrid fight seen in the streets between two women, not one of the bystanders interfering in what was a common occurrence. Now it has all changed. The police superintendent says he has seen a very marked improvement during the past 16 years and there had been a noticeable decrease in drunkenness.

Father Murray said that time after time he had been face to face with financial ruin. He had thought the work must stop but in the end their prayers had always

been answered and their faith justified. Why? Because they had learned to give
something - themselves. Sometimes it had been said, 'I cannot afford to go to St
Chad's, the religion there costs too much.' This was one of the best testimonials
he had had. For that which costs little was worth as much as it cost.

A week later saw the funeral of Alfred Mear on a memorable date, the 11 11 1911. He
was a partner in the firm of Stephen Mear, timber merchants of Longton, the father of
Stephen Mear, the churchwarden of Holy Trinity who lived at Weston Coyney House.

It was a measure of the popularity of the church and its social calendar that frequently
the demand for a particular event outstripped the supply of tickets. Christmas in 1911
was such an occasion.

> *The Meir Boy Scout patrol will benefit by about £10 as a result of a whist*
> *drive and dance held in the church institute on the 10th inst. The Institute*
> *was crowded and several failed to gain admission.*

In a final flourish during the season of Advent, the congregation from the Church of the
Holy Evangelists were treated to a musical delight:

> *The organ of Normacot parish church was reopened on Thursday afternoon*
> *after being improved and enlarged. The work has been carried out by*
> *Messrs Key & Steel of Burslem at a cost of £120. A number of new stops*
> *have been introduced, tracker action has been superseded by tubular*
> *pneumatic action and 4 new composition pedals have been introduced. At*
> *the reopening service the preacher was the Rev G T Birch, rector of*
> *Bucknall. An organ recital was subsequently given by Mr C Perkins,*
> *organist of Birmingham Town Hall and the University of Birmingham.*

And the builders of the chancel of Holy Trinity could spend a happy festive season
secure in the knowledge there would be plenty of work on their return in the New Year.

> *Messrs Tompkinson & Bettelley have been awarded the contract for the*
> *remodelling of Longton Town Hall. The contract price is £7375. The*
> *architect is to be Mr J H Beckett ARIBA and the aim of the work is to*
> *enlarge the size of the assembly rooms by no less than 80%.*

The rector of St John's passed another milestone; the Rev George Oliver had clocked
up 35 years in the Diocese of Lichfield of which 16 had been at Longton.

At St Mary & St Chad's, the Rev T L Murray followed closely, having been at the
helm for 21 years, and his anniversary was marked by an appeal to clear the £300 debt
from the church:

> *At a presentation to Rev T L Murray in February, he received a cheque for £165:*
> *for in his time at St Chad's, he had raised £30000 of which £18000 was spent on*

the church. The mayor, in making the presentation, said, "When Father Murray came to Sandford Hill there was no church in that neighbourhood. Now on every side they saw evidence of active churchwork-a beautiful church, boys & girls institutes, mens and womens' rooms."

In acknowledging the gift, Father Murray remarked that in his early days, he dreamed of great mission work in South London where he received his training, but he was induced by Mr Smith to throw up his London work and come to Longton. Longton would forgive him for it was not so true now, as it was then, but he thought he had never seen a filthier hole in his life. A few months after he came, he was asked to take charge of the forlorn hope of Sandford Hill.

Life often appears to move in circles. In early 1912 Captain Scott and his four companions had perished in the bitter wilderness of the Antarctic. Days later, 400 miles off the coast of the eastern United States, the Titanic, steaming at full speed towards New York, struck an iceberg and sank. The captain, locally born Edward Smith, went to his death along with over 1500 other souls. Many years later, a statue of the mariner was sculpted and it now stands in Beacon Park, Lichfield within sight of the spires of the cathedral. At the base of the effigy on its granite plinth is the signature of the sculptor. It is that of Captain Robert Falcon Scott's widow, Lady Kathleen Scott.

Evidence of the growth in the village of Meir was in the rapidly increasing numbers attending the church:

The annual meeting of the Holy Trinity church, the Meir was held on Tuesday evening (7th May 1912), the Rev A A Brooks presiding. Mr W J Taylor, financial secretary, submitted accounts showing a credit balance at the beginning of the year of £22 11s 2d had been increased to £42 19s 11d. The result was very satisfactory. The Sunday School had doubled its numbers in recent years and the fact they had no less than 312 communicants at Easter was a record. Mr Stephen Mear was nominated vicar's warden and Mr J H Barlow, people's warden.

Whilst on the sporting front, the men of the green baize from the church had demonstrated their prowess once again:

In the course of the social gathering which was held at the Meir Institute on the 20th inst, gold medals were presented to the members of the Institute's billiard team who last year gained the championship of the second division of the North Staffs Church Institute Billiards League. During the whole of that season the team did not experience a single defeat. Mr J H Barlow made the presentation and the following were recipients; A Donkin, A Harrison, H Colclough, S. Smith, G Ballance and G Donkin

One event always eagerly anticipated was the local holiday called the 'Wakes'. For many the arrival of a circus or fun fair on spare ground at the end of the street was an occasion talked about before and afterwards for many weeks. These were times of few holidays beside the sea and the rector of a Longton church (Rev G Oliver) put it into focus in the St John's magazine:

A Wakes Picture

Ordinarily speaking, society is divided into many parties. There are the Conservatives, Unionists, Liberals, Radicals, Socialists, Suffragists and many other kinds of 'als' and 'ists'. It is all very puzzling. But at Wakes Time differences sink and only 2 parties remain. They are; 1. Those who have gone away for a holiday and are glad they have and, 2. Those who have not gone away & are sorry they haven't. In other words the Idle Rich (for the time being) & the Deserving Poor (also for the time being, we hope).

Benevolence was bestowed on the not so well-to-do through numerous Associations, Clubs and Funds. One of these occurs frequently in the press - Pearson's Fresh Air Fund, through which many youngsters got an all too infrequent treat of a day out in the country or a park. Therefore spare a thought for about 750 excited children in August, as they looked out to see the weather ruin their special day. Indeed the month as a whole was very wet with over 8.2" of rain falling in Yarmouth and in Wales. Pembroke had barely one third of its monthly sunshine total. The summer of 1912 was a stinker!

Life was improving in many ways. Not only did Holy Trinity Church have a bowling green and access to a golf course, it was now to have tennis courts:

A whist drive and dance in connection with the Meir Church Institute Tennis Club was held on the 27th ult. with the object of meeting the costs of laying out the new courts. There was a good attendance and the prizes were won by Miss R F Atkinson & Mrs Bould, Mr G Ballance & Mr J Siddall. The prizes were given out by Mr Bowers, Mr Richard Amor and Mr Guy Murray. Mr Brain's band provided music for the dance which took place subsequently. 5th October 1912

There must have been some misgivings then, about choosing this particular time to leave a parish clearly so well-endowed, but the die was cast and for Rev A A Brooks, it was off to pastures new:

At the annual Martinmas gathering in connection with the Holy Trinity Church, the Meir, a presentation was made to the former curate-in-charge, the Rev A A Brooks, who has been appointed to the living of Wheaton Aston cum Lapley, near Stafford. The proceedings were presided over by the Rev H M Fowler, the vicar of Caverswall who was supported on the platform by the Rev A A Brooks, the Rev A H Bird, Messrs J H Barlow, F H Heath, J M Philips and S Leese. The vicar said they were gathered to mark their appreciation of five years faithful service of Mr Brooks at the Meir. He greatly valued the loyal co-operation which he had always received from Mr Brooks and he was delighted that the Meir people were to show their practical appreciation of his services.

The presentations were made by Mr J H Barlow, one of the wardens. He said the parishioners greatly appreciated the good, sincere and Christian work which Mr Brooks had done. He asked Mr Brooks to accept a purse of gold as a token of their genuine appreciation. On behalf of the Tennis Club, he also presented Mr Brooks with a handsome brass table lamp and shade.

Mr Brooks said he thanked them all for their tangible proof of their love, affection and respect and he should always have a warm place in his heart for the Meir.

The vicar said he had appointed the Rev Ralph Creed-Meredith, at present curate of St Andrews, Dublin, to succeed Mr Brooks.

It was to prove to be an inspired choice.

With the festive season on the way, the last place the vicar would wish to spend the festival was on his back:

The Rev T L Murray has sustained a fracture of the thigh bone when he slipped and fell over on the vicarage steps. He was conveyed to the Cottage Hospital and examined by means of X-rays. A year or two ago, Father Murray fractured the same leg whilst skiing in Switzerland. The present injury is a little higher up the same limb.

After all his many wanderings, he had finally come unstuck in his own backyard!

At a special ceremony in January 1913, the new vicar for Holy Trinity presented himself in the Meir to be warmly welcomed. What must he have made of this small rural parish tucked away in a corner of North Staffordshire after the hurly-burly of city life in Dublin?

The annual supper was held on the 31st ult. - the vicar, the Rev H M. Fowler presiding. A hearty welcome was afforded to the President of the Institute and curate-in-charge, the Rev R Creed-Meredith, the vicar remarking that he was confident that Mr Creed-Meredith would be for the good of the district. As regards the Institute, it afforded a meeting place for social advantage but they had an opportunity of doing definite religious and social work in the district. Mr Creed-Meredith said he should look to the men of the Institute to rally round him and back up that work. The supper was followed by a whist drive.

The 'social advantage' was a polite expression for teaching those who were unable, to read and write.

Wasting no time he got to grips with the finances and in late April at his first vestry meeting there was an early encounter with the church's 'profit and loss' accounts:

The annual vestry meeting was held on the 25th ult. in connection with the Holy Trinity church, the Meir, the curate-in-charge, the Rev R Creed-Meredith presiding. There was a credit of £3 against a surplus of £43 at the commencement of the year. There had been an extraordinary expense of £41 11s, it having been spent on laying out a bowling green as an adjunct to the Meir Institute.'

Notes.
1. Potteries and Newcastle Directory, 1912.
2. This raised over £250.
3. The church, closed for repairs in the 1980's due to subsidence from local coal mining, was reopened with a lowered roof line and other modifications.

Caverswall Castle, Courtya

Caverswall Castle, originally constructed in Norman times, has had various additions throughout the centuries. The wing on the right hand side was by Mr William E Bowers in about 1890. The scene today is not far removed from 80 years ago. It is only two miles from the noise of the crossroads at Meir. *Priestley Collection*

The entrance to Caverswall Castle was used by Oliver Cromwell's forces during the Civil War from 1649 to 1660.. The Castle was at the time owned by Matthew Craddock.

When Mr. William Bowers returned from honeymoon with his second wife in 1909, they drove through an illuminated arch saying 'Welcome Home' and the staff greeted them with a torchlit procession. *Priestley collection*

112

This is Weston Road (A520) in about 1915. The Meir Villas were originally a row of terraced houses. Alf Gunn's tobacconists' shop is now the office of the Staffordshire Building Society with three more shops beyond mixed in with one or two private homes. Very few non-business premises are left in the heart of Meir eighty years later, and it seems likely that this area will be the town's main shopping centre in the future.

Author's collection

MEIR RD LONGTON. 295-5.

This unique panorama of the western end of the Meir where it joins Normacot was taken standing in Utoxeter Road which disappears right with the tram lines. The period is after 1910 but before 1928. The Normacot Methodist Chapel, at the extreme left in Meir Road, is visible standing across the road from the old "Iron Chapel". The latter is situated just beyond the two men standing on the right hand pavement. Travelling past the lady with a pram, Meir Road descends and passes Normacot Church and Longton Cottage Hospital after half a mile or so. The shop, right of centre, has a notice board fixed to the brickwork on the left of the window which reads, "United Methodist Church, Normacot. Next Sunday Morning 10.30am. Evening service 6.30 pm and the name Mr T Ratcliffe. Usual Offertories. Hearty Welcome". During the 1930's the shop was owned by the legendary Ewart "Ewie" Hollinson and this junction was known as "Hollinson's Corner". He retired forty years later with the building still going strong. However, the demolition ball claimed it, along with the rest of this picturesque corner of Meir for the A50 improvements.

Priestley Collection

CHAPTER 10
1913 -.1915
'Blow out, you bugles, over the rich Dead!

Rupert Brooke 'The Dead' 1914

The Royal visit to the city by King George and Queen Mary took place during the week 19th to 26th April and many from the Meir would have seen their majesties in Longton, in Market Street, Anchor Road and Mr Colclough's works in Goddard Street.

Typically, that May of 1913 was *'cold and unseasonable'*, but wild horses would not have kept many from the special events scheduled for the holiday that spring. Many spent a day at the 25th Annual Fête of the two day Whitsuntide holiday, the 12th & 13th May, at Queen's Park, Dresden. The entrance fee was a whole shilling, children under 12 paying half price (12.30pm till 5 pm) but it was 6d from 5.30pm until the park closed at 11pm.

Some of the acts appearing were stupendous. The Great Rollo, King of the Air, in his sensational performance on the aerial slack rope and La Belle Duchess, the celebrated Australian with her troupe of performing horses, ponies and dog 'comedians', were all great attractions. However the man they had all flocked to see, the star of the show, was Mr Gustav Hamel, the aviator who had recently flown from England to Germany. Many who marvelled at his prowess that day would scarcely believe that, in a very short while, men would be shooting at each other from these flimsy, string and fabric machines in a terrible war which was the complete antithesis of the adjective 'Great'.

The aerial convulsions were a huge success. During the two days of the fetes, admissions totalled £385 on Monday and £195 on Tuesday, from which were deducted the expenses of the aviator (£200), variety artists (£90), fireworks (£40) and at the bargain price of £42, the band, which left them with cash to put in the bank.

After a welcome, the sort for which Potteries people have always been noted, Rev.Creed-Meredith must have been gratified to have settled in at the Meir so quickly. He was, it appeared, a man of innovative ideas; so much more than an ecclesiastical 'new broom'. With a highly original appeal, he went straight to the root of any clergyman's problem, ie getting people to listen to what he had to say. *"Come in your working togs and bring your pipes. I'll bring the baccy along,"* ran the invitation given by the new curate-in-charge, and some 170 responded to his delightfully unconventional request to come to a church social. In the course of the evening, he appealed to the men to help forward the work of the church at the Meir. It was undoubtedly something of a minor miracle that this man of God could see, let alone talk to, the smouldering gathering as they puffed away - the sight of 170 pipes all belching forth must have been an awesome spectacle and probably why the offer was never repeated. Later in the month, it was the turn of the thriving tennis club to hold centre 'court' in the events calendar - and pipe smoking on court was not encouraged. The tennis club was another example of the church creating situations that encouraged worshippers to meet for fellowship other than just at church times:

> *The Tennis Club in connection with the Meir Church Institute was opened for the season by Lady Meredith, mother of the Rev R Creed-Meredith, curate-in-charge. The opening games were played by the Rev H M Fowler (vicar of Caverswall) & Miss F Dayson vs Mr Guy Murray and Miss A Radford. There was a large gathering and the company was entertained to tea, after which a hearty vote of thanks was passed to Lady Meredith for her presence. Mr J H. Barlow observed that at the Meir they were out for all that tended to further the social interests of the people, which he considered true Christianity. For this reason, the church council had by a loan, originally financed by the Tennis club (and now that loan had been repaid), laid out a bowling green which he hoped to see in use very shortly.* 24th May 1913

But the religious side of church was also very strong and the two came together with what was the first local wedding at which Holy Trinity's new curate officiated, only he was 'playing away' at Caverswall:

> *The Rev R Creed-Meredith presided at the wedding in Caverswall at St.Peter's of Mr Hubert R Lawson B.Sc, eldest son of Mr & Mrs Lawson of the Meir & Miss Agnes E Heath, daughter of Mr F Heath of Prospect House[1], the Meir. The bride was attired in soft white satin trimmed with old lace and a lace veil over a wreath of orange. The Rev R Creed-Meredith was assisted by the Rev H M Fowler.*

Autumn brought the final fête of the year with the redoubtable Ralph 'pressing the flesh' with one hand and rattling the collecting tin with the other:

> *A successful fête organised on behalf of Holy Trinity church, the Meir was held on Thursday in a field lent by Mr Hood. The opening ceremony was performed by Lady Feilden of Dilhorne Hall[2]. In the presence of a large*

gathering the Rev R Creed-Meredith, priest-in-charge, in extending a hearty welcome to Lady Feilden explained that the net proceeds would be divided between the new organ fund and the Lads' Institute fund. There was a decorated bicycle parade and an admirable programme of music was rendered by Mr Glover's Military Band. A pierrot troupe gave performances in the afternoon and evening.   6th September 1913

As if this was not enough, soon after came the fête to end all fetes, a two day test:

Considerable activity has marked church work at the Meir, since the Rev R Creed-Meredith took up his duties as priest-in-charge of Holy Trinity church[3]. In order to raise funds to pay for a new organ & to build a Lads' Institute, a two day gymkhana and fête was held last week. The members of the church entered wholeheartedly into the effort and as a result considerably over a hundred pounds was raised. The fête was opened by Col F G Goodwin of Silverdale, head of the Church Lads' Brigade movement in North Staffs. The Rev R Creed-Meredith who presided, referred to the proposed Institute and said they all felt the need for work amongst the lads which would form a connecting link between the school and the mens' classes. Col Goodwin, in opening the fête referred to the recent camp at Rhyl & said that he was sure that the combination of military discipline and religious training was good for the lads themselves, good for the future, good for the church and good for the future of the country.

The situation was ironic, that a military man should preside at a fête which would be the last in the parish before the curtain came down on their genteel, if hard, way of life. 1914 was a watershed in many ways. The early months ticked away like a slow fuse, the combatants assembling their military might about them. The same was happening at the Meir but on a distinctly smaller scale:

Members of the church lads' Brigade & Boy Scouts Organisations associated with the Meir church held their annual supper on the 8th inst; the Rev R Creed-Meredith, curate in charge presiding. Amongst others present were Col F G Goodwin (Silverdale); Brigadier General Loney; Captain Johnson and Mrs Johnson (Eccleshall); Capt C. Heath and Mrs Heath ; Mr & Mrs Amor; Mr & Mrs J M Philips & others. The chairman acknowledged the cordial assistance which he had received during the twelve months he had been working at the Meir. During that time they had been able to undertake and complete the erection of a new organ at a cost of £400-500. With the new year, they must enter on fresh schemes and the provision of the Lads' institute was very desirable. For this they had £50 in hand. It was originally intended to erect a tin building which would cost £400 and whichever scheme was adopted, he thought that by the end of the year, an institute would be erected and paid for. He appealed to the parents to back up, by a healthy home influence, the work which the officers were doing amongst the lads, often at inconvenience to themselves.

A familiar cry, then and now! To give the fund impetus, a sale of work took place the following month:

> *A sale of work last week produced upwards of £50 towards the fund for the building of a Lads' Institute in connection with the Meir church. At the opening ceremony on the 19th inst, the Rev R Creed-Meredith, curate-in-charge presided and the sale was opened by Mrs Alfred Mear.* 24th February 1914

Was it luck or just bad timing that 'moving pictures' had begun to appear in the county in 1914? They allowed a release to an unknown world and had a dramatic impact upon a population which, to be blunt, was still very naive.

Some cinemas or 'picture palaces' were grander than others. The Stafford Picture House, if their advertising patter was to be believed, was *'always delightfully cool in the hottest weather'*. And nothing was too much trouble; *'Tea will be served free to adults in the 6d, 9d and 1s seats at all the matinees'* and very welcome it must have been during a showing of 'Anthony and Cleopatra'!

Normacot, less than a mile from the Meir had its own cinema, the Alhambra. Surprisingly it had some connection with Holy Trinity church since it was built by Messrs Tompkinson and Bettelley. The first reels turned in May 1914 with their flickering black and white shapes, along with the piano music that accompanied them. The licensee, T C Wild, had a younger brother, master potter J S Wild, who lived at the Beeches in Uttoxeter Road.

In the summer before the world went mad, an auction at the Crown & Anchor, Longton saw several local town houses come under the hammer:

> *At the Wednesday Sale at the Crown & Anchor, Longton: 6 dwelling houses numbers 29 to 39 Bright Street, the Meir, together with a plot of freehold land at the rear producing a grand annual rent of £53 6s were sold for £505.*

War was declared and dreams faded. Much was to change but just how much nobody knew. The good folk of the Meir, within a fortnight, had decided they were not going to just sit back and take it on the chin:

> *On Monday evening (17th August 1914) residents of the Meir met at the Church Institute under the chairmanship of the Rev R O Walker[4] to discuss methods of alleviating distress which might arise during the war. As a result, the ladies present formed themselves into a sewing committee to provide garments for the Red Cross and the gentlemen present constituted a committee to raise funds.*

There was perhaps an unspoken thought that some of their own relatives could soon be in desperate need of help as troops of the Staffordshire Regiment left for Burton on Trent at the start of the conflict. A trickle of young men from the area were caught up in the early euphoria which quickly broadened into a flood. Just what they were letting themselves in for they could not in their wildest dreams imagine, but the scene at the recruitment station in Longton Town Hall was being repeated all over the country:

Young men have been coming forward faster than the authorities could cope with them. On Wednesday (30th August) 128 took out papers and between Saturday and noon on Thursday, 452 had enlisted.

This rare view of men of the Royal Field Artillery was taken in 1914. They are passing the portals of the old King's Arms public house on their way to Burton, 24 miles away.

One local man who had volunteered again for duty was Band Sergeant James Sturgess, 6th Company North Staffs Regiment who had previously fought in South Africa and been wounded 16 times in the battle for Spion Kop, having part of his skull blown away. This required the surgical insertion of a silver plate and he had been invalided out to Netley where he was at death's door for some time. He was lucky to have survived.

And yet with war in the air, it was ironic that someone should relinquish his life on his own doorstep, almost casually:

A porter, George Elwell from Meir Station was killed on the track as he went to fetch some pears from a shop in Weston Road.

The Lads' Institute at Holy Trinity was completed and the customary honoured guest was wheeled out:

On Monday evening (5th October) Mr G Rittner of Weston Coyney Hall opened the Lads' Institute which has been erected as an adjunct of the church Institute. The formal opening was preceded by a service in church conducted by the Rev R O Walker, curate in charge. The vicar of Caverswall, the Rev H M Fowler presided at the opening ceremony and pointed out the growth of work at the Meir necessitated an extension of their parochial organisations. The new hall would be used for drill and recreation and on Sunday, for Sunday School purposes. Mr Rittner wished the organisation every success and commended the extension of church work in the district. A short musical programme was gone through and an ambulance exhibition was given by the Boy Scouts

But the war would not go away. Belgium fell and was in chaos. Ask any local to write down all they know about Belgium and it's a safe bet Belgian refugees would not be near the top of the list. But that year displaced Belgian nationals were brought to Longton where two houses were set aside for them. Safe at last, they would now only have to worry where the next meal was coming from. The news that bread was up by a halfpenny for a four pound loaf at 6d for 'best' and 5d for 'seconds' and beer was 4d a pint would probably for them be almost inconsequential.

But the needs of 'our boys' at the front were pressing. Within the first few days of the new year, the good people of the Meir had decided to add their help to the war effort:

The Meir is to have its own Civilian Training Corps. At a meeting on Monday evening in the church institute presided over by Mr J H Barlow, Mr S A Griffiths, secretary of the Longton Corps, explained the movement and what had been done locally and in other parts of England. The chairman said it was the duty of every man who was unable to join the Regulars[5] or the Territorials to assist these forces as much as possible should the necessity arise, hence the Civilian Training Corps. The proposition to have a local corps was made by Mr Charles Heath and seconded by Mr Ney. Messrs A V Bowden and J D Weaver were appointed secretaries pro tem.

In truth, the area had an outstanding record when it came to recruiting volunteers. In early 1915 between 3000 and 4000 Longton men, some from the Meir, were in the services. A remarkable example of patriotism was when twelve members of one Longton household 'joined the colours'. Mrs Mooney of Goddard Street, East Vale must have found cooking the evening meal and doing the washing a lot

o.   **n.**

ROYAL FLYING CORPS.

RECRUITS, SKILLED or UNSKILLED (the latter must be clerks, storemen, etc.), men of almost any occupation, are wanted at once for the various branches of the Royal Flying Corps.

Men of military age and up to fifty years of age accepted. Corps rates of pay.

Apply personally or in writing to the nearest Recruiting Officer, who will put applicants into touch with the Special Recruiting Officer of the Royal Flying Corps in this district.

GOD SAVE THE KING.

easier with all her family away in France - but a lot more worrying!

The clergy also assisted with recruiting and Rev T L Murray did his duty in this way. And some members of the cloth went further and were inevitably injured:

Canon Tyrwhitt,[6] former vicar of Fenton now rector of Bolleston and chaplain-in-ordinary to the King was wounded while under fire.

It was all a matter of being in the wrong place at the wrong time and for one family, it must have been particularly hard to bear:

Lieutenant Geoffrey V F Monckton of the 1st Scots Guards of Stretton Hall was killed in action, the second son to die in the conflict.

Some did duck at the right time and live to tell the tale. Private A. Long, formerly of the Staffordshire Advertiser returned and received a warm welcome from his colleagues. *"Guess who's here? It's Arthur - you remember, Arthur Long. Good old Arthur."*

But it was far too early to celebrate anything yet. At the church of the Holy Evangelists, Normacot, a memorial service to Lieutenant Schofield RN was conducted by the Rev E C Hipkins. And the vicar of Uttoxeter's son, Lieutenant B A Knight-Smith was lost on 4th September 1915 aged just 20 years.

A cold realisation was beginning to dawn that the war would not be over by Christmas after all!

As a result of many fathers being absent from home, it was a noble gesture for someone to think of the welfare of their children and typical of the country in wartime:

Treats for Soldiers and Sailors Children: 1300 children of those serving in the forces were treated to an entertainment in the Town Hall. They were entertained by the proprietors of the Alexandra picture palace and the Longton Picturedrome

While elsewhere:

The bad weather forced Pearson's Fresh Air Fund indoors to Queensbury schools.

There was a brighter side to the situation when:

they were treated to a two hour picture show at the Alhambra picture palace Normacot, through the kindness of the proprietors.

But war or no war, life went on. The annual supper of the Institute and Bowling Club took place with the Rev H M Fowler and the Rev R O Walker, curate-in-charge of Holy Trinity, presiding.

Concern was expressed when in April, Aubrey Bowers, the son of the late Mr & Mrs Bowers of Caverswall Castle, applied for a commission in the 3rd Battalion of the North Staffs Regiment to do his part for King & Country. The battlefields of France would be a far cry from the recent celebrations he and *'a party from the castle'* had enjoyed in Caverswall Village. But the future inexorably beckoned him with countless others.

It was the year of Galipoli and Ypres. At home, there was a wedding between a local girl and a former curate in charge at Holy Trinity the Meir:

THE REV. R. CREED MEREDITH.   MISS SYLVIA ANYSLEY.

The Rev R Creed Meredith   **Miss Sylvia Anysley**

The marriage took place at St Peter's, Forsbrook, on Wednesday 22nd April between Miss Sylvia Aynsley, the eldest daughter of Mr & Mrs Joseph Aynsley of Blythe Bridge and the Rev R Creed-Meredith, son of the late Sir James Creed-Meredith LLD and Lady Meredith of Dublin; Miss Meredith was one of the bridesmaids. Mr W Sherratt, the organist played Lemarc's 'Andantino in D flat' and the 'Bridal March from Loehengrin'. The ceremony was performed by the Rev H S Woollcombe, vicar of Armley[8], assisted by the Rev E W Bridgwood of Forsbrook, the Rev F H W Archbold, cousin of the groom and the Rev H M Fowler, vicar of Caverswall.

The bride was dressed in an exquisite gown of ivory satin de Paris with a bodice of Chantilly lace and pink chiffon, the waist being held up with a cluster of orange blossom and myrtle. The train, suspended from the shoulder was lined with draw pink chiffon and had in the corner a spray of silver flowers embroidered with love knots. The veil of plain silk, set with silver roses was worn with a coronet of orange blossom and myrtle.

The combined choirs of Meir and Forsbrook were present - the concluding hymn being 'Come Gracious Spirit, Heavenly Dove' - and as the newly married couple left the church, Mr Sherratt played Mendelssohn's Wedding March.

The bride went away (to Torquay) in a costume of blue gaberdine with a collar of ivory capricieus embroidered in oriental colours and a blouse of crepe viora. She wore a french sailor hat of a pretty shade trimmed with a blue ribbon and small clusters of shaded roses.

Caverswall's own Rev H M Fowler and Mrs Fowler gave the happy couple a silver toast rack whilst Rev R O Walker and Mrs Walker handed the twosome Hymns Ancient & Modern, which was the equivalent of giving a carpenter a tenon saw for his birthday!

This would turn out to be the final ceremony for the Rev Herbert Metcalfe Fowler, the vicar of Caverswall. The incumbent of St Peter's since 1902, had been offered (and accepted) the living of Holy Trinity Church, Hereford.

Now, in addition to the Civilian Corps formed earlier in the year, there was also an active First Aid movement in the Meir. Anyone injured at church could find themselves bandaged from head to toe if they were not careful:

The Meir Division St John Ambulance Brigade carried out field work in the grounds of Weston Coyney Hall on Saturday, by kind permission of Mr & Mrs Rittner. The work was examined by Dr Allan and Lieutenant Brewer RAMC while tea (an essential part of any patient's recovery) *was provided by Mrs Barlow. the ambulance division was later inspected by Captain GH Rittner.*

BRITISH FARMERS' RED CROSS FUND.
MEIR SALE. JAN 6TH 1916.

Sections of the community staged a variety of events to collect money. Here an auction sale at the Meir sale yard possibly at the rear of the Saracen's Head or King's Arms for the British Red Cross who ministered to servicemen wounded in the Great War and sent food parcels to those in prisoner of war camps in Germany. The woman to the right is Mrs Rittner of Weston Coyney Hall followed by Mr Claude Hill with starched collar and Mr C Averill. Opening the sale, Mrs Rittner asked her audience to keep before them the words *"Duty, faith and endurance, during the coming year and if they lived up to that, she was convinced they would see peace in their midst possibly very much sooner than many of them expected."* The final figure raised reached £700.   *Priestley collection*

These were not the only section of this close-knit community who decided to help the conflict. The Meir, still truly rural in 1915, had a thriving farming fraternity:

A large and enthusiastic meeting of the farmers and butchers who attended the cattle market at Blythe Bridge and the King's Arms Hotel, the Meir on Tuesday (9th November) to consider the availability of holding a jumble sale by auction, the proceeds to be given to the British Red Cross Fund.

The Lusitania, 'the greyhound of the Atlantic', was torpedoed and sunk on her return to Liverpool from New York, eight miles off the Head of Kinsale, County Waterford Ireland. Over 1400 men women and children were lost from a compliment of 1,978. The neutral American government was outraged. Casualties included Alfred Vanderbilt, millionaire and close friend of President Woodrow Wilson and 127 of his fellow countrymen. Local people Mr John Walker and Winifred Barker, aged 9, were drowned, as well as Arthur Wood who was art designer to W H Grindley of Tunstall.

Galipoli added to the despair with the slaughter of 25,000 men, with 76,000 wounded and 13,000 missing - and the parting of the ways for one, Lieutenant Rupert Brooke:

If I should die think only this of me,
That there's some corner of a foreign field
That is forever England. There shall be
In that rich earth a richer dust concealed;
A dust whom England bore, shaped, made aware,
Gave, once, her flowers to love, her ways to roam,
A body of England's, breathing English air.
Washed by the rivers, blessed by sons of home,
And think, this heart, all evil shed away,
A pulse in the eternal mind, no less
Gives somewhere back the thoughts of England given;
Her sights and sounds; dreams happy as her day;
And laughter, learnt of friends; and gentleness,
In hearts at peace under an English heaven.

Although the war raged, social problems at home still needed attention and the Rev George Oliver involved himself in politics and the Shops Closing Order. Hours worked in shops were very long and the new hours suggested closing times of 8.30pm on Monday; 8pm on Tuesday and Wednesday; 1pm on Thursday; 8.30pm Friday and 10.30pm on Saturday.

The shortening days of Autumn meant for the villagers of Caverswall and the Meir milking cows in the dark and cold. The harvest festival at the Meir that year was notable not only for its fine produce but for a collection plate which contained no less than 399 farthings! The long awaited announcement of who was to be their new vicar was made:

The Rev F Barton Horspool of St Michael's, Bournemouth has been appointed to the living of Caverswall by the preferment of the Rev H M Fowler to Holy Trinity, Hereford. He is to take up his duties early in November. Rev Barton Horspool is a Devonian by birth and began his career as a journalist. He then went on to study at a theological college on the Isle of Man.

The ceremony proper took place in the stillness of Caverswall village, days before the celebration of Christmas.

The Rev F Barton Horspool was instituted to the living of Caverswall in succession to the Rev H M Fowler by the Lord Bishop of Lichfield in the parish church on Tuesday afternoon. There was a large congregation present including the local clergy. The service was conducted by the Rev R G Plant. the first lesson was read by the Rev R O Walker and the second by the Rev W G Mayne (rural dean of Cheadle). The Bishop delivered a most impressive address from the text Rev xix. 11. At the conclusion of the address an offertory was taken on behalf of the Lichfield Candidates Ordination Fund which amounted to £3 13s

Notes.
1. Prospect House is situated in Weston Road at its junction with the Avenue (now Penfleet Avenue). It is used by a dental practice.
2. The lodge was for sale in 1993 and the hall is now a country club.
3. R Creed Meredith was never priest in charge, only curate in charge.
4. Walker, Robert Osborne, Curate of Caverswall, including Meir, 1914-16.
5. There was no conscription until 1916; until then everyone who joined did so voluntarily.
6. He accompanied Princess Henry of Battenburg and the royal party when her Royal Highness opened the Fenton Town Hall Bazaar in November 1906.
7. Now Times Square, Longton.
8. Rev Ralph Creed Meredith had moved to Armley in 1914.

The Alhambra cinema, Normacot in Upper Normacot Road was owned by T C (Thomas Clarke) Wild. Built by Tompkinson & Bettelley, it brought the delights of the outside world to a population whose horizons were limited.The stone window facings, gabled pediment and circular leaded window over the impressive entrance, are all pleasing features while the electric light bulbs around the window frames are a novelty. Before the advent of Meir's own cinema, many would have walked down the hill after work to spend an hour or two in the flickering make-believe world. Taken on a June day after 1914, the forthcoming attractions on the billboard are Mon, Tues & Weds, 'Escape of Jim Dolan' and Thurs, Frid & Sat, 'Black Spot'. There appears to be no Sunday show! All the houses and the Alhambra were demolished by the Highways Agency for the A50 in 1994.   *Lovatt collection*

From 1915, this scene from Weston Road (A520) shows Station (now Stanton) Road on the left and Bright Street behind the figure on the right. This part of old Meir is virtually untouched in over 80 years; all the buildings on the left along with most of those on the right are original. A feature to note is the large number of mature trees close to the junction with Uttoxeter Road (A50) in the distance.   *Author's collection*

126

Unlike Holy Trinity, the church of the Holy Evangelists, Normacot had a vicarage from the 19th century. This view was taken by J A Lovatt. Formerly known as the Furnace Inn, it stood behind Mill Farm and was sometimes called Church House. A stone at the back of the house has a crown and coronet dated 1817. With its manicured lawns and expansive grounds it was a very fitting residence for the incumbent of the parish. Normacot church is visible to the left above the high hedge around the private garden. *Lovatt collection*

A charming shot of Rev E.C.(Edwin Charles) Hipkins, the vicar of Normacot, his wife and their grandson with some of his treasured toys, on the lawn of the old Normacot vicarage. Rev Hipkins was first a curate at St James' in Longton before becoming vicar of Normacot in 1892 where he stayed until his death on the 27th July 1929. *Lovatt collection*

This elegant house,Weston Coyney Hall, 3 storeys high, was situated a mile from the crossroads in Meir, and stood in spacious grounds which in later years would be partly occupied by Lautrecs public house in Weston Road (A 520) It was the home of Captain & Mrs Rittner (see Farmers Red Cross Fund in 1916) who were involved in many local charitable events. Like many of the magnificent residences found locally, it has regrettably been demolished.

Hill collection

This is the later Normacot vicarage taken by JA Lovatt. Extensively covered in either ivy (or virginia creeper) with the elegant bargeboards and singular street lamp, together they all combine to add charm to this view from 1939.

Lovatt collection

The Empire theatre had a chequered career before this photograph was taken. Originally built in 1888 for £8000 and called the Queen's Theatre, it was redecorated and re-upholstered at a further cost of £4000 in 1890. Burnt to the ground in September 1894, it rose from the ashes in 1896 after further expenditure of £17000. A mile or so from the Meir, it was a popular place of entertainment and the location for many Christmas pantomimes towards the end of the 19th century. Acquired by Leon Salberg of The Alexandra Theatre, Birmingham and promptly closed for refurbishment during 1917, it reopened on Christmas Eve with the appreciative audience seated in a sumptuously appointed blue and old gold auditorium. Designed by Frank Matcham, it was mysteriously gutted by fire in 1992 and despite gallant attempts by many groups, one by Ellis Bevan, it was alas deemed beyond redemption and largely demolished. Longton, with so few remaining buildings of worth, could little afford to let this piece of Victoriana slip so casually through its fingers! *Author's collection*

Taken at his shop at 71 Weston Road Luke Bennett with his grandchild; at the time, he was one of Meir's oldest residents. He originally had a shop on the old King's Arms car park where he mended watches and sold sweets. When Meir Cottage was demolished and the King's Arms rebuilt in 1934/35, he made 71 Weston Road (today Hyland's) into a shop. It stood on the junction of Weston Road and Station (now Stanton) Road with Weaver's the bakers on the other corner on the same side. Luke Bennett is listed in Kelly's Directory for 1936. *Bennett collection*

Probably taken in the early 1920s, this is the young Arthur Bennett in the garden of Meir Cottage. Many local cycling clubs were formed, despite the hilly terrain.and it was not uncommon to see a line of twenty or thirty cyclists heading for the coast during the 1930s. *Bennett collection*

This rustic view of old Meir was taken almost 70 years ago. It depicts Meir crossroads with the 'Toll Cottage' nearest the camera. The building behind it is the old Saracen's Head which stood opposite in Sandon Road. The road that runs straight through the photograph is the A50 with Blythe Bridge in the distance and Longton over the shoulder of the photographer. Sandon Road, formerly Lewis's Lane, joins this road by the gas lamp in the middleground. It is interesting to compare this shot with later views after the Toll Cottage had been demolished after 1928. No traffic lights, Pelican crossings or air thick with traffic fumes: it was wall-to-wall countryside.   *Bennett collection*

This photograph helps untangle the view above. Taken at the same period it shows the relationship of the Toll Cottage nearest the camera, to that of the old Saracen's Head behind it. Sandon road runs from lower left to middle right, while Meir Lane (Uttoxeter Road 1995) runs parallel to the front of the Toll Cottage. The poster, just visible, is for the Alhambra cinema, Normacot, showing the film 'PARIS'. Due to road widening, both these buildings were demolished by the mid 1930's.

Bennett collection

CHAPTER 11

1916 - 1922

'He that finde his life shall lose it: and he that lose his life for my sake shall find it.'

Matthew 10 v39

News of the fighting was carefully controlled by the War Office and the idea that 'right would prevail' slowly seeped into the conscience of a population that desperately wanted to hear some good news. This was perpetuated by some of the local dignitaries in a meeting in the Meir:

The annual gathering of the Meir Church Lads Brigade took place at the Church Institute and subsequently Col. F G Goodwin, commanding the 11th Lichfield Division gave an inspiring address to the lads on the work of the Church Brigade. Col. Goodwin said he was getting some returns from the War Office and when he had all the figures, the result would show that no fewer than EIGHT HUNDRED AND FIFTY MEN had gone from their battalion into the army quite apart from the attestations under Lord Derby's scheme. Four or five of their members had gained the Distinguished Service Medal(DSM) and they had secured a great number of commissions.

Lance Corporal Ernest Bailey of the Royal Welch Fusiliers whose home was at 11 Pitt Street, Sandford Hill, Longton was awarded the Military Medal *'for bravery in the field'*, as was Corporal John Wyatt of the Sherwood Foresters who lived at 17 New Hall Road, Normacot, not far from the Alhambra cinema.

And, although not a Meir man, Private James Grundy of the Grenadier Guards of Fenton was recommended for the Victoria Cross for *'selfless gallantry of the highest order'* by Major-General the Earl of Cavan, commanding the Guards.

But the fighting was a long way away and if you tried hard you could forget it very easily:

A social gathering was held at the Meir Church Institute when a hearty welcome was extended to the Rev Barton Horspool and Mrs Horspool. The company numbered more than 300. Dancing, music, games and cards were provided. The Rev R O Walker, curate-in-charge presided and observed that their vicar had come amongst them to help Meir quite as much as the mother church at Caverswall. It was essential for the work of the church that they should be united as a parish. The vicar, in reply, said "we are living in times when the church had to give a lead to the nation to help make this country a happier and holier place after the war". They, as a parish, could do their share by trying to bring the people back to the God of their forefathers.

In addition to the usual government agencies, voluntary organisations contributed to the war effort in innumerable ways. A prime example was the Silk Nursing Association which by its endeavours in April 1916 from the sale of flags, raised £46 9s 9d for the purpose of treating the injured and wounded. And for those interned abroad (at this time 19 Longton men were held in camps in Germany), a flag day for the Longton Prisoners of War Society collected money for parcels to be shipped abroad to them. One recipient was Corporal Horace Woods, *'who before joining the army in 1915 had been for several years a member of the Stoke-on-Trent Borough Police Force stationed in the town'* who had been reported missing before it was established he was being held captive: *'Corporal Woods has written to his wife who resides at the Meir that he is now at an internment camp in Germany.'*

But for some, there was the shock of learning the loss of their husband was permanent - 'he had given all for King & Country'. The death of one of Caverswall's more notable sons was an event that shattered the composure of the solitary country village:

> *Lieutenant W Aubrey Bowers, son of the late Mr & Mrs Bowers died from wounds received the following day in the great battle in France, July 1916.*
>
> *Lieut Bowers joined the 5th North Staffs Territorial Regiment in April 1915 and went to France early in the present year. He was the only son of the late William Bowers, the 'Squire of Caverswall'. He was born at Barlaston Hall a little more than 29 years ago and educated at Manchester and New College Oxford. He married Miss Vera Annie Latham three years ago.*
>
> *Mrs Bowers was staying in Eastbourne with her one infant daughter when the sad news was communicated to her from Caverswall Castle.*

A tragedy, one of many for thousands of families throughout the land whatever their station.

In that terrible battle at the Somme, during one day, the British had 60,000 casualties and by nightfall, some battallions numbered barely a handful of men. It was fervently hoped that the new Prime Minister, David Lloyd George, would fare better than Herbert Asquith[1] in the quest for victory. But there was a quiet realisation that things would never be quite the same again.

This was true for the family of Major Cecil Wedgwood DSO along with countless others whose photographs adorned the papers. All were personal tragedies, but even in these hours of individual misery, ran the thread of the British class system: *'Stafford Grammar School Boy Killed'*, while there were many attempts with prose straight from the pages of 'Boy's Own'. *'Popular Lichfield Sergeant Killed'*.

The year changed and 1917 saw the loss of Longton's perpetual Catholic parish priest. Only a few months earlier he had been the recipient of his parishioners heartfelt gratitude:

> *A magnificent testimonial to the work of the Rev J Stringfellow, rector of St*

Gregory's Roman Catholic Church, was paid him by his parishioners on Sunday when he was asked to accept a purse containing six hundred pounds.

The venerable rector has been at Longton through four decades:

The death of Father John Stringfellow of St Gregory's Roman Catholic Church, Longton for 45 years has occurred at the age of 75 years. Son of a Liverpool builder, he was educated at Birmingham and ordained a priest in 1873, serving at Stafford, Walsall and Caverswall before going to St.Gregory's. He is succeeded by Dr E Goodwin of Banbury.

A memorial to Aubrey Bowers was commissioned at Caverswall in the church amongst the winding lanes where he had spent so many sunny afternoons:

LIEUT. W. AUBREY BOWERS KILLED.

A wide circle of friends in North Staffordshire will deeply regret the death of Lieut. W. Aubrey Bowers, of Caverswall Castle, near Blythe Bridge, which occurred on Sunday evening from wounds received in the great battle in France on the previous day.

Lieut. Bowers joined the 5th North Staffordshire Territorial Regiment in April, 1915, and went to France early in the present year. He was the only son of the late Mr. William Bowers, "the

THE LATE LIEUT. W. A. BOWERS.

Squire" of Caverswall, and succeeded to extensive agricultural and colliery interests in the

Choir stalls of oak with a brass mural tablet to the memory of 2nd Lieutenant William Aubrey Bowers of the North Staffs Regiment who died from wounds in action on July 2nd 1916 were dedicated by the Bishop of Lichfield (Dr Kemp Thorne) at Caverswall Church on the 13th inst. The tablet bears the following inscription, "To the Glory of God and in ever loving memory of William Aubrey Bowers of the North Staffordshire Regiment, Caverswall Castle. Born January 22nd 1887. Died July 2nd 1916 of wounds received in action at Gommecourt, France on July 1st. This tablet and choir stalls in the chancel are erected by his widow." The inscription goes on, "And whosoever will lose his life for my sake, shall find it."

Churchwardens Mr Stephen Mear and Mr J Barlow from Holy Trinity Church, the Meir were present as was the Rev H M Fowler, now of Holy Trinity, Hereford - formerly vicar of Caverswall for 13 years, the Rev F Barton Horspool, vicar of Caverswall and the Reverends Maurice Davies and T Caleb. 22nd September 1917

The Rev T L Murray at SS Marys and Chads Sandford Hill expressed his anxiety over his church's finances as a consequence of the conflict:

Opening a sale of work, the Rev T L Murray had said that as a result of the war, the church had had to borrow £400 from the bank. He mentioned that he

had completed 27 years in Longton, during which time buildings which were worth £16000 had been erected!

That Christmas of 1917, there was scarcely a family in the kingdom that had not either lost someone or knew a family who had. Spirits were flagging. The Empire Theatre, under new ownership, offered an opportunity to set aside life's realities for awhile:

The Empire Theatre has been acquired by Mr Leon Salberg of the Alexandra Theatre, Birmingham. The present theatre, formerly known as the Queen's Theatre, was built following a disastrous fire which destroyed an earlier building in 1894. It was designed by Mr Frank Matcham, a leading theatrical architect of the day, and built by Mr Peter Bennion at a cost of about £20,000. The original opening took place on 18th May 1896 when Miss Fortescue a popular actress of the time supported by a powerful company appeared in 'Pygmalion and Galatea' by the late WS Gilbert.[2]

As the first days of another year dawned, the feeling was that, surely this time we would see victory. To support 'our brave boys', in January 1918 a Tank Bank Week was held locally. And while some chose to channel their energies into increasing our mechanised might, others helped in another manner. An advertisement exhorted all to:

Remember our brave lads in the trenches are standing between you and the Germans. Stand behind them with your money!!

Newspaper photographs told the familiar story of local men who had gone 'over the top' never to return. But for those who did return, much was done to assist sick, wounded and permanently disabled soldiers in May 1918:

Mrs E Durber of the Dorothy Café, Stafford Street, Longton kindly entertained a party of about 100 soldiers from the Stoke War Hospital on the 2nd inst. The Rev Gilbert Oliver (rector of St John's) met the soldiers and accompanied them to the Edensor Road Picture Palace.

Closely followed in June by:

a concert arranged at the Empire Theatre to raise money for our prisoners of war in Germany.

The formation of the Royal Air Force from the ashes of the Royal Flying Corps and the Royal Naval Air Service on April 1st 1918, marked their evolution to a modern fighting service. A glance back at the string and wire aircraft of the time only fuels one's admiration more. The men who actively sought to fly *and* fight were held in awe and the Meir had its own champion:

It has been announced that Mr Kenneth J Wolfe Dennitts, younger son of Mr & Mrs L Dennitts of the King's Arms Hotel, the Meir has been awarded a commission in the Royal Air Force.

The fragile marvel of a First World War 'fighter plane'

Given that three years earlier his elder brother had lost his life in France, it was even more courageous. Despite all the odds, some got away with it, while others did not; to pay the ultimate price so close to the trumpet's victory blast was the ultimate irony. The parents of 18 year old 2nd Lieutenant W J Brian, who lived quietly behind the net curtains at 'Holmlea', Meir Road, saw their world fall apart when his death was belatedly announced at a time of national celebration of victory.

The price of victory was immense - the lives of three quarters of a million men from Britain[3] together with 200,000 from the Empire; and as elsewhere, for the people of the Meir, it was a sacrifice borne with courage. The photographs of the soldiers killed before the Armistice continued to appear periodically and joltingly in the press.

One activity that grew in the years 1914-18 was the allotment movement: Many grew vegetables and potatoes to supplement a meagre diet, but this required land that was convenient for the members' houses. During 1917 Stoke Corporation had taken over land from the Duke of Sutherland's Estate to turn it into allotments at Shrubbery Lane. It soon had its imitators:

> *An enthusiastic interest has been displayed of late in the allotment movement and last week a food production society was formed in the village, a strong committee being appointed. Mr J H Barlow (from Holy Trinity church) has been elected the first president and Messrs D Cartlidge and C Swift appointed secretary and treasurer resp. It has also been arranged to hold a show during the present year.*

The Potteries was also suffering the effects of a bread famine and to stave off the shortage some newspapers gave detailed directions on "How to bake bread at home".

January and February 1919 brought more news of returning soldiers. The Military Medal was awarded to Sapper H Shaw of the Royal Engineers of 6 Russell Street, Dresden. In Longton, a matinee was held at the Empire in aid of blinded soldiers and sailors for St Dunstans; £608 was raised. And in Longton, there was a dinner for 228 repatriated prisoners in the Town Hall; a further £500 was collected. The appreciation and admiration of the heroes in Longton and the Meir, as elsewhere, knew no bounds. In March, a local presentation was made:

> *An interesting gathering took place at the Heathcote Arms Hotel[4] Longton on Wednesday evening, the Meir Division of the St John Ambulance Brigade being entertained to dinner by Mr J H Barlow JP and the superintendent of the Division, Mr F H Heath. During the proceedings, the chairman presented the Croix de Guerre to Corporal A. Gunn of the North Staffs Regiment who has been twice wounded and twice mentioned in dispatches. "Meir," observed Mr Barlow, "had produced a VC and several Military Medallists in addition to the winner of the Croix de Guerre."*
>
> *It had also been intended for Private Tom Bradbury of the Duke of Cornwall's Light Infantry to receive the Military Medal from the hands of Mr J R Hey (District Officer of the St John Ambulance Brigade) but it was explained that Private Bradbury was still suffering the effects of gas poisoning and was at a convalescent home.*

EGERTON, Ernest Albert
Corporal (later Sergeant)   16th Bn., The Sherwood Foresters (The Nottinghamshire and Derbyshire Regiment)
Other Decorations: —
Date of Gazette: 26 Nov. 1917
Place/Date of Birth: Longton, Staffordshire — 10 Nov. 1897
Place/Date of Death: Stoke-on-Trent, Staffordshire — 14 Feb. 1966
Memorials: Buried at Forsbrook, Stoke-on-Trent
Town/County Connections: Longton, Staffordshire
Remarks: —
Account of Deed: On 20 Sep. 1917 south-east of Ypres, Belgium, during an attack, visibility was bad owing to fog and smoke. As a result the two leading waves of the attack passed over certain hostile dug-outs without clearing them and enemy rifles and machine-guns from these dug-outs were inflicting severe casualties. Corporal Egerton at once responded to a call for volunteers to help in clearing up the situation and he dashed for the dug-outs under heavy fire at short range. He shot a rifleman, a bomber and a gunner, by which time support had arrived and 29 of the enemy surrendered.

The Meir's recipient of the Victoria Cross, reproduced from 'England, their England' by kind permission.

St Chad's at Sandford Hill had a belated Victory Bazaar some twelve months after the last rifle shot:

> *A bazaar at the church of St Mary and Chad's has raised £900! The amounts*

raised each day of the three was: £508: £231 and £160 on the 3rd day.

With characteristic innocence, the Rev T L Murray used the last day's takings for a six month holiday to alleviate his health - he needed time to think. When he returned, his mind was made up:

> He has decided to give up the living of St Mary and St Chad, Sandford Hill in
> August and will act as a missionary in the diocese for the Bishop of Lichfield.
> He has been at SS Mary & Chad's for 30 years.

The man who with fortitude and against opposition from miners and pottery workers on 'The Hill', had succeeded in building up the parish with its beautiful church overlooking the filth and squalor of Longton, had now had enough.

For many the year went from bad to worse. Where was the 'Land fit for Heroes' they had all been led to expect? The creditors of Harold Fernihough of Meir Farm, the Meir had little chance of getting their money:

> The first meeting of the creditors was held at Stoke on Trent. Liabilities
> amounted to £1045 while assets totalled £5 12s.

It reflected life for many in Meir and Longton at the time. National and local politicians tried hard to repair the country's battered and bruised economy. What, though, of the 'lost generation', the men slaughtered during the war?

> A positive remembrance of all their sacrifices was proposed by a memorial for
> Longton against which £650 has so far been collected.

Surprisingly, the roughness of people's existence was no reflection of their generosity. North Staffordshire had at that time a convalescent holiday home at Llanfairfechan in Wales and with running costs considerable, voluntary cash was essential:

> Longton that had the distinction of collecting the largest sum of money in any
> of the Potteries towns on the occasion of the recent flag day effort for the
> North Staffs Health Home at Llanfairfechan. Of the £85 17s 8d raised no less
> than £63 4 s 7d was collected in coppers.

Most of the working people of the area had little or no chance of ever changing their station in life. For those at the bottom of the ladder it was nigh on hopeless. But just occasionally, someone would perform little 'miracles' for them:

> Mrs W Langford JP, whose work among the poor of Longton is widely known
> added yet another to her acts of generosity on Saturday when, at her
> invitation, thirteen hundred of the poor children of Longton enjoyed
> witnessing a matinee performance of "Beauty & the Beast" at the Empire
> Theatre[5]. The children, many of whom were entering the theatre for the first
> time, manifested a great interest in the proceedings. Each was presented with
> a bag of chocolates on leaving the theatre.

It was not the first or the last time that the Empire Theatre would throw open its doors for good causes. It had been the venue during the preceding month for the staging of a concert for the welfare of the many caught in the 'no-man's land' between honest poverty and complete destitution.

> *A concert was held at the Empire Theatre, Longton in aid of the Boot Fund.*
> *Over £62 was given over to the Longton Schools Child Boot Fund and with*
> *another £40 provided boots for four and fifty children.*

The fact that so many Longton and Meir children had no boots and shoes was a symptom of North Staffordshire life at the time. Housing in the Longton area had caused grave concern among the Medical Officers of Health for years and there was a priority to demolish insanitary dwellings (of which there were acres) and to rebuild them 'in some luxury' elsewhere. One 'elsewhere' was in the clean air and open fields at the Meir. The Leason Road[6] estate was the first of two housing commitments the City undertook in the 1920s.

In Spring, the Rev Prebendary George Oliver of St John's died at the rectory in Longton, leaving a multitude of bereaved parishioners and an estate worth £2222.

The efforts and achievements of Longton and Meir's clergy were at that time chronicled in minute detail. Odd, therefore, that little was written of what the congregation of Holy Trinity thought about their priest, the Rev T Caleb until he was about to go, although the registers at the church do signify his presence throughout his stay (save for one Christmas Day when he was ill).

Without a doubt, the most notable incident which coloured his whole incumbency was the infamous choir strike of 1916. Did the whole affair have its origins at the Rural Deanery Choirs Festival where choirs from Caverswall, East Vale, Werrington and Kingsley took part in the service? The registers from the church, written in ink, (not blood), indicate the 'little local difficulty', with the Rev Theophilus Caleb penning, *'Holy Trinity church abstained owing to my appointment as curate in charge.'* But passions were inflamed after lads stationed outside Holy Trinity Church told worshippers, *'Not to go in. Please miss; don't go in that church![7]'*

This course of action was not wholly successful and they finally resorted to the ultimate weapon, a choir strike. But at the end of September, tempers had cooled: writing in a mood bordering more on retribution than reconciliation, the Rev Caleb wrote in the registers. *'Choir strike finished. Most unsatisfactory. It would have been better had they never come back.'* adding and emphasising, *'never'*.

In spite of this, a lot of water had flowed under the bridge when it came time to leave six years later and the bitterness had been assuaged:

> *Evidence of the regard in which he was held by his parishioners was*
> *forthcoming on Sunday, when the Rev T Caleb, curate-in-charge for the past*

six years of the Holy Trinity church, Meir bade goodbye to his friends. A crowded congregation on Sunday evening heard Mr Caleb's farewell sermon and there was also a large attendance at a farewell meeting in the Sunday schools over which Mr G C V Cant presided. Mr Cant said they were gathered together to bade farewell to Mr. Caleb and to offer him their hearty congratulations of his preferment to the village of Norman's Heath. He paid a tribute to Mr Caleb's ministrations at the Meir and expressed the hope he would have happiness and success in his new sphere of work. A series of presentations were made to the departing minister during the evening. He received an illuminated address and a handsome pot and pedestal from the members of the Stoke, Fenton, Longton and Meir Royal Antediluvian Order of Buffaloes Lodges, a purse containing £23 13s 9d from the members of the congregation and a number of smaller gifts from the Mothers' Union, Girl Guides and Sunday School.

If there had been disunity during his sojourn at the Meir, it certainly did not show.

Notes
1. Herbert Asquith was to lose a son in the fighting.
2. W S (Schwenk) Gilbert, of Gilbert & Sullivan fame, died from a suspected heart attack at the age of 74, whilst swimming.
3. The total is equal to all the supporters at the Cup Final for 10 years.
4. Shown on page 81.
5. The theatre at this time was owned by Cartwright & Edwards.
6. Named after Alderman Leason
7. From the registers of Holy Trinity Church, Meir.

A beautiful photograph taken from the nave at St Peter's Caverswall, towards the altar, in 1903 or earlier. Notoriously difficult to capture, JA Lovatt has brought out the peace and timeless solemnity of the church .
The glass in the chancel windows has been replaced since by scenes of the Crucifixion and Ascension. On the left in the chancel is visible one of the superb figures by Sir Francis Legatt Chantrey, whose work also complements and adorns the interior of Lichfield Cathedral. The choir stalls were later dedicated to the memory of W Aubrey Bowers of Caverswall Castle.   *Lovatt collection*

This memorial over a communal grave in Longton cemetery shows the final resting place of three of the priests from St Gregory's Roman Catholic church. The last name is that of Rev John Stringfellow.
Author's collection

A crisp and detailed photo of the Chantrey figure in the chancel, St Peter's Caverswall. It was taken probably before 1903. Sir Francis Chantrey (1781-1842) became one of the greatest sculptors of his time inspite of being orphaned at the age of 12. On his death, his fortune was left to the Royal Academy for the purchase of works of British Art.

The inscription reads *"Interred with him (Sir Thomas Parker) is his daughter, Martha, wife of Sir John Jervis, afterwards created Earl St Vincent for his great naval victory over the Spanish Fleet off Cape St Vincent in 1797. The lovely figure to her memory erected in 1818 by her husband is the work of the sculptor, Chantrey"*.   *Lovatt collection*

Sporting a bowler and overcoat, this is J A. Lovatt who took all the photographs bearing his name - except this one, which was taken by Salopian J R Pugh, almost 90 years ago in Woodpark Lane(formerly Bog Lane), Lightwood. Each leg of the tripod has only one extension, so even when it was closed, it would be cumbersome to carry. Note also the focusing cloth on the camera
                    Lovatt collection

Travelling west, half a mile down the Uttoxeter Road, the traveller came into Normacot with its bustling and vigorous shopping centre. The atmosphere further down this road in Longton was anything but clean, judging from the stained and blackened brickwork of the houses. Most of the shops on the right are still standing 70 years on, although their business has changed. Billy Bettelley's is seen on the far right where the woman wearing a white cloche hat is holding the hand of a child. Like so much of the city, much of the property on the left side of the road has now gone; however the shops on the corner, in front of which a horse and cart is moving, still hang on. A50 road widening has decimated the area. *Warrillow collection*

After entering Dresden, continuing a little way along Belgrave Road leads to the junction with Trentham Road. A policeman on horseback is leading a military band and a large procession towards the gates of Queen's Park, Longton some quarter of a mile away. Did this take place after the end of the Great War or were the men marching off to battle? Many who lived in the Meir would have walked down to see this celebration perhaps then strolling on to the park. A large proportion of the buildings shown here are still in evidence today, save for the Lord John Russell public house which straddled the corner close to the right hand tram pole - it was demolished for road improvements along with two adjacent houses and their position is now the site of a car park. Most of the housing along Belgrave Road and towards Dresden Church was ripped out in the same development. Nearly everyone pictured here is wearing a hat: something which 80 years on, looks strange.

Lovatt collection

Meir Lane and Meir Road joining from the left, 1925/6. Horse drawn trams appeared in the City in the last quarter of the 19th cent. Electric trams came to this junction at first then later right into Meir. The final tram to Meir ran in July 1928. The terraced houses are still there, but the shop at the fork is gone (Ewart Hollinson owned an ice cream parlour on these premises from the 1930s).

Hill collection

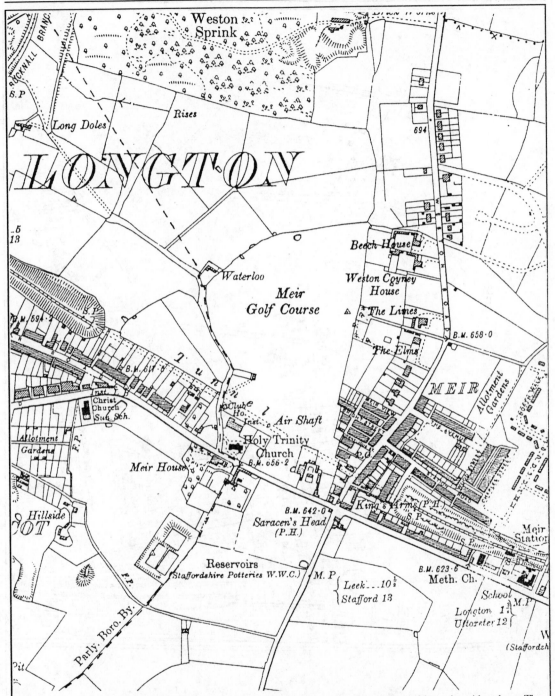

Meir 1925. based on OS map.The pace of development since the end of the first world war is evident here. The town centre is larger and there have been the additions of the golf course, bowling greens and tennis courts. Note the farm close to the crossroads on which in the 1960s was built a Kwik Save and the Barclays bank. Towards Longton, the ribbon development of large terraced houses and grand villas either side of the A50 can be seen.

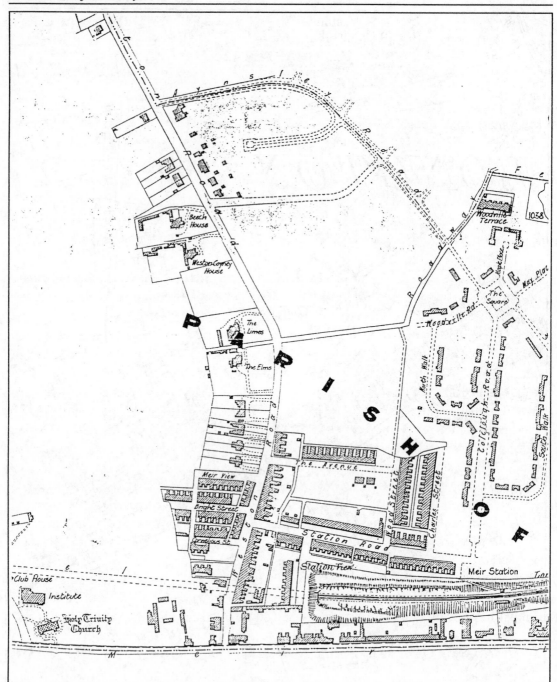

Based on 1926 parish map, this shows Meir at the time it broke away from Caverswall. Some roads were to later change their names. The Avenue became Penfleet Avenue, Station Road became Stanton Road along with Wood Street and Charles Street. Note how close the houses hug the A50 and A520. It also shows how close to the Meir centre the parish of Normacot comes.

CHAPTER 12
1923 - 1929
In this best of possible worlds, all is for the best
Voltaire.

Five years has slipped by since the end of the Great War. For those who had never hesitated in the hour of their country's greatest need, the promise of 'jam tomorrow' seemed further away than ever. Any opportunity of a 'treat' was seized gleefully:

The annual entertainment for the children whose Fathers had fallen in the Great War was held on the 5th inst. by the NFDDS & Services at the club premises in Lovatt Street, Stoke. Mr Arthur Argo performed his ventriloquial act to great amusement and on leaving each child was presented with a toy from an enormous snowball.

It was fortunate they had patrons like a Mrs Brown and her friends at Shelton Church Institute, for it was they and their colleagues who looked after four thousand poor children from Hanley. Many were dependent upon the Herculean efforts of a few private benefactors. Generally, there was an awareness that the physical and mental health of young people was linked to their environment but this once a year treat did nothing for the other 364 days.

The need to get children away from insanitary housing and create areas in which they could play was important and was beginning to be given a high priority. The Victorians had initially bequeathed this city several parks with intricate boathouses and lodges, but there were few, if any, playground facilities. Children would hang around street corners and 'the backs'[1]. But in May 1924:

The Stone Road (later Lightwood Road)[2] Recreation Ground was opened at 3pm on 30th inst. by his Grace, the Duke of Sutherland. A musical accompaniment was performed by the band of the 5th North Staffs Regiment and to mark the occasion, school children in the area were given a half-day's holiday.

Channelling the enterprise and initiative of youngsters was a thread running through the Boy Scout movement, which was world wide, and not without a 'whiff of empire', but it must have been a pleasant surprise when some overseas visitors 'dropped-in':

Rhodesian scouts were entertained to tea by the 1st Longton (Earl of Harrowby's Own) scouts at St Mary & St Chad's Institute, Sandford Hill. Longton.

An act of bravery over the border in the principality did not go unnoticed by the local papers who were always keen to praise this human attribute:

There was an award to Scout Tunnicliffe for helping a colleague who had fallen down a mountain at Penmaenmawr on August 5th. It was presented by the District Commissioner, Mr Ronald Copeland.

The spiritual and moral needs of the population were never far away from the scrutiny of the Watch Committee in 1924:

> *Authority was given to the Borough Police Court on Monday for picture shows on Good Friday at the Empire Theatre[3], the Alexandra Palace[4] and the Royal[5], subject to conditions laid down at the Watch Committee that only suitable pictures be shown.*

Just what constituted suitable is not explained.

During the final week before the feast of the Nativity, a memorial to a once ever-present cleric was begun.

> *A Memorial window to perpetuate the memory of the late Rev Preb George Oliver, Rector for 26 years at St. John's, Longton is being constructed. The light has been designed by Mr Gordon Forsyth and is being executed at the Longton School of Art under his personal supervision assisted by Mr A J Lovatt.*

The immense opportunities of aviation were slowly being realised by many. Unfortunately Stoke Corporation was not amongst them! The location of an airport in the City would inevitably improve links for both trade, pleasure and travel, but the city Fathers 'cast the runes' to make a decision that would have far reaching implications for Stoke on-Trent's position in Britain's internal air network. The proposal for a North Staffordshire Flying Club at the Meir must be seen as a golden chance to expand the city's commercial base and industrial profile.

The Corporation, as so often happens, were otherwise occupied with the appalling housing that afflicted such great areas of the city. The 2nd to the 7th of May was designated National Rat Week. Many needed no reminding of rats: they lived with the problem 52 weeks every year! Whole areas needed razing and rebuilding and as a 'stop-gap' measure the Housing Commission of the Stoke-on-Trent Corporation had proposed a revolutionary solution - steel houses. It sounded a good idea at the time, especially one suspects to the miner who lived with his wife in a railway carriage:

There will always be tragedies close to home. Three such were reported in quick succession. The first a woman run down by a train:

> *"What was she doing on the line sir?"*
> *"I - I can't say.......she was.....," his voice trailed away.*
> *"May I express my hope for a speedy recovery, sir."*
> *"Yes, yes, thank you for your concern., I've no idea why she was there."*

Mr Joseph Ward of Weston Road, the Meir would be asked the same questions over and over again until he was weary with explanations.

"My wife was just crossing the track when she was knocked down by a light engine."

"Yes, but what was she doing there?"

In the second tragedy, Mrs Caroline Wood, a 70 year old widow of 12 Smith's Buildings, the Meir, was burned to death whilst reading by candlelight when her bedding caught alight. And the life of John Francis Leese, the son of a garage proprietor of 49 Meir Lane, was lost when he was struck by a Potteries Electric Traction bus on its way to Blythe Bridge in the spring of 1925.

The air of notoriety that had on various occasions surrounded the previous parish priest[6] at St Mary & St Chad's seemingly had not deserted his successor:

The Rev Douglas Cooper, vicar of St Mary & St Chad's, Sandford Hill, Longton was summoned for "failing to stop his motorcycle on request". Two constables gave evidence that the defendant drove out of Anchor Road, Longton without stopping.

In his defence he stated, 'He didn't know he had been asked to stop.'

The case was dismissed on payment of costs.   7th March 1925.

With summer, the 'pageant and fête' season for worthy causes returned; surely none was more deserving than the hospitals:

The annual fête and pageant in aid of funds for the North Staffordshire Royal Infirmary was held on Saturday in splendid weather. A procession headed by the Dilhorne Brass Band (under Mr J. Beardmore) paraded through the village to a field adjoining the Red House Hotel, Caverswall. The prize winners in the fancy dress competition were: 1. Mr. J Holmes, as a crossword puzzle. 2. Mrs Joynson, as a tea cosy.

In the Fancy Dress for children competition, the winners were: 1. Winnie Sergeant, as a book of matches. 2. Ethel Edwards, as a fairy.

The prizes were distributed by Mrs Bowers, who was president of the pageant.

During the afternoon, a programme of Maypole and country dancing was given by the children of the Catholic and Church of England Schools.

Simple country pleasures for country folk. The heartache and agony suffered during the Great War put to one side on an idyllic summer's afternoon.

Miles away from this frivolous jollity, a local man had beaten the world by his skill and genius and a moment of history was unfolding:

The Supermarine monoplane designed by Reginald J Mitchell won a prize for his firm of £8000 by designing an amphibious flying boat. The Supermarine monoplane will be flown by Captain C H Baird who won the cup in 1922.

And as the aroma of ripening apples and bounteous vegetables filled the still air for the harvest festival in Meir, a ceremony took place that was to leave the church with one of its more enduring memories:

The stained glass memorial light in the east window of the Holy Trinity Church, the Meir, to perpetuate the fondly remembered services of the late Mr Frederick Henry Heath was unveiled at a simple little ceremony on Saturday afternoon. The late Mr Heath, whose death took place in 1914, had been a chorister at Meir church from the time it was opened for public worship up to the time of his death. In later years he took up the duties of choirmaster and had also served as church warden. The church was his religion and apart from his church work he was widely connected with public and social organisations.

The ceremony attracted a large congregation which included, in addition to the members of the family, a host of persons who had been associated with him in his various public and social interests. There were present a representative gathering of the Etruscan lodge of Freemasons and also the Longton China Manufacturers Association. The Rev H C Sheldon, priest in charge of Meir church, conducted the service, assisted by the Rev R O Walker of Sleaford, Lincs, who was formerly priest in charge. Following the rendering of the hymn by the church and congregation, Mr F H Heath, son of the deceased, unveiled and formerly handed over the gift to the church. The gift was accepted by the churchwarden (Mr JH Barlow) and dedicated by the priest in charge.

The address was delivered by the Rev R O Walker who said that although 11 years had passed since Mr F H Heath's death, his memory was still as fresh as though he was still with them. He was one of the very first worshippers of the church and he laboured ungrudgingly for 25 years to serve it. It was mainly through Mr Heath's work that the church at the Meir was founded and it was fitting that it should be adorned by something which was meant to keep his memory fragrant. In coming back to the Potteries he, (the speaker) was confronted by a picture of grime, soot and squalor, but beneath it all was hidden wondrous beauty of kind hearts such as the late Mr Heath possessed. The late Mr Heath's life, he concluded remained as a lasting memorial and as an example to those who followed. The light which has been given by the widow, is one of the highest quality glass which considerably enhances its beauty. It occupies the central position in the east window and represents 'Christ knocking at the door of the human heart.'[7] The panel is surrounded by a rich architectural canopy of the 14th century style, empanelled with figures and angels, one of which is holding the inscription.

If the city as a whole was looking to house its population in more sanitary conditions, Holy Trinity church was also thinking in the same vein. Curates had lived in Weston

Road for years but the need for purpose-built accommodation for the clergy 'nearer the job' was pressing:

> *The annual sale of work in connection with the Holy Trinity church, Meir was opened on the 10th inst by Mr Edwards, when the proceedings went towards the funds for the erection of the new vicarage. The opening ceremony was presided over by the vicar[8] (Rev H C Sheldon) who was supported by Mr J H Barlow (people's warden), Mr T. Hull (secretary) and the Rev E W Bridgwood (vicar of Forsbrook) and many prominent church workers. The hall had been artistically arranged and the efforts of those responsible were amply rewarded.*

The Duke of Sutherland, with providential foresight, had some years previously donated a plot of land for this very purpose, adjacent to the church.[9]

The year 1926 was a watershed for Holy Trinity. Up until this time the church, had merely been a daughter of the mother church of Caverswall, the latter having supplied all the curates for the former parish. The term 'conv. distr.', meaning a conventional district, appears frequently in legal documentation from about 1919. When a town begins to grow rapidly, perhaps due to new housing, then as a precursor of creating a new parish, that town or area may be termed a 'conventional district'. It is an agreement between the bishop and the clergy of the parishes concerned. By doing this, the town or area is removed from the incumbent's charge; the bishop licensing a 'curate in charge' who works towards a legal separation from the 'mother' parish. The legal position of the parishioners is unaffected and the obligations to marriage, burial, etc are unaltered.

The area or town, now on its own, can organise itself into a complete parochial unit which has its own PCC (Parochial Church Council) and electoral roll. Simply put, it is 'church speak' for the breaking away of a parish church like Holy Trinity, from its maternal roots.

An agreement as to the right of presentation to the living was made by deed dated 16th July 1925, in which the incumbent of Caverswall who was previously entitled to appoint the minister at Meir, with the agreement of William Parker-Jervis, the patron of Caverswall, conceded the patronage should transfer to the Bishop of Lichfield.

When the Rev H C Sheldon took over the reins from the Rev Theophilus Caleb in 1923 his CV included the same terminology. However all that changed in 1926. The documentation for this was presented at Court on June 28th 1926. The Meir had come of age. From that time forward, Holy Trinity, serving its devoted congregation, would be on its own; the first vicar of Meir being the Rev Harry Christie Sheldon.

The extent of the Meir parish at this moment is revealedby the the map at the beginning of this chapter. What is striking is the acres of open space, which would prove to so tempting to building developers. But the estate off Broadway was still years

AT THE COURT AT BUCKINGHAM PALACE,

The 28th day of June, 1926.

PRESENT,

THE KING'S MOST EXCELLENT MAJESTY IN COUNCIL.

WHEREAS the Ecclesiastical Commissioners for England have, in pursuance of the Act of the 8th and 9th years of Her late Majesty Queen Victoria, Chapter 70, of the Act of the 14th and 15th years of Her said late Majesty, Chapter 97 and of the Act of the 19th and 20th years of Her said late Majesty, Chapter 55, duly prepared, and laid before His Majesty in Council, a Representation, bearing date the 15th day of April, 1926, in the words and figures following, that is to say :—

" We, the Ecclesiastical Commissioners for England, in pursuance of the Act of the 8th and 9th years of Her late Majesty Queen Victoria, Chapter 70, of the Act of the 14th and 15th years of Her said late Majesty, Chapter 97, and of the Act of the 19th and 20th years of Her said late Majesty, Chapter 55, have prepared, and now humbly lay before Your Majesty in Council, the following Representation as to the assignment of a Consolidated Chapelry to the consecrated Church of the Holy Trinity, Meir, situate within the Parish of Caverswall, in the County of Stafford and in the Diocese of Lichfield .

from construction. Behind the Institute and Church, note the Club House which has also sadly gone. The scattering of large houses with their expansive gardens are evident along Weston Road. They would, within four decades, all be razed to make way for rows of modern housing in Yarnfield Close and Dene Close. The home of the churchwarden, Mr S Mear, was not far from the tolling of the tuneless church bell. Some road names no longer exist, lost during municipal reshuffling; The Avenue now renamed Penfleet Avenue, Aynsley Road (later Leason Road), Wood Street and Charles Street are prime examples. The Old King's Arms Hotel still stood on the corner of Meir Lane (at its meeting with Weston Road) whilst stretching towards Blythe Bridge terraced properties lined the side of Meir Lane out to the Methodist Church to the east. The Meir Square estate was not fully finished. Northwards there was the Weston Coyney Brickworks and to the west of Holy Trinity, properties ran all the way down to the Station Hotel[10] in Normacot. Virtually all this has been destroyed in the intervening years.

The year 1926 would make its mark on history as the year the working man most completely showed his disaffection with employers and employment conditions. At midnight on May 5th, the first General Strike in British history began, the TUC voting to throw their weight behind the miners following a breakdown of negotiations. Barely a week had passed before the TUC called off the action. Many of the middle classes, male and female had beaten them while playing out childhood fantasies working on the footplates of locomotives, driving lorries and being special constables. The determined miners carried on with their strike until November.

Elsewhere, Hobbs and Sutcliffe helped England recapture the Ashes in the Test match against Australia and Alan Cobham[11] flew out there and back covering 28,000 miles in his De Havilland 50 biplane. A A Milne revealed to the world Winnie the Pooh, the 'bear of little brain', while Agatha Christie, missing for several days, was spotted at a Yorkshire hotel by an observant maid, doubtless a devotee of the genre and an ardent reader of the local newspapers.

Locally, the Meir lost a devoted servant in the shape of Nurse Proctor aged 84, of 96, Station Road, Meir whilst at Alton Towers they got out the 'best china' for a visit from the Bishop of Lichfield. He was followed a week later by the Longton Town band. It would cost you a 'bob' to get in but when postmen earned 1/3d an hour, this was still a bargain.

The suspicious and remarkable demise of some of the city's 'Houses of Entertainment' by fire were mysteriously unexplained. Was it 'spontaneous combustion' or were the patrons just plain careless when they dropped their 'dog-ends' on the best axminster of the auditorium? The Queen's Theatre (the Empire[12]) had gone up in smoke in 1896, and now another was set to join it:

> *A fire in Longton at the Alexandra Picture Palace has reduced the building to ashes. All performances have therefore been cancelled. Nobody was injured.*
>
> 25th August 1927

The main local newspapers, the Sentinel under the hand of Barrett Greene JP and the county paper, the Staffordshire Advertiser continued to keep the community abreast of the news with fascinating stories, like 'Foot and Mouth in Bedfordshire', and 'Profitable Poultry Keeping' and for sheer exhilaration, 'Judging Bottled Fruit'. News now also came from the radio to which listeners were shackled for hours by their earphones and trailing flex.

The growth of car ownership had begun to intrude on the way of life in the Meir. From photographs of that era, it is impossible to guess that in the years ahead, the car would ultimately be responsible for the destruction of their pleasant way of life.

The infamous cross roads where the A50 and A520 dissect the town, soon became the site of many crashes and near misses. It was difficult to see why, as visibility seemed limitless on this former Roman thoroughfare. But in early 1928 the careless action of one motorist landed him 'up before the beak':

For driving a motor car (which he had hired) in a dangerous manner at Meir crossroads, William Turner, London Road, Stoke was fined £4 and costs at Longton Police Court on Monday. It was stated that the defendant appeared to have had some drink but was not unfit to drive a car and that he almost collided with a motor car belonging to the Lord Mayor of Stoke on Trent. The defendant was also fined for having no driving licence (£1).

If you were going to almost collide with someone it was better not to be the Lord Mayor. But not everyone did miss: a few weeks later at the same spot, the sound of rending metal filled the air:

In a crash at the Meir cross roads, the wife of Dr C Burgess of Chaplin Road, Normacot was thrown from her husband's car which was travelling towards Blythe Bridge.

Mercifully she was unhurt, save for a few bruises. Traffic offences proliferated at a great rate and fines were exacted for what seemed trivial offences - the case of the 'boy cyclists' was a perfect example; *'4 local youths were fined for furiously riding pedal cycles down London Road, Chesterton.'* And it was suggested that *'bus companies had somehow cajoled their driving staff to put their foot down'*:

William George Ash of School House, Blythe Bridge and Albert Smith 25, Arthur Street, Longton by driving 'buses in a dangerous manner by RACING at 25 miles per hour on the Meir Road were fined £5 each at Longton Police Court.

At the hearing of another case, the chairman of Hanley Police court, Mr H Coates was heard to comment on speeding buses (22 to 30 mph); *"The speed at which these buses travel in this district has become a disgrace."* If only they could travel that quickly today!

In Spring, the City had a distinguished visitor, invited by the City Fathers. Would it be perhaps the red carpet, a fanfare of trumpets, a civic lunch, champagne and a guided tour of the borough? But wait a minute - this was Stoke on Trent!

There was a visit to Stoke by the Prime Minister, Stanley Baldwin and his wife last week.. They were met by the Town Council at 11.15am along with others at Etruria Gasworks.

The final year of the twenties saw unemployment escalate, so much so the regular office was overwhelmed and another opened to meet the demand.

Longton Town Hall is to be used as a temporary Labour Exchange as the 'new' Labour Exchange in Stone Road, has been totally inadequate.

It is often said that lightening does not strike the same place twice. To prove it does, the strange case of the 'unpleasantness at Caverswall' in January 1929 is a case in point:

> *As a result of a dispute between the vicar of Caverswall (the Rev J R McNamara) and the members of the choir at St Peter's church, the latter have resorted to a strike. They have absented themselves from the services for the past two Sundays and so far, there are no signs of a settlement. It appears that some time ago, the choir held a supper at a well-known local hotel - a revival of an old custom which had been in abeyance for 5 years. It is understood that the vicar took exception to the function for some reason or other and shortly after the supper was held, he informed Mr Adams of Blythe Bridge, who acted as organist and choirmaster, that he would have to resign. Having no alternative he did so and was succeeded by another organist. Owing to the vicar's action the choirmen registered a protest against deposing their leader and refused to attend the service the following Sunday. On behalf of the vicar, it is stated that his strongest objection was to the choirmen arranging the supper without in any way consulting him or the church officials on the matter. In the meantime the choir is being carried on by the boys and female volunteers.*
>
> 26th January 1929

The outcome of the altercation at St Peter's is not stated. Choirs it seemed, were not the angels they were purported to to be, as a further incident demonstrated:

> *Eleven youths, several of whom were members of a church choir, were brought before Longton Magistrates on Monday for playing a game of cards called 'nap'. The case was dismissed but the boys had to pay 5 shillings.*
>
> 7th September 1929

At that time the punishment meted out by the courts for what today would seem to be regarded as trifling offences might seem harsh but it surely reflected a genuine respect for the person and society:

> *A man was sent to prison for 1 month's hard labour for conning a widow out of £2 and Ben Roberts was fined £2 for ill treating a horse.*

The death of the vicar of Normacot in August 1929 saddened the parishioners more than words could express:

> *The death has been announced of the Rev Ernest Charles Hipkins, the vicar of Normacot, who was the Lord Mayor's Chaplain for many years. He was a curate under the Rev Adam Clarke of St James' Church, Longton, who in his turn, was responsible for the inauguration of Longton Cottage Hospital in 1868.*

The Rev Mountford replaced Rev Hipkins, who had been at the church of the Holy Evangelists for thirty seven years, by any reckoning, a long time, reflecting the total commitment so many of the clergy displayed to the church.

The new vicar was a talented man; much like the Archdeacon of Stoke on Trent who put his free time to good use and at the end of the decade, staged a one man art show of the city, painted in watercolours. The Venerable Malcolm Graham *"who pursued his hobby of painting in water colours with unobtrusive assiduity was an artist of some skill and talent. The sale of his work realised £50 which he gave to the fund for the North Staffs Royal Infirmary."*

And at Forsbrook, a parcel bearing a particular coat of arms on the outer packaging must have made more than one person inquisitive when it was delivered in December 1929. The sender was Queen Mary, who had donated a coffee set to the Forsbrook Church Bazaar to be held on the following Thursday and Friday. Was it stamped 'by appointment' and what eventually happened to that regal crockery? The reason for the patronage is unclear, but her generosity would have brought many people through the doors, swelling the coffers.

The roaring twenties were fast running out. The country had staggered on from the 'victory' of War and had seen the advancement of science and medicine and great improvements in public health, housing, sanitation and transport.

But the last of these was was beginning to make its mark in unpleasant ways. In a telling outburst, the East Lancashire coroner, Mr F Rowland, stated that *'in three weeks, over three hundred people had been killed on the roads of this country'*. The love affair with the internal combustion engine would change the landscape and the lives of Britain forever, especially those in the Meir and for some the change would be sudden and final.

Notes
1. The 'backs', in terraced housing, which were common in the City, occurred where two rows ran parallel to each other and shared a common rear entrance.
2. This children's playground was destroyed by the Department of Transport in building Phase 1b of the new A50 in 1994-5.
3. Destroyed by a suspicious fire in December 1992
4. Demolished for Phase 1b of the new A50 in 1994-5
5. The Royal was situated half way up Sandford Hill, Longton and ended its days as a warehouse.
6. Rev Thomas Lawrence Murray 1887 - 1948.
7. The actual painting on which it is based is 'The Light of the World' by W Holman Hunt, 1827 - 1910.
8. There was not yet a vicar of Meir.
9. Over 1000 square metres of this land was compulsorily purchased in 1994 by the Department of Transport for the A50 improvements.
10. Demolished in September 1994 after being destroyed by arsonists whilst awaiting demolition for the new A50.
11. Meir's connection with aviation is immortalised today by the naming of a road in Meir after Alan Cobham.
12. Used by the Longton Garrick Club in March 1928 to give a performance of 'Gamblers All', in aid of the local District Nursing Association, whose president was Mr J H Barlow of Meir

Spitfires flew from, and crashed around the Meir during the Second World War. This Roll of Honour shows an early indication of the ability of aircraft designer R J Mitchell. He was ultimately responsible for designing 24 different types of aircraft including the Supermarine Seaplane which went on to victory in the Schneider Trophy Air Races during the early 1930s and from which the famous fighter evolved.

Reginald Joseph Mitchell was born in Butt Lane, Stoke-on-Trent in 1895. A few months after his birth, the Mitchell family moved to 87 Chaplin Road, Normacot, Longton. He married Florence Dayson, headmistress of Dresden Infants' School "at the Meir Church in the village just beyond Normacot" at the end of the Great War in 1918. He died in 1937, unaware of the tremendous debt this country owed him and the Spitfire aircraft which had such a pivotal role in winning the Battle of Britain against the might of the Luftwaffe. Photographed at Fenton Technical School.   *Lovatt collection*

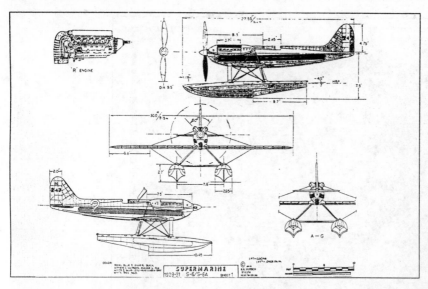

A few of the many machine drawings for the Supermarine S6-S6A, made by the Vickers design team, of which Mitchell was Chief Designer.

Right: Locally born Reginald J Mitchell, seen here with Sir Henry Royce at the Southampton-based Vickers Supermarine

Left: A Supermarine seaplane of the type flown by Boothman and Stainforth when they claimed the World Airspeed Record, along with the famous trophy named after a French arms manufacturer, Jacques Schneider.

This photograph from 1925-1927 was taken looking down Sandon Road into Weston road; the Saracen's Head pub is to the right and the King's Arms behind it. Both were owned by John Joule & Sons of Stone. The A50 runs left to right across the view; Weston Road (A520 Leek to Stone) runs into the picture from the photographer standing in what today is Sandon Road.

By the telegraph pole opposite the Saracen's Head is 'Bloor's' Toll Cottage - a relic from the days when the A50 was a toll road, the last toll keeper being John Poole in 1875. The chimneys of Meir cottage can just be seen above the roof of the Toll Cottage far left. Further down Weston Road are Weston Road Cottages followed by Gunn's hairdressing shop with the off-licence shop wall in white beyond (on the corner of Cornelious street). The Morris motor car in Weston Road belonged to Herbert Pearson and is parked outside the shop of Luke Bennett. There are a few changes to notice in the 25 to 30 years which separate this photograph and the one on page 52. Gas lamps are evident outside the Saracen's Head and in Weston Road. The signpost on the left points the way to Longton 1 mile, Stoke 4 miles to the left and Uttoxeter 12 miles to the right. *Bennett collection*

159

This photograph was taken at the same time as the on page 159. It shows Meir crossroads viewed from fields up and to the left of Sandon Road. In later years the shops in Sandon Road from Meir Takeaway and L J Hart, Accountants, to Crooks & Partners, Veterinary Surgeons would be built on these meadows along with the Broadway cinema on the corner on the far side of the large tree. The A50 runs left to right across the middle of the picture: Blythe Bridge to the right, Longton to the left. The Saracen's Head pub, with its many outbuildings, is in the right foreground. Almost all of the front facade of the King's Arms Hotel is seen with 4 upper storey sash windows on the opposite corner of the road. The dark building, centre, behind the far right hand side of the tree canopy, is Bloor's Toll Cottage whilst left, and actually across the road, is Meir Cottage, the home of Luke Bennett and his family. Continuing left on the same side, the last set of buildings belong to a farm; a site 70 years later occupied by Kwik Save and Barclays Bank.

Bennett collection

A close up shot of Meir Cottage in 1928/30, with its ornate barge boards and sash windows, standing on the corner of Meir Lane and Weston Road. It was demolished in 1932/33 for road widening: 'Crossroads' Farm is to the left. The right hand road sign points left to Longton and Stoke and right to Uttoxeter. The left hand sign shows the road to Hilderstone 6 miles away, to Cellarhead, 4 miles and to Leek, 10 miles. Note the sign for Leese's Garage of Meir Lane which sold Raleigh Steel Bicycles, on the corner. The tree immediately to the left of the cottage is the same tree which now stands outside Kwik Save in 1995 *Bennett collection*

Nothing remains of this view in 1995 save perhaps for the odd tree. Taken in Meir Lane before 1928, the road running from the foreground into the distance is the A50. Blythe Bridge is behind the camera which is looking west, whilst Longton lies directly ahead. Sandon Road (A520) is clearly seen joining from the left between the Toll Cottage and the gas lamp. Weston Road begins by the signpost to the right. The familiar Meir Cottage is on the right, the not so familiar farm and outbuildings are next door towards Longton in Uttoxeter Road. The loneliness and isolation of this village scene can only be marvelled at when compared with the road traffic and fumes of 1995.

Bennett collection

In this scene at Meir crossroads, the road running into the distance is Sandon Road:the marathon runners have just come from Longton on the right. Blythe Bridge is to the left. The Toll cottage on the right is opposite the old Saracen's head public house on the other corner of this lonely junction. Note there are no buildings whatsoever in Sandon Road. The figure at the right hand side of the view is a policeman who was shielding the camera from the sun on this changeable day nearly 70 years ago. *Bennett collection*

With the ghostly presence of the Sutherland Institute in Stone (later Lightwood) Road glowering over the immediate surroundings, the workmen, using horses and carts, are preparing and levelling what would become Stone Road Recreation Ground. Stone Road runs obliquely left to right into Longton whilst Webberley Lane, in which was situated St James Church school, attended by Havergal Brian, runs at right angles to the Stone Road passing in front of the houses to the right of the Institute. *Lovatt collection*

A timeless study with figures caught in an empty landscape. Incredibly this is the Meir between 1928 and 1932. The camera is looking east with Blythe Bridge straight ahead in the distance and Longton behind the lens. The Toll Cottage has been demolished leaving the old Saracen's Head as the solitary building on that corner of the A520 & A50. This was before the building of the Broadway cinema in 1935/1936. Sandon Road joins the A50 from the right in front of the public house: Weston Road is directly opposite. The two men in the centre field have had to walk in the road to avoid a cart and an excavation in the pavement outside the farm on the left. Taken in the afternoon, is it the walk home from work?

Bennett collection

Shot from Stone Road (now Lightwood Road), looking towards Longton (left), this view of the preparation of the Stone Road Recreation Ground in 1927/8 shows the enormity of the task. The only earth moving equipment available seem to be shovels and picks. The roof of St James church school can be glimpsed on the far right in Webberley Lane, which runs off the main road at the point where the houses are situated.

Lovatt collection

Lying on the cusp of Uttoxeter Road and Meir Road(A50 & A5035), Normacot Methodist church was built by Messrs Bennion at a cost of £2567. This was without fixtures and fittings which increased the final bill to a figure in excess of £3000. It was erected as a replacement for the so called 'Iron chapel'built in 1880 at a cost of £350. They co-existed for many years until a 'kamikaze' motor car embedded itself in the walls of the 'Iron Chapel' after which the building was declared unsafe and demolished

Lovatt collection

J A Lovatt took this panorama from an elevated position when work to construct the Stone Road Recreation ground was in full swing. The camera is pointed towards Normacot on the left with numerous bottle kilns; Meir and Lightwood are on the horizon. Note the horse and cart travelling along the A5005 Stone Road, bottom, right of centre. Tragically the Lightwood Road Recreation Ground was completely excavated for the new A50 in 1994/5: another amenity lost forever to the motor car.

Lovatt collection

St John's Longton. Impressive and grand, the bells in this brick church, built in the middle of the eighteenth century, would ring out across rows of terraced housing in Longton or Lane End (literally Meir Lane End). The bells, cast as a thanksgiving for the victory at Waterloo, were renovated many times during the late 19th and this century. The church has unfortunately nowbeen demolished.

Priestley collection

A portrait of Prebendary Edward Fenton Woodward MA of SS Mary & Chad's Church, Sandford Hill, Longton, taken in later life. He was instrumental in consolidating the pioneering work of Rev T L Murray and raised the profile of the church throughout the Diocese of Lichfield. Ridiculed by many of the working men in the area in his early days, he earned their respect and admiration through his reasoned and intelligent logic. A good organiser who was served by a willing and loyal congregation. Not one to suffer fools gladly, nevertheless, a man of towering personality who often spoke his mind; the outburst in the parish magazine critiscising the unsuitability of the Old Vicarage in Pitt Street was a case in point. One several occasions he journeyed to Holy Trinity, Meir as the celebrant at church services. He died in 1973. His brother, Tom Woodward, was chief photographer for many years of the Staffordshire Evening Sentinel.

CHAPTER 13
1930 - 1934
'Make haste, slowly.'

Emperor Augustus 63 BC-AD 14

In local cinemas, the clipped tones of the Pathé News pronounced the age of prohibition in the USA, mobsters with machine guns (who indeed achieved cult status through the new medium), the R101 airship disaster, Amy Johnson's[1] flight to Australia and unemployment causing riots in mean streets.

In England unemployment was also the root from which social unrest sprang. Locally[2] it was twice as bad in 1930 than in 1929; the outlook was familiarly depressing. The endemic poverty that afflicted the Potteries towards the end of the 19th century was still rife and with little in the way of state aid - many years before Lord Beveridge would unveil his plans for the welfare state - many lived life very precariously. Charities continued to take some little corners off life's rough edges:

The Henry Hill Charity took place at Longton Town Hall on Saturday. One hundred and seventy aged people received four shillings each from the hands of the Lady Mayoress and were addressed by the Lord Mayor, who wished them, somewhat belatedly, "compliments of the season".

Houses were going up in the Meir, in what was basically still a farming community, albeit one in rapid decline. Building stalwarts Tompkinson and Bettelley, who had constructed the chancel of Holy Trinity and many other triumphs, were busy on a small development below the church called Meir Residential Estate[3]. One of the first occupants were Mr & Mrs Hill who lived in Warwick Avenue.

With timbered gables and pantiles, the houses were markedly different from anything in the town at that time and were in direct contrast to much of the housing of late Victorian terraced running along the length of Meir Lane and Uttoxeter Road. There were still some grand houses; Meir House, the Elms, Weston Coyney House, the Limes and Beech House, and several large Villas in Weston Road too, nudging into Meir, cheek by jowl with the more humble houses.

One of the local community, which in 1931 numbered 3,682, a dental surgeon William Lawrence Ferguson, bought a large piece of farming land at the top of the hill almost opposite Meir House where he built Highfield House, next door to Holy Trinity Church, overlooking its lawns. It is one of the few houses close to the town centre still standing sixty years later.

With Holy Trinity, Normacot & Meir Methodist churches and the old School, the town had a feeling of equilibrium. But the growth which had already meant the need for further school buildings in Colclough Road, now brought increased traffic and the enlargement of Meir Lane from a cart track into a proper road.

The number of clergy in the UK in 1914 had been 18,180. By 1930 it had declined to 16,745 whilst conversely, the general population in the decade had ballooned from 1911 by almost two million.

Quite suddenly, in January 1930, the prospect of an airport took a step nearer to becoming a reality:

'Stoke-on-Trent Municipal Aerodrome at the Meir:
Representatives of the National Flying Services arrived on Wednesday (22nd January) to discuss with the City Surveyor's Department who will survey 180 acres and the first planes should be using the aerodrome next spring.

And other sounds began to punctuate the rural tranquillity of the Meir with familiar regularity. With the popular Singer 6 saloon costing £199 10s at Olympia in Birmingham (taking into account a saving of £75 10s 0d from the list price, but only if you were sharp about it!), the motoring age was dawning with a vengeance. Collisions at Meir crossroads carried on with monotonous regularity:

James Bottomer of Victoria Road, Longton and James Thomas Smith of Green Farm, Caverswall were involved in a crash at Meir crossroads. Neither of the men was injured but one car was extensively damaged!

Frederick Beard of 4 Smith Buildings, the Meir, was fined for, *'being a nuisance with a motor horn between eleven o'clock and midnight.'*

But when it came to record breaking, nobody could hold a candle to the 39 year old Vincent Riley[8] for court appearances. Quite simply he was in a league of his own. Appearing for the one hundred and first time and fined for being 'drunk and disorderly' Riley was sent down. Today an enlightened society would have suggested a course of treatment for his alcoholism.

August in Caverswall saw the second Mrs Bowers carrying on the family tradition of fund-raising activities in the parish. The horticultural show needed her undivided attention and along with the head gardeners from Caverswall Castle and Dilhorne Hall, she had the unenviable job of deciding who had won. It obviously all went well:

During the evening service at Caverswall church on Sunday, (17th August) the vicar, the Rev J McNamara, announced that £284 was the gross amount realised by the bazaar recently held in celebration of the seven hundredth anniversary of the church, this sum being not far short of what was asked for.

Non-existent parish funds like the National Debt are always with us: St Mary and Chad's, Sandford Hill was no exception. To swell the coffers before Christmas the Operatic Society got out all the old coats and wigs to give a performance of the operetta, 'Aladdin-in and Out'. For their trouble, these amateur thespians were thanked by the priest-in-charge, the Rev Edward Fenton Woodward - for their enthusiasm above all else.

The year marked the retirement of Dr Harris[9], the headmaster of Longton High School, still then in Trentham Road, Longton, and the conclusion of an illustrious scholastic career. He had been responsible for the inspiring 'school song'.

The yuletide weather was turbulent; on December 27th a gale battered the city for several hours. Later in January, bad weather or not, Caverswall elders were being treated:

The annual Old Folks treat at Caverswall was held at the Red House, Caverswall last week. All who attended had a splendid feast and came away having had a happy and most enjoyable evening.

Anyone who has actually seen Caverswall will know that basically it is a small square in the centre of which is a tree around which lie most of the buildings, spread out like the place settings at table. And there was the nub of a problem. There was nowhere for the children to safely play. In early March 1931, a plan was put forward:

At Caverswall, the parish council unveiled a £1000 scheme to provide somewhere for the children of the village to play as they had nowhere else but the streets.

With finances as fragile as ever they had been, it was a bold plan.

Then the bombshell struck. Caverswall Castle was to be put up for sale; the reason being 'health considerations':

An Historic Mansion: Caverswall Castle, near Stoke on Trent, for a number of years the residence of Mrs V A Bowers, has been placed in the hands of Messrs Hampton & Sons of St James Square London SW for sale at auction in the early autumn. Mrs Bowers, whose work as County secretary for the Girl Guides is well known, has been indisposed for a considerable period and considerations of health have prompted her to take up permanent residence in the south of England. It is in these circumstances and in view of the stringency of modern times and the consequent burden of high taxation that Mrs Bowers felt it necessary to relinquish possession of Caverswall Castle and its estate of 93 acres.

The history of Caverswall Castle dates from medieval times. It is recorded that a castle was erected there by William de Caverswall during the reign of Edward II and it is believed that a still earlier castle was erected in the time of King John. Legend has it that a Lady of Caverswall alone, of all the beauties assembled at the court of the Round Table at which King Arthur himself presided, was able to wear the girdle of chastity while on the shoulders of all the other ladies in attendance, the charmed mantle

171

withered. Legend apart, it is certain from the time of Richard I to that of Edward III, Caverswall was the stronghold of a knightly family. Subsequently the mansion passed to the Montgomerys and later came into the possession successively of the Giffords, the Ports and the Earls of Huntingdon. At the beginning of the 17th century the estate was purchased by Matthew Craddock, who rebuilt the mansion. Craddock was the son of a Stafford wool merchant and clerk of assize for the county. He preserved the outer wall and moat, the latter being crossed by a stone bridge. In the Civil War, the Craddocks took the side of the Parliament for whom the castle was garrisoned. From the Craddocks the property passed into the possession of the Jollifes and from them, by marriage, to William Vane, Viscount of Ireland.

Early in the 19th century the mansion was the property of the Hon Booth-Gore, who in turn sold it to Mr Brett, a banker from Stone. From this gentleman it was leased by Mr W H Coyney of Weston Coyney acting on behalf of the sisterhood of Benedictine nuns from France. For over 40 years Caverswall Castle was run as a nunnery by the sisters, known locally as the 'Black Ladies', who conducted a school for about 30 young ladies. In the late 1850s the property was purchased by Sir Perceval Ratcliffe, who caused a statue to be erected in the grounds of the Roman Catholic Church dedicated to St Philomena, and had the moat converted into beautiful lawns and gardens.

The estate was purchased in 1889 by the late Mr Bowers, who carried out further extensive improvements to the property including the laying out of a beautifully appointed cricket ground now used by Caverswall Cricket Club. The castle, which possesses features of great architectural interest and is in an excellent state of preservation, occupies a commanding position at the point where the River Blythe, a tributary of the Dove takes its rise.

The demise of Caverswall Castle was perhaps in its way an end as stark as that of local author Arnold Bennett, who died at the same time in Paris of typhoid fever after drinking water to prove 'it was safe'. It was ironic that he had travelled far from the corner of Hanover and Hope Streets in Hanley, where he was born at his father's drapers and pawnbroker shop, to succumb in this way. With David Garrick & Havergal Brian, Bennett formed a notable trio of Staffordshire artists at the time.

Discussions over the viability of an aerodrome for the Meir had smouldered on during 1930. There had been rumours and counter rumours but in the early summer, a demonstration of the real thing did far more to enthuse a feeling of interest in the local population. In May 1931:

> *An exhibition of gliding at Meir aerodrome has been given by Professor C H Lowe-Wylde and attracted visitors from as far away as Wrexham, Manchester and Nottingham.*

Politically, the area was in ferment. Lady Cynthia Mosley MP for Stoke, Longton and Fenton said that she would resign her parliamentary seat and put up as candidate for a new (Mosley) Party at the next election[10]. It was a high risk strategy. Sir Oswald Mosley had formed the Mosley party on February 28th with the avowed intention, as he put it, *'to harness modern machinery and ask for the mobilisation of energy, vitality and manhood to save the nation.'*

The year had two moments of great achievement. At the start of the year, Sir Malcolm Campbell had driven 'BlueBird' into the record books at Daytona Beach at

245 mph, and in September, the aircraft designed by Reginald Mitchell succeeded in winning the Schneider Trophy for England It was a proud moment but there must have been very few who suspected the significance it would have in the coming years.

Undercurrents of discontent in Germany at the mounting economic crisis had led to the National Socialists increasing their representation in the Reichstag from 12 deputies to 107, to become the second largest political party. The victory had thrust them into the world spotlight along with their leader Adolf Hitler, and from this triumph, he used his skill as an orator to pander to the nation's fears of inflation, unemployment and economic uncertainty, to bring Germany together as never before, eventually united, powerful and heavily-armed.

The first Burslem and District Co-operative Wholesale Society branch had opened in 1901 and the society had mushroomed in little over 20 years to 25 branches and a membership of 29,000. By using a simple yet effective marketing ploy, each customer had a number, so each time a purchase was made, a small amount was added to a personal 'rolling total' and a dividend or 'divvi' was calculated periodically. Many who participated could reel off this Co-op number without hesitation. In due course, the Meir joined the chain with premises in Weston Road and the unique aroma of ground coffee, freshly baked bread and a system of suspended wires which whizzed the cash overhead to a kiosk at the back of the store with unerring accuracy. It was a time when staff could rattle through a list of groceries as long as your arm and still get the final bill right every time!

Among the Meir community, there was the demise of William Bartlam of Waterloo Farm who along with his extensive farming interests, was a respected horse dealer. There was still an emphasis on farming in the local papers and exciting articles like *"Forming a National Pig Policy"* were read with enthusiasm.

1932 was the year the city had its first lady Lord Mayor, Miss F A Farmer, and while Dr Dawes from Denbigh House in Battison Crescent, Longton died from typhoid fever in Buenos Aires, Lord Ampthill, speaking at the autumn meeting of Baird Television Limited mentioned talks of transmissions with the BBC and the growth of broadcasting. In September, the new fangled 'wireless' came to the city:

The BBC has arranged to broadcast a service to be conducted by Archdeacon Crick from Stoke Parish Church from 8am to 8.45am on Sunday 18th September.

The threat to the Meir's peaceful isolation was growing daily. Deaths from car accidents had climbed alarmingly. The car had developed into a social evil despite all the upbeat advertisements. The volume of traffic was minuscule but the machines that travelled the highways and byeways left much to be desired from the safety point of view. Car deaths in 1930 reached 4069 in this country, with a still alarming 3631 in 1931. Meir had its fair share; more than fair some would say!

One event that inspires more prayers than any other is the annual fête - praying for fine weather! The image of bedraggled parishioners trudging across rain-swept lawns to have 'one last go' on the tombola are indelibly printed on the mind. So the arrival of the day and its coincidence with the barometer set to 'fair' is a cause for great joy. So it was in July 1932:

> *Favoured by fine weather the annual village carnival in aid of Caverswall &*
> *Weston Coyney Playing Fields Scheme on Saturday proved an unqualified*
> *success. High revelry reigned throughout the afternoon and evening and the*
> *colourful fancy dress parade provided numerous novel and original costumes*
> *and tableaux. The attractions included a display of dancing by the*
> *schoolchildren, a first aid demonstration by the Adderley Green Ambulance*
> *Corps & a musical programme by the Longton Town Band and a baby show.*

Vincent Riley, of no fixed abode, appeared in Hanley Police Court on Monday charged with being drunk and disorderly once more:

> *I am very sorry sir but it was my birthday. said Vincent Riley, I had been*
> *steady for weeks & I promise you faithfully, it will not happen again!*

Inspector Appleton said the defendant was making his 110th appearance. Mr Walton Stanley, magistrate, said, *"He has apparently had 110 birthdays!!!"* Riley was fined ten shillings. It was worth a try!

Riley's physical demeanour no doubt matched much of the housing in the city, which in 1932 was still in a lamentable condition. In the previous year, many of the city's 276,619[11] population were living in an abominable state.

> *The Bishop of Lichfield has denounced the poor living conditions of the*
> *working class population of 239,000 in the City of Stoke on Trent; one out of*
> *every five persons is living in housing unfit for human habitation.*

It therefore is incredulous, coming as they did from such a city, that two young men would take on the best in the world and not be found wanting:

> *RH Leivers, a 17 years old from Longton High School[12] who with Norman*
> *Wainwright, has been chosen to represent Britain in the Olympic Swimming*
> *Championships to be decided in Los Angeles this month.*

The New Year brought the Biggles Brigade down to earth with a bump. The aerodrome at the Meir[13] was beginning to look like an albatross around the neck of the good citizens of Stoke on Trent; the figures presented were startling. In late January, Mr G B Rogers said he had opposed the municipal aerodrome project at the Meir from the start.

So far it had cost £29,180 while the income for the past year had amounted to £234 16s 6d and the expenditure was £2,632 10s 10d.

In view of the hostile rumblings from Germany and the need for the country to have an airborne defence, perhaps other opinions won the day on this occasion? At any rate, a city the size of Stoke on Trent with a population of a quarter of a million, surely needed an airport! In a typical about-turn twelve months later, one of the city's civic big guns re-emphasised that Stoke on Trent should be to the fore:

The City of Stoke-on-Trent has gained control of the lease for £150 of Meir Aerodrome which was bought from National Flying Services. At a meeting of the council the future of the aerodrome was debated. "It was right that a city with a population of close to 300,000 should not be left out of the air ring." stated the Lord Mayor, Alderman A Hollins. Countering, Mr G B Rogers said that he thought it (Meir Aerodrome) should be converted to a building site seeing the corporation would have to spend from between £40,000 - £50,000 before it could be made available for the purpose for which it was intended. Agreeing, Mr J Mooney added that he believed that somewhere about £32,000 had already been spent on the aerodrome.

Soon Railway Air Services Limited would be flying within easy reach of Meir aerodrome on their journeys from Manchester and Birmingham and as if to underline the opinion of the sagacious Alderman Hollins, a celebrated royal visitor to the area called at the Meir on his way to an appointment:

Prince George[14] arrived and left from Meir Aerodrome on his tour of social service centres in Staffordshire!

As spring gave way to summer and long warm evenings, a hint of frustration crept to the surface in a acerbic critique delivered by the vicar of Dresden. He had put into words what every clergyman thinks but then bites his tongue and decides to walk a couple of times round his church instead. Letter in the Parish Magazine in Dresden, from the vicar:

PARISH NOTICE
This church will be closed for divine service during the
Summer months except on wet days when it is not fit for
people to spend the Lord's Day in pleasure!

Probably taking this as his cue, the parish priest at SS Mary & Chad's, Sandford Hill, the Rev Edward Fenton Woodward put pen to paper to give vent to his feelings in a measured outburst about a long standing grievance:

I have laboured conscientiously among you for 4 years. During that time upward of £750 have been passed and spent on the church and its furnishings & £100 on the church hall. Although my predecessor & his wife warned me I should find the vicarage a hopelessly cumbrous & costly proposition and that my first work should be to secure a new house, I have stuck it for four years because I could not conscientiously go forward with such a scheme, while the church and church hall were in such dire straits. But now I am at the end of my tether and quite frankly it does mean a new presbytery or a new priest.

At the risk of boring you, I will present in some detail a few reasons why the present house is impossible. It was condemned at the last Diocesan Survey (1929) as thoroughly unsuitable for habitation. That sums up what the Diocesan Authorities think about it.

The windows of the rooms most used nearly all face north. We never get sunshine. As a result, the house is cold even in the summer. In the winter it is a draughty refrigerator. It is built 'in a hole' below the level of the garden. Consequently the foundations are water-logged and having no damp course, the whole house is shockingly damp. Downstairs there are 6 rooms and 4 pantries. They are fitted with no less an 23 doors. My study has 4 doors; one in each wall. The rooms are divided by 3 passages comprising in all a length of 20 yards. You can imagine how cosy and warm it is in winter. The passages act like elaborate flues and the numerous doors like dampers in a huge range. There is a bewildering system of first rate draughts. Although my coal bill averages £1 a week in winter, one is invariably done to a turn on one side and frostbitten on the other. The house is a standing joke so far as those arrangements go.

It is a day's march from the dining room to the scullery and you have to turn three corners in transit. A passage separates the kitchen from the scullery. Of the 3 pantries in use (all are poky, damp and insanitary) one is just inside the back door; one is next to the scullery and one is in the front hall. The last cook we had described the house as a "hell-hole'. I forget whether there was a heat wave on at the time for she can't have been referring to the warm of the atmosphere. Altogether the house is old, expensive and comfortless. The doors won't latch and the knobs come off in your hand. The electric lighting system is antiquated and doesn't function although last June I spent £20 on renewals.

Occasionally in the dining room and lounge we get a smoke barrage which just ruins everything. This is a mystery. The latest explanation is that it rises from old workings beneath the house. This morning at breakfast I was informed that before we can begin the winter fires, at least 3 hearths want relaying. All the rooms need redecorating. They are a disgrace to Pitt Street.

Incidentally, the back door is at the front and the front door is at the back. To reach either entrance, you must pass the old stable, the ash bin and the lavatory. The garden won't grow (only lettuce & we can't live on that) and the fence is falling to bits. I would tell you more but you'll think I'm being funny. It isn't a joke, it's a tragedy. We are all dreading the winter and its rigours. We all know what that means so you see the need is genuine and something must be done about it.

The Sale of Work in December is our first big effort to solve the problem. Do you want to see your clergy decently housed? If so, do something now. Don't wait until the middle of November. Please realise I am being very serious & I do feel the matter very keenly.

It was clearly 'make your mind up time' for the parishioners 'on the hill'.

The roads in Meir were still as dangerous as ever, as illustrated by an accident in October 1933. The name of the defendant has been omitted:

Accident at Meir Crossroads: Mr. X was fined £50 and banned for 5 years (the maximum fine). While driving in the Meir he hit a man in his car on 7th October at 5.40pm. The man, Thomas Trathowen, 59, was crossing from the

Saracen's Head[15] side and had got to with in 6 feet of the other side when he was struck by the car. The defendant was coming down Sandon Road.

The magistrate had taken a serious view of the offence and imposed a huge fine bearing in mind a new car cost about £200 as well as levelling a five year ban. Was it was because injuries caused by driving were reaching epidemic proportions?

Mr Fenn Sherlie, writing in Pearson's Magazine some months later declared:

In the past 14 years some 1.8 million men women and children have been killed or injured on the roads of Great Britain, a figure equal to 70% of the total casualties of the Great War!

The demolition of Old Longton continued unrestrained. Just before Christmas 1933, an area not far from the Police Station was razed under instructions from the Ministry of Health.

A great number of properties were cleared from Sutherland Road and High Street in Longton but excluded the factories. About 953 people were re-housed. Some were settled at Gom's Mill in Blurton, which was about 1170 yards away. Altogether 178 houses, 6 shops with houses attached (213 children and 221 families) were demolished.

For them a new start in a new place - but the poverty would stay the same.

Captain F G Goodwin died in February 1934 at the age of 68 after a long association with the Meir Church Lads Brigade. Many times throughout his long life he had encouraged young men in the Meir to play their organised part. It is debatable whether he would have approved though, of what was taking place on his own doorstep on the 25th March 1934:

The Potteries branch of the British Union of Fascists was held at Longton Town Hall on Sunday night when an address was given on the policy of the organisation by William Joyce, area administrator from London Headquarters.

Little did those who heard him that spring evening realise they were listening to a voice that would become a part of everyday life in the dark days of the Second World War as he tried to demoralise the nation as Lord Haw Haw.

William Brooke Joyce was born in New York on 24th April 1906, the 'Brooke' being at the insistence of his English mother, Gertrude Emily Brooke, a doctor's daughter from Lancashire. She had married Irishman Michael Joyce on 7th May 1905 in New York State, where they lived for three years. In 1909, Michael Joyce went to County Mayo in Ireland, followed by his wife and son shortly afterwards. They never returned to America.

William came to England in 1921, and after completing his education at catholic

177

schools, joined the regular army in the Officers Training Corps at 16 years of age. Leaving Battersea Polytechnic for Birkbeck College, he became President of the Conservative Society in September 1923 while studying for a degree in French, Latin, English and History.

Violently anti-semitic, he joined the right wing group formed by Miss R L Linton-Orman; the British Fascist Party. Such was the feeling engendered towards this party, violence was never very far away. On the evening of the 22nd October 1924 at a street gathering in London, Joyce was attacked and slashed with a razor from the corner of his mouth to behind his right ear.

Sir Oswald Mosley[16] founded the British Union of Fascists in 1932, which robbed the British Fascists party of its members, one of whom was William Joyce. During the carefully staged meetings of the British Union of Fascists, any dissenters would be surrounded by Mosley's 'blackshirts'[17] and escorted from the hall where they were beaten, often so severely that they required hospital treatment.

When Mosley was ill in 1934 it gave William Joyce a golden opportunity to appear as the chief speaker at rallies. Joyce's orations were so powerful, they left those that had heard them with indelible memories. One such man was the writer Cecil Roberts, who attended a meeting at the Park Lane Hotel, London in 1933 when Joyce spoke:

Never before in any country had I met a personality so terrifying in its dynamic force, so vituperative, so vitriolic. The words poured from him in a corrosive spate. We listened in a kind of frozen hypnotism to that cold stabbing voice.

Joyce believed that the model for the British Fascists should be Hitler and not Mussolini. A frightening portent indeed, considering too the fact that Joyce was a monarchist and a staunch admirer of Edward VIII.

The expenses of the British Union of Fascists approached nearly £3000 a week, largely met from the private fortune of Sir Oswald Mosley. In an attempt to cut costs, he reduced his staff by 80%, one of whom, Joyce, then formed the National Socialist League in 1937.

Cultivating support through the politics of fear and ignorance, Joyce polled 2,564 votes in an election at Shoreditch, London. Fascism was declining, however, with the Italians attacking Abyssinia, the Spanish Civil War and Hitler's speeches and actions alienating liberal British opinion. Out of work and with slender prospects, he decided to try another tack. Along with MacNab, a fellow fascist, they set up as tutors under the title of John Angus MacNab BA (Oxon) & William Joyce BA (Lond) LCP, at 83 Onslow Gardens, London SW7.

William Joyce married for the second time[18] in February 1937 and after an aimless existence for a period, he and his wife found themselves in pre-war Berlin. Before long he had secured a position with German radio, his first broadcast being on the 11th September 1939. Joyce's repugnant reputation began to grow and throughout the whole of the Second World War, he would broadcast on the 150kW transmitter at Bremen, described as Radio Hamburg - although Cologne, Zeesen[19] and Hilversum were also used - to what remained of Free Europe.

His clipped nasal tones had a sinister appeal and to him was attributed the soubriquet 'Lord Haw -Haw' by Jonah Barrington in the Daily Express. *'He speaks English with the Haw-Haw-get-out-of-my-way variety and his strong suit is gentlemanly indignation.* One wonders if there is any one still alive today in Meir who remembers this diminutive man with a distinctive scar appearing at Longton Town Hall, who by his treasonable action secured himself such an infamous place in history?

Notes.
1. Amy Johnson, the aviatrix, married fellow pilot Jim Mollison in the 1930s. He is remembered in the streets of Meir by Mollison Road.
2. The population of Stoke on Trent was about 276900.
3. These photographs, from the Olive Hill collection, depict the houses (in 1994 numbered 658 Uttoxeter Road along with 656 and the entrance to Warwick Avenue) just after completion
8. After his death it was revealed that Vincent Riley was the holder of a First World War Military Medal for 'gallantry in the field'.
9. Dr Harris's successor was employed at a salary of £700 per annum.
10. In October 1931 the Labour Party was routed in the General Election, losing 236 seats.
11. The population was 267,647 in the 1921 census.
12 Built in 1885, demolished November 1993. Situated in Trentham Road, Longton.
13. Meir aerodrome had been the headquarters of the North Staffs Aero Club since 1925.
14. This was the Duke of Kent, killed on active service in 1942.
15. The Saracen's Head was situated at the cross roads.
16. Mosley visited Stoke in 1932.
17. In later years, the Public Order Bill forbade the wearing of political uniforms on public occasions and gave the police powers to forbid processions if they considered them against public safety.
18. Margaret Collins.
19. 'A chap I'd like to meet is moaning periodically from Zeesen.' Jonah Barrington of the Daily Express was later to write of Lord Haw Haw.

These houses formed part of a development built by Tompkinson & Bettelley called Meir Residential Estate. This photograph was taken in 1932 by the husband of Mrs Olive Hill, who for over 50 years lived in Warwick Avenue; the start of which can be seen in the centre of the picture. Longton is to the right and Meir to the left. With pantiled roofs, half timbered gables and wrought iron work fixtures, they characterised the optimism felt in the Meir during those times. In 1994 the Highways Agency demolished virtually all these homes for the new A50. On the left, using 1994 numbering (they were renumbered in the 1950s), is 658 Uttoxeter Road. *Hill collection*

Like the photograph above these are houses in Meir Residential Estate, in the early 1930s. During the 1950s they were renumbered: 658 Uttoxeter Road being on the far left with the Hill residence, the single fronted semi-detached house in Warwick Avenue,on the left hand side off the road. Longton is to the right and Meir town centre to the left. Note there is no house after that in Warwick Avenue and the trees of Meir House can clearly be seen on the extreme left. Meir at this time was still full of trees and green open spaces. *Hill collection*

Taken in 1928/29,in Meir lane (now Uttoxeter Road); the camera looking eastwards along the A50 towards Blythe Bridge. Visible are Meir Cottage (extreme left) and the King's Arms Hotel (centre left). Terraced houses and shops stretch along to what is today Terry Atkinson's, Swedish Car Care and Meir Methodist church, next door, beyond the two telegraph poles and the tall chimney. These are the only buildings left standing in this row almost 70 years later. The Saracen's Head, outside which a cyclist and a friend nonchalantly pass the time of day, is on the right in Sandon Road. The Toll cottage in Sandon Road had been demolished. Note the white posts on the right hand side. Further back on this corner, A V Shenton built the Broadway cinema, which opened in December 1936. Note the oversized arrows on trestles to direct traffic around the roundabout and the oil lamps to point out the obstacles. The amount of traffic on the A50 is very light: 60 years later there were 50,000 vehicle movements a day at this junction. The flat-capped cyclist casually negotiating the bend did not appear to be in much danger, but incredibly a decade later in this country, over 6500 people died as a result of road accidents.

Hill collection

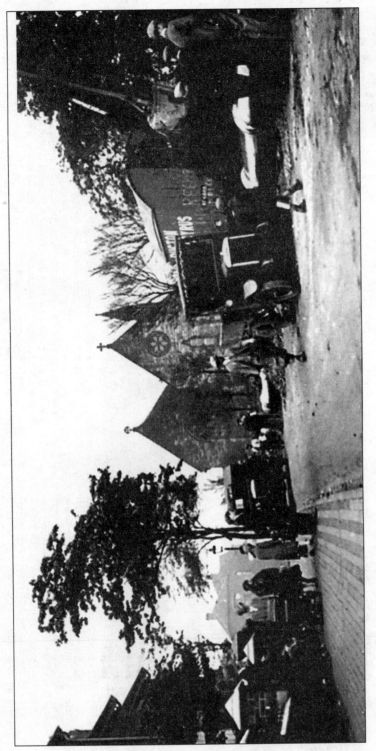

A scene of industry in Meir Road outside the Church of the Holy Evangelists, Normacot. A crane (registration number RF 6888) is lifting sections of pipe into place assisted by the usual crowd of onlookers and helpers.This church is higher up the road from, and on the same side as, Longton Cottage Hospital. A bus, (registration number UR 2271) travelling from Meir to Longton is beginning to negotiate the excavations with some care so as to miss the gentleman in the plus fours rounding the stationary truck. The pavement, made of blue brickettes, is a hard wearing and almost indestructible paving which was later ripped out in favour of flagstones. Now in 1995, brickettes (blue or otherwise) are in fashion for pedestrianised areas once more. It is inconceivable that people could casually stroll around what is now a heavily used through road for heavy goods vehicles making for Derby and the M1.

Lovatt collection

182

Prince George, Duke of Kent was the brother of King George VI. The Prince, here with his wife, Marina, Duchess of Kent and their two children, was the son of George V and Queen Mary and lost his life on active service in 1942.
Author's collection

In this shot of Joyce in later life, taken during the mid thirties, with cigarette in one hand and stick in the other, he is sporting the terrible scar inflicted on him after an attack with a glass bottle at a rally. The policies of the Fascists often aroused great animosity and the 'blackshirts', a type of Praetorian guard, present at many meetings would often beat dissenters severely. *Author's collection*

William Joyce as a young man proudly wearing his black shirt. He was to speak in later years at the Town Hall, Longton, in an attempt to win converts for the Fascist movement. Literate and highly persuasive he was an understudy to Sir Oswald Mosley, whose first wife, Cynthia, was Labour MP for Longton for two years from 1929. She died in 1933. At one time, Stoke on Trent had the largest branch of Mosley's Party with over four hundred members. *Author's collection*

A snowy scene of farm buildings and hedgerows in Meir before 1932/33, looking westwards from Meir towards Longton. This scene was taken from the second storey of Meir Cottage, from a position 5 yards to the right of the line of the A50, across the back of Crossroads Farm towards Holy Trinity church. In front of this, No 719 and Highfield House, Uttoxeter Road can be seen, very shortly after completion. Blythe Bridge is behind the photographer and Weston Road on the right..   *Bennett collection*

Taken probably 1932/3, looking up Meir Bank; Blythe Bridge is over the brow 2 miles away; Longton behind. Holy Trinity Church stands at the top left. Dr Heath's house, The Beeches far left, is behind snow covered trees. Behind the elms on the right are the chimneys of Meir House once occupied by Charles Harvey in the 1850s and surrounded by an enormous six foot wall. At the side were stables and a coachhouse known as Boardmans buildings. Arthur Bennett garaged his car here in the 1930s. Meir House was demolished in 1947. The buses seem to have stopped running as many are walking home and who is the brave soul in the open topped car?   *Hill collection*

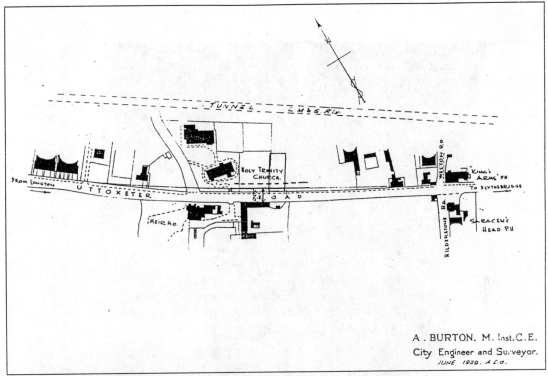

A . BURTON. M. Inst.C.E.
City Engineer and Surveyor.
JUNE 1920. A.C.O.

A view of Meir Cottage taken from the A50 showing the tidy curtains and intricate wrought iron fence. The wider angle gives an unusual glimpse of Weston Road to the left, with possibly Smith's buildings visible extreme left in the middleground. It was taken before 1932/33. The signpost on the corner points to Hilderstone whilst the road to Leek follows the line of Weston Road into the picture. *Bennett collection*

Built of Hollington stone and a mile from the Meir, the Town Hall in Longton is one of the town's architectural delights. This photograph from 1934 was dated by the S type bus, acquired by the PMT from Stevenson's Omnibus Service. William Brooke Joyce (Lord Haw Haw) once came here and addressed a rally in 1934/5. After the collapse of the Third Reich, Joyce was captured and brought to England, where he was tried and found guilty of treason. He was hanged at Wandsworth in 1946.

Hill collection

This series of maps taken from the OS map of 1938 shows the dramatic growth of the Meir since the maps of 1925/6 on pages 145 and 146. There has been a huge expansion of housing towards Caverswall. The City of Stoke on Trent Council built the Meir Square and Harrowby Road estates between 1925 and 1938 to clear large areas of 'slums' in Longton which had been declared unfit for human habitation.

The 'golf course' houses, Oak and Elm Place and Poplar Grove, had also appeared replacing the Golf Course! There was no direct link between this private estate and the housing in Waterhead Road - the fence that separated them was removed in the late 1930s. Ludwall House, built before 1832, can be seen off Sandon Road. It was the home of William Webberley, owner of the large Hanley bookshop that still bears his name. A large proportion of the old 'quality' houses are still present even at this relatively late stage. Meir House opposite Holy Trinity was an extensive mansion and was demolished in 1947.

Below are also shown tables which show the dramatic increase in life expectancy and the co-existent growth in the population of Great Britain over the past 150 years.

TABLE OF LIFE EXPECTANCY, POPULATION AND INFANT MORTALITY IN GREAT BRITAIN 1800-1993

YEAR	POPULATION	LIFE EXPECTANCY (YEARS)	INFANT MORTALITY
1993	57,649,000	76(m) & 76(f)	8 PER 1000
1963	53,274,000	68(m) & 74(f)	23.5 PER 1000
1943	46,467,000	N\A	63.9 PER 1000
1923	42,769,000	56(m) & 60(f)	76 PER 1000
1903	37,829,000	49(m) & 52(f)	110 PER 1000
1883	30,426,000	43.7(m) 47.2(f)	139 PER 1000
1863	23,753,000	41(m) & 45(f)	151 PER 1000
1843	19,016,000	40(m) & 42(f)	148 PER 1000
1823	14,681,000	39(m) & 39(f)	600 PER 1000
1783	8,410,000	N\A	N\A

(source: Independent on Sunday 1993)

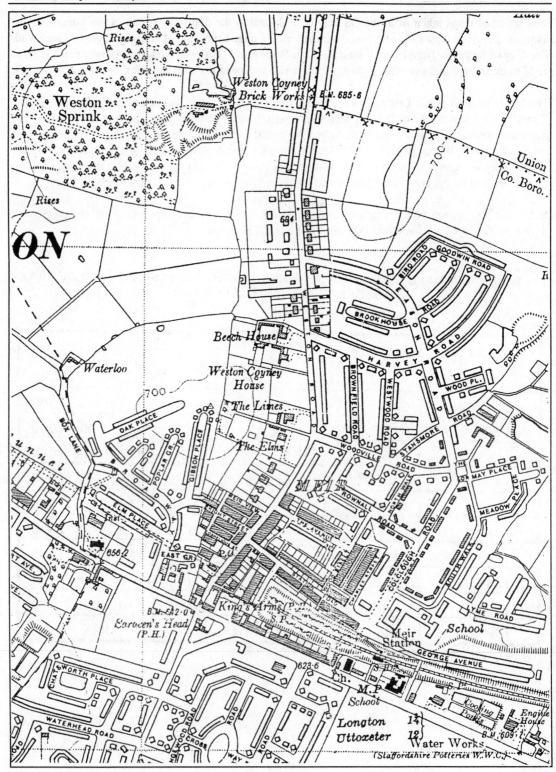

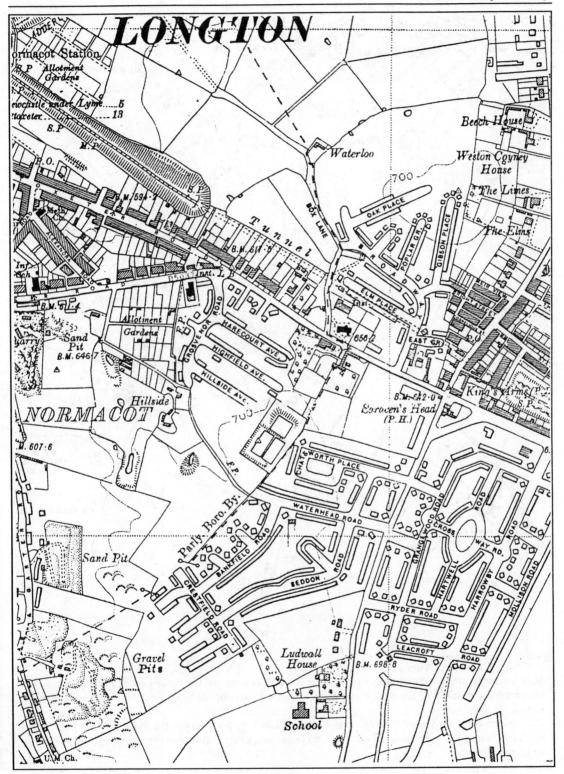

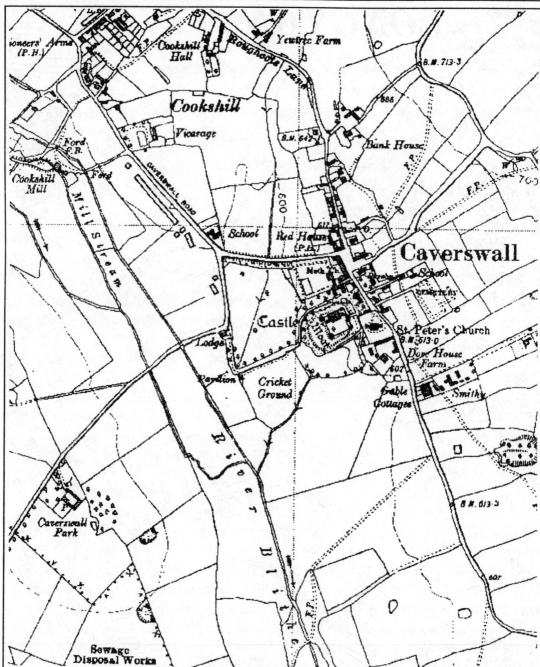

Meir was barely worth a shout in directories in the late 19th century and Caverswall dating back 800 years was the prominent member of the pair. While Meir blossomed over the 40 years from the turn of the century, Caverswall stood still.

The comparison of the map of 1901 (p.17) and 1938 indicate very few changes, the addition of a sewage works and a few houses along Roughcote Lane. Even 60 years later, today, Caverswall remains a tiny village with an air of tranquillity.

CHAPTER 14
1935 - 1939
'Farewell, a long farewell to all my greatness.'
Henry VIII

Virtually at a stroke, the old Meir vanished like the morning mist. With the construction of several large buildings which came to dominate the town, its demeanour changed radically during the space of just five years. These buildings characterised Meir's 'Golden Age' of expansion and progress. Meir was going somewhere and its inhabitants had basically all their needs on their own doorstep; even the town's drinkers were amply catered for!

The first of these buildings, the new Kings Arms Hotel, for John Joule & Sons, opened in 1935 on the same spot as its predecessor. The Broadway Cinema, built by AV Shenton on the opposite corner of the crossroads, was put up in response to the demands of an increasing population. It opened its doors to movie goers in December 1936. Some months later it was joined by the Territorial Army Drill Hall, with which it was to rub shoulders for nigh on thirty years and the new Waggon & Horses, moving from across the 'Blythe Bridge side' of Uttoxeter Road to its new site; whilst up Sandon Road, the rebuilt and enlarged Saracen's Head and Longton High School completed the picture.

However in 1935, the problem which concerned many was unemployment. Crude numbers, facts and figures fail to tell the whole story. Misery and depression does not after all, appear easily on balance sheets. Unemployment in the area (Stoke and Newcastle) at 29,579 on the 23rd January 1935, was an increase from 28,024 on the 17th December.

But however bleak the future seemed, there were crumbs of comfort. The policy[2] to remove Longton's slum dwellings and rehouse the town's population in something fitting to the 20th century continued. During this phase, residents of Edensor were transplanted to Meir.

It was evident that this urban renewal was succeeding in many perhaps unforeseen ways. The Medical Officer of Health was bullish and rightly so! Writing in an annual report, Dr Alan Wotherspoon, the Medical Officer for Stoke on Trent said that:

Infant mortality was now 85 per 1000 compared with 89 in 1933 and an average of 98 per 1000 between 1922 and 1931. The child population of Stoke on Trent from 1 to 5 years of age was estimated at 17140 [1]and plus the births under 1 year gave an estimated population of 21250 under 5 years. Deaths of children from 1 to 2 fell from 1219 in 1919-1923 to 469 from 1930 to 1934 while for those 2 to 5 years of age fell from 1374 to 345 during the same period. There had been a great improvement in the health and vitality of the surviving children.

It was certainly not before time. The land 'fit for heroes' had been a long time coming.

The wound within the city council concerning the aerodrome at Meir had developed into a running sore:

> *The proposed visit to the Stoke on Trent municipal airport at Meir of a squadron of the Royal Air Force on Empire Day (May 25th) was hotly debated by a meeting of the Stoke on Trent City council on Thursday. The whole incident was not unanimous because the RAF were proposing to bring their biggest bomber, bombs and machine guns which did not meet with universal approval by the members.*

But some were for it and said so vehemently: '*I have never heard so much bosh talked as I have in the last half hour,*' said Mr AJ Hewitt. '*The country today owes everything to the Army, Navy and Air Force.*'

The visit was cancelled; people had very short memories, it seemed! Though in a prophetic rejoinder, a letter in April from Air Commodore J A Chamier (Secretary General of the Air League of the British Empire) concluded by saying, '*An opportunity of strengthening the North Staffs Aero Club will have to be lost!*' Before the month was out, the perfect example of what might in future be at stake occurred, almost on cue, at the start of that perfect summer:

> *The Rt Hon J A Lyons, the Prime Minister of the Dominion of Australia, visited the Potteries on Saturday when he came to fulfil his engagement to declare open the bazaar by members of St Gregory's Roman Catholic Church Longton, at Longton Town Hall. Accompanied by Mrs Lyons, the distinguished visitor travelled by air from London to Meir Aerodrome where he was met by the Lord Mayor (Ald AC Harvey) & escorted to Stoke Town Hall for a luncheon.*

25th May 1935

But it was not only national politicians who set foot on the runway at Meir. In August, Harry Taylor, the Town Clerk and Miss F Farmer were the first passengers from Meir to London when a Railway Services de Havilland 4-engined aircraft touched down on its way south from Scotland. Planes would call on demand at the aerodrome at 11.50 for Manchester, Liverpool, Belfast and Glasgow. Additionally, there was a rail link at Croydon for those who were going on to the continent, while at Manchester it connected with the Manx Airway Section of Railway Air Services. The fare for the 75 minute trip to London or the Isle of Man was £4 1s return and £6 11s to Glasgow - a snip!

Just as the public in Meir were getting used to the noise of aircraft engines rattling the ornaments in their china cabinets, in the week before Christmas, the perils of flying were exposed with dramatic results:

> *A plane piloted by Miss Dorothy Clive, the daughter of Col and Mrs Harry*

Clive, of Willowbridge, Pipe Gate, has come down in bad weather. The passenger in the aircraft, her cousin, Mr Roger David Clive of Hyde Park Street London who was a stockbroker was taken to Longton Cottage Hospital. The crash was due to a snow storm as the plane was attempting to land. Blinded by the snow the pilot tried to climb above it but hit a tree in her 90 hp Miles Hawk aircraft.

The festive season approached and it helped those in Meir (and elsewhere) to forget their immediate worldly worries. The notion that all was not well was reinforced by an announcement that the Home Office had decided to circulate pamphlets on air raid precautions!

Meir in 1936 was a vibrant, bustling and confident place full of shops of various trades, several churches, pubs and a cinema plus a Co-op (which for attempting to burgle, three men had been sent to prison the previous year). The area was blessed too, with a number of professional men and would have one of Staffordshire's first supermarkets - the shape of things to come - whilst Weston Road was a major shopping area:

Barlow, Jas, The Elms, Weston Road.
Mear, Stephen, Weston Coyney House, Weston Road.
Burslem & District Industrial Co-operative Society, Weston Road.
Chadwick, Elizabeth Ann Mrs, Grocer 32 Weston Road.
Adderley, Frank, Chemist, 41, Weston Road.
Aldridge, Mary Alice, Milliner, 65 Weston Road.
Parks Pharmacy, 66 Weston Road.
Cappers Limited, Grocers, 69 Weston Road.
Bennett, Luke B, Watch and Clock Repairer, 71 Weston Road.

It also had its medical men:

Griffith, Michael Joseph, MB B Ch BAO, Physician/Surgeon, 106 Weston Road.
Heath, William, BA MRCS LRCP, Physician/Surgeon, The Beeches Uttoxeter Road.
Ferguson, William Lawrence, Dental Surgeon, Highfield House, 717 Uttoxeter Road.

As well as the first landlord of the newly opened public house:

Johnson, Robert Arthur, King's Arms Public House, Meir.

And not forgetting:

Capper, Edith Mrs Grocer, 249 Uttoxeter Road, Longton.
Massey Arthur, Farmer, Uttoxeter Road.
Nixon John, Farmer, Uttoxeter Road.
North Staffs Aero Club (Leslie Irving Hon Sec), Uttoxeter Road, Longton.

The year was a year apart not just at home. King George V died early in January (his passing was to usher in a period of constitutional turmoil and uncertainty), but abroad the Nazis entered the Rhineland, fascist rebels set alight the tinder box of civil war in Spain, Il Duce (Mussolini) proclaimed *'Italy at last has her empire'* and the Olympic

Games in Berlin were a triumph for the young black American athlete Jesse Owens, in the face of Hitler's expectations.

The simmering abdication problem returned throughout the year. Prime Minister Stanley Baldwin had the unenviable job of telling His Majesty, the choice was between the crown and his relationship with Mrs Wallace Simpson, an American divorcee. He chose the latter. At the end of it all, on December 12th, King Edward abdicated and sailed into exile.

Away from the constitutional crisis, for those with more mundane expectations, buying a home of their own came top of the list. Meir was expanding; Hillside estate off Grosvenor Road built by Messrs Tipping was begun and the typical price for a detached house, 1 Harcourt Avenue, was about £475. Many took out a mortgage from a building society:

Leeds Permanent Building Society Rates at the time:

Advance (Over 12 years) (£)	Weekly Payments s d	Monthly Payments £ s d
100	2/7d	1 11 3
200	5/2d	1 2 6
300	7/9d	1 13 9
400	10/4d	2 5 0

Whatever the weather, farmers will always complain, but 1936 a phrase that entered the topic of conversation in the new King's Arms was simply 'the worst in memory'[3].

The death of Thomas Swynfen Parker-Jervis occurred during the autumn. He had by virtue of his Father, Col William Swynfen Whitehall Parker-Jervis, a link back to the time when he, the patron of Caverswall parish, relinquished the hold on Holy Trinity. He was related to one on England's greatest admirals, John Jervis[4] (Earl St Vincent after the famous sea battle in February 1797) who was born at Meaford Hall, Stone. His Father, Swynfen Jervis, was a barrister and his mother was sister to Thomas Parker, Lord Chief Baron to the Exchequer.

Christmas finally came, but as often happens was not a happy time for everyone:

Mrs Jane Wood of 12 Grangewood Road, Meir, in the vaults of the King's Arms, Meir at 7.50pm on Saturday night (19th December 1936), said, "The deceased asked for half a pint of bitter beer & after drinking part of it, she felt in her handbag and drew out a small bottle wrapped in brown paper and drank the contents. Deceased then asked the witness to fetch a doctor and she immediately called for assistance. The bottle was labelled POISON. Dr F R Oliver said at death was due to an irritant poison.

The Broadway Luxury Cinema opened in December 1936 bringing the thrills of the silver screen to the Meir and emphasising its growth in size and importance. The architect of the classical 1930s art deco building was Mr A Glynn Sherwin and the builders were Messrs Shenton of Longton. With its luxurious furnishings and sophisticated amenities, it must have seemed the acme of modernity. The souvenir brochure and the pages from it are reproduced at the chapter end.

One thing that remained very popular in Meir despite the new cinema was football, either watching or playing. Matches played around the Christmas break were extensively supported, drawing large crowds. What better then to work off an excess of Auntie Elsie's 'homemade mince pies' than to take the bus from Meir to the Victoria Ground four miles away and spend the afternoon cheering Stoke City (the 'Potters'), with 20 year old Stanley Matthews playing.

Stoke City FC[5] had matches on Christmas Day and Boxing day (Saturday). In the first match against Chelsea they won 2-0 watched by a crowd of 25,000, while 39,000 at the second game saw Stoke draw 1-1 with Liverpool, with gate receipts for Stoke City in the region of £4000 for the two games. In the Chelsea match there was a glimpse of the young maestro at his best:

> *Then we saw the real Matthews. Again and again he ran past 2 or 3 men at good speed with the ball at his toes leaving these would-be tacklers behind one after the other. It was sheer sleight of foot and the openings he made for his colleagues on his left, ought to have produced a crop of goals. Once he went on to shoot himself but made a hash of it.*

Shame on you Stan lad!

In January 1937, Dr Kempthorne, Bishop of Lichfield, gave notice of his intention to stand down due to 'advancing years'. The new King, George VI, appointed the Rev Edward Sydney Woods MA as the new Bishop of Lichfield at the end of the year.

Nearer home there was a more humble appointment but for his parishioners still a proud moment: The parish priest from Meir was amongst those at the induction:

> *The institution of the new vicar of Fenton (Rev Jesse Howse) has taken place. Present at the ceremony were the Rev B Paton Jones (Vicar of Dresden); Rev R W Bell (Vicar Of Holy Trinity Church, Meir):Rev G Goater (SS Mary&Chad, Sandford Hill); and the Rev A F Dodd (St James, Longton).*

In Meir, the military preparations reflected those throughout the country:

> *As a result of the changeover from an infantry to a mechanised searchlight unit attached to the anti-aircraft branch of the Territorial Army, the War Office has issued instructions for the erection of three new Drill Halls to meet the changed requirements. These new halls are to be built at Burslem, Cross*

Heath and Meir, Longton. In the planning of the new buildings, the comfort and scientific training of the men is to be specially studied. There will be classrooms for technical instruction, writing rooms and many recreational facilities which were unknown under the old order of things.

Patriotic feeling swept Britain; everyone was willing to play a part:

The company of Veteran Motorists (it did not specify whether the adjective referred to the car or the drivers!) offered a plan it had to register all 35000 members, who, in an emergency (military or civil) are willing to lend their services to the Government.

Unwittingly the local papers rekindled the argument about Meir aerodrome in April. Readers throughout the length and breadth of the land scrutinised their maps to find out where 'Meir' was!

It has been announced that Meir Airport is to be the "turning point" in the King's Cup Air Race to take place on Friday and Saturday 10th &11th September 1937. The North Staffs Aero Club were anxious for Meir to assume importance as a control point. In the Coronation year, the Royal Aero Club have decided the race shall take the form of a circuit of Britain. Taking off from Hatfield, Herts, turning at Cambridge, Skegness, York, Scarborough and Whitby via Newcastle on Tyne to Aberdeen, the course then lies south west over Perthshire to the Glasgow control and from then onto Newtownards in Northern Ireland, finishing at Phoenix Park Dublin, where they will spend the night. Those who succeed this 780 mile eliminating contest, will leave Dublin the next day to Newtownards and fly round a "turning point" at Carlisle, St Bees Head and then Stanley Park Aerodrome, Blackpool. The machines will pass over MEIR, "another turning point" 369 miles along the course from Dublin. The next turning point will be Leicester and then on to Cardiff before crossing the finishing line at Hatfield.   24th April 1937

The Spanish Civil War raged on and the Royal Navy lost eight of the crew from HMS Hunter in the Mediterranean when it struck a mine.

But one might be forgiven in Meir for overlooking the gathering storm in Germany; the local papers were preoccupied with another menace. Farmers were advised to '*go into action on the Home front and tackle Charlock and Wild Radish before it became a problem'*. It was certainly nice to get your priorities right!

The motor car was making great strides in popularity and was available from local dealers like Leese's garage in Uttoxeter Road, Meir. A new Morris Saloon cost £172 10s for the fixed head model and the coupé version was yours for a mere £215 0s 0d. For the economy minded, the Austin Ruby 7 saloon at £125 afforded miserly travel, while the Austin Ascot at £210, the Goodwood at £235 and the Cambridge for £178 in May 1937 gave one a difficult choice. All very British in name and the 'Buy British' slogan was clearly visible beneath the advertisements.

Inevitably, there was a proportionate increase in casualties; the toll of road deaths in Great Britain in 1935 was 5690 (with 178,864 injured), soaring massively to 6561 fatalities in 1936 and still further to 6591 in 1937.

The coronation of King George VI and Queen Elizabeth took place on 12th May 1937. The country would need a popular King and Queen in the dark days around the corner, to share in their triumphs and failures and inspire them with their courage.

The old order was also changing locally as demonstrated by the sale of Meaford Hall, the home of W S W Parker-Jervis, the former patron

of Caverswall church. The sun was setting on an age of opulence in which the chasm between the housing of the rich and that of the poor had been immense. Modern buildings were going up but Stoke's monumental housing problems would need a Herculean effort before inroads would be noticed.

But some things never changed and Vincent Riley was still in trouble with the police:

> *Vincent Riley made his 161st appearance in court on charges of 'being drunk & disorderly' and was sent to prison for 1 month.*

The incumbent at St Peter's, Caverswall also fell foul of the law and was duly castigated by the courts: mercifully the punishment was not as severe as Riley's:

> *The Vicar of Caverswall was summoned for failing to stop at a Halt sign. He pleaded guilty. He was fined £1.*

The completion of two important building projects were celebrated three weeks before Christmas: '*The consecration of St Gregory's, Longton*' and at the same time: '*the opening of the senior department of the new school took place last week.*' 4th Dec 1937.

The theme was reinforced a few months into the New Year by the Archdeacon of Stoke on Trent:

> *The Venerable Percy Harthill and the school managers are to launch a programme for the reconstruction and enlargement of Church Day schools in*

the area; the cost of which is estimated to be £24000.

Many churches saw the correlation between school and church and tried diligently to effect the link. Numerous examples abound in the city, although, regrettably, with the passage of the years, schools and churches have been demolished or turned over for community purposes. Irony indeed as the government would later insist religious education be taught as part of the curriculum.

1937 was almost at an end; the year that saw the manufacture of the first gas masks; the annual expenditure for Staffordshire County Council set to exceed £3m for the first time and a visit to the Victoria Hall Hanley by Gigli.

And trade reports from 1937 were optimistic for the local economy:

The pottery industry in 1937 experienced one of the best trading periods since the post war boom and at the moment there is a distinctly cheerful note as to its future.

Further cheerful notes came aplenty during the next year, a year that would see the appearance of two giants of the musical world on the local scene:

Sir Thomas Beecham and the London Philharmonic Orchestra are to appear at the Victoria Hall, Hanley on 17th January. Prices are 7/6d centre balcony, or arena 3/6d or on the platform (limited accommodation) for 2/-.

The second artist was not only a world class composer but a world class performer as well. His appearance was a never to be repeated experience for local music lovers. Once described as *'Six and half feet of majestic indifference'*, he appeared at the Victoria Hall, Hanley, on the 17th March. The prices of the seats were, Balcony 10/6d to 8/-; Gallery 5/6d to 3/6d. The Evening Sentinel music critic (F.B.) could not praise him highly enough although he did have a moan about the attendance:

It would have been nice to see all the arena seats occupied on so memorable occasion but Rachmaninoff can never have played to a more exemplary audience. Genius was listened to with rapt attention.

Rachmaninoff died in Beverly Hills, California on March 28th 1943[6].

If trade was getting better, the weather certainly was not and this time it was not just the vicarage tea party that was under threat:

Bad weather conditions which caused cancellations of displays in several parts of the country, curtailed the Empire Air Day programme arranged on Saturday by the North Staffs Aero club at Meir Aerodrome. Of the 30 RAF machines expected, only 16, including the 46 (Fighter)

*Squadron (Gloster Gauntlets) from Digby, Lincolnshire, were able to reach
Stoke on Trent but the large crowd was rewarded with some spectacular
flying.* 4th June 1938

An Avro Anson coastal reconnaissance machine, an Airspeed Oxford trainer and a
Hawker Fury were open for inspection and were a continual source of interest.

In connection with the display, a demonstration was given by members of the city
ARP under Mr R G Totty. Major H M. Powell commanded a contingent of the 41st
Anti-Aircraft Battalion RE which also gave a display.

The RAF personnel were entertained to a luncheon with the Deputy Lord Mayor
(Ald A J Dale), who extended a civic welcome to the visitors. Undeniably, an amazing
volte face by the city's civic deputy.

But within a short time the sabre-rattling of Empire day would become just a pleasant
memory and a more purposeful air force would have to take its place:

*The RAF Volunteer Reserve Training School which has been established at the
Stoke on Trent Corporation Aerodrome at Meir was opened on Monday and the
instruction will shortly commence of the first batch of 25 volunteers. In much the
same style as the TA, instruction will be given by qualified RAF instructors in the
evenings and at the weekends. The school will have a complement of 25 training
planes for use in the instruction of that number of volunteers - to be drawn from
the Stoke on Trent area - and the full course will extend over three months. In this
way the school will be able to turn out 100 qualified pilots each year. In
connection with the Air Ministry scheme for the training of the Civil Air Guard,
the North Staffs Aero Club which also operates from Meir, have received nearly
300 applications to join, many of them from women and they have completed
arrangements for the commencement of training on September 1st.* 6th August 1938

To allay the fears of the Great British Public, resident in Stoke on Trent:

*The Air Raid Precautions (ARP) are
going on full steam in Stoke on
Trent - the scheme is as far
advanced as any.*

So they could all go on their hols
without worrying:

*North Staffs Exodus: Throughout
Saturday, the stream of travellers
continued by road and rail with
special trains on Sunday to take
people to the Welsh Coast and*

Lancashire.

Caverswall Castle was in the papers with the sale of a piece of its history in September:

> *A portrait of Matthew Craddock who was a member of Parliament for Stafford from 1544-1555 has been sold for 105 guineas; Matthew Craddock owned Caverswall Castle in the Commonwealth period 1649-1660 when it was garrisoned for Parliamentary troops.*

Christmas was approaching fast. Even if the City council did not think much of Meir's aerodrome, Santa Claus was definitely not of the same persuasion, his ride doubtless raising the expectations of many wide eyed children who watched his journey through the town. Tragically, for many it would be the last family Christmas for seven years - and for many, forever.

The worsening political situation cast a shadow across celebrations of the new year. The Air Ministry had always had its critics but no one could censure them for their thoughts in the first days of January. Hitler's rantings were increasingly bellicose and a state of readiness was in force at our Training Centres.

The work of the RAF Volunteer Reserve stationed at Meir Aerodrome was the subject of an address to members of the Stoke on Trent Rotary Club by Colonel P Y Birch. It was to be hoped there were no spies among his listeners:

> *The total establishment of the school at Meir would be about 213 and present requirements were for another 70 pilots, 37 observers and 75 wireless operators. Recruiting for the ground section had not yet begun. He dealt with the training of entrants and said after each satisfactory year of service, a pilot received a training fee of £25; in other sections the fee was £20. Recruits, he said were being drawn from Cheshire, Staffordshire and Shropshire. In the event of war, recruits would NOT be sent to fight at once. They would be assessed and be sent as occasion demanded to advanced service training schools.*
>
> 8th Feb 1939

Civilian preparations progressed and ration cards appeared. Throughout June and July, the sabre rattling rose to a deafening clatter; the 'Empire Displays' would never be more significant than now - and the 'coming of age' of the Royal Air Force was getting close:

The admission to the Empire Air Day Display on May 20th 1939 would be 1s for adults and 3d for children. They would be held at 78 aerodromes in the UK; including 63 RAF stations, 11 civil aerodromes, where personnel are being trained by the Royal Air Force, the Auxiliary Air Force and the Royal Air Force Volunteer Reserve. The remaining four are purely civil aerodromes. Stations will be open from 2pm until 7pm. The public will be afforded the opportunity of witnessing the performance of the latest types of monoplane fighter.
15th April 39

Time slipped by like sand through an hour glass, but desperate as things were, there was still the downright absurd, like the excuse given locally by a motorist caught by the police exceeding the speed limit. *'I was in a hurry to get home to hear Hitler's speech."* No; that did not work either; Robert Ernest Siegwialt of 'Sun House' Trentham Road, Longton was fined £2!

As war waited in the wings, it seemed bizarre to be passing round the hat for new buildings at a time when many could soon be blown to smithereens:

The Rev Brookes has made an appeal for cash to repair the fabric of St John's Church, Longton it being pointed out that the roof needed immediate action. On Good Friday morning the rector found a £5 note and £1 note in his letterbox pushed through by anonymous donors.
15th April 39

And in what was to be the last month of peace for nearly six years, a simple ceremony near the Common signified their act of faith in the future:

The foundation stone of St Francis's church at Rough Close was laid by the Bishop of Lichfield last week. Those present applauded warmly as Dr Woods ceremonially began the construction of the new building in these trying times.
5th August 1939

Notes.
1. The estimated population of Stoke on Trent in the middle of 1934 of 274,750 declined to 272,800 in 1937, according to the Medical Officer of Health.
2. Clearance order No 27, Longton, for Sheaf Passage (Webberley Lane) was carried out in December 1936.
3. Rainfall in 1936 of 29.22" was recorded by Major Moat at Johnson Hall, Eccleshall, Staffs.
4. A bust of Earl St Vincent, sculpted by Sir Francis Chantrey, embellishes the mausoleum of St Michael's Church, Stone.
5. Sir Francis Joseph retained the presidency of Stoke City Football Club in 1937.
6. Rachmaninoff became even more popular and widely known when his Second Piano Concerto was used by Noel Coward in 'Brief Encounter' with Trevor Howard and Celia Johnson: a favourite post-war film.

KINGS ARMS, MEIR

A fine view of the King's Arms public house. The Saracen's Head, which stood on the opposite corner, was relocated about a mile away, higher up Sandon Road. These two buildings, together with the Weston Coyney Arms in Weston Coyney, built at the same time, are all typical of the elaborate but intriguing designs of the mid 1930s. The houses on the left hand side in Weston Road have all given way to a development, altogether too large for its own good, along with the ubiquitous windswept car park. The large Sycamore is still standing (1995) outside Thresher's and the offices of HGC Hulse and Co, Accountants.

Bennett collection

A familiar photograph in the late 1930s of a well-loved cinema standing at the crossroads of the A50 and A520 in Meir. The photographer is standing in the A50 with Blythe Bridge at his back and Longton, a mile away, straight on. Sandon Road (A520) joins from the left, at this 'untidy' roundabout - it was later replaced by a complex tangle of traffic lights and Pelican crossings. Behind the Broadway (to the right and left) are the buildings of the Territorial Drill Hall. These were demolished in 1994 for the new A50. The shops to the left in Uttoxeter Road are still trading in 1995. Of the originals depicted here, Duncan Ross(Chemists) which opened for prescriptions in 1937 and La Marguerette the florists are still going strong. As Meir rapidly grew, the need for entertainment on the doorstep provided the impetus for the building of the Broadway. Opened in December 1936, it was tragically demolished in 1972 for the aborted Derby Way road scheme thereby necessitating a lengthy ride to Festival Park Etruria for devotees of the silver screen.

Author's collection

Part of the souvenir edition of the programme to commemorate the opening of the Broadway, Meir. This large and luxurious cinema embodied the spirit in Meir in the 1930s of progress and enthusiasm, something which has perhaps evaporated in the intervening years. *Author's collection*

THE BROADWAY LUXURY CINEMA
MEIR, STOKE-ON-TRENT,
SOUVENIR BROCHURE DECEMBER 1936.

FOREWORD

The development of Meir as a "bedroom" suburb of Stoke-on-Trent, particularly of Longton,has proceeded rapidly and large scale housing both by the Corporation and by private enterprise has resulted in a satellite town springing up.

The new population, forsaking the gloom of the older towns for the clearer atmosphere of the immediate countryside, have found among the obvious advantages of the location of their homes certain minor disadvantages, one of the chief of these being the definite handicap of the journey back to the city for an evening's entertainment.

The older residents of the district in considerable number have likewise suffered under the disadvantage, and it is to supply a need which is felt by new and old alike that the erection of the Broadway cinema has been undertaken. It is hoped by the directors that in every way this cinema will be found to afford complete satisfaction and that it will contribute in no mean manner to the social and artistic life of the Meir.

It was realised by the directors with their intimate business knowledge of the Potteries that here was a magnificent and commanding site on a main crossroads, in a district which will grow in importance with the inevitable progress and development of the City Aerodrome.

It is not the purpose of this foreword to justify the cinema of today, or to speak of its influence upon current art and fashion.

Suffice it to say that by careful choice of matter and style the directors of the Broadway Cinema intend to present an ever changing programme of uniformly high quality and it is hoped that the combination of fine films and of the comfort and elegance of the house itself will be reflected in the support of a wide circle of patrons.

THE CINEMA CREATED FOR YOUR COMFORT AND ENTERTAINMENT

THE DIRECTORS OF THE BROADWAY CINEMA

1) Herbert E. Clewlow: A native of Hanley and a partner of the firm Charles Knight and Sons, Removal contractors and former 'bus proprietors. For a number of years he was connected with the Roxy Cinema Hanley of which he was also a director. He has always been actively engaged in the removal business of Charles Knight and Sons and was greatly responsible for the construction of the Broadway being built. Served during the war with the Northumberland Fusiliers and King's Own Yorkshire Light Infantry and was awarded the Military Medal.

2) G Harold Wright: Also of the removal business of Charles Knight and Sons of which he is a partner. Like Mr HE Clewlow is a native of Hanley and was formerly in the 'bus business and greatly responsible for the erection of the Broadway. Served during the war with the 5th Lincolns.

3) Lawrence AV Plumpton: Comes from Melbourne, Australia but has resided in this country for many years. He has been in the cinema trade since 1919 in which he is well

known. Was the manager of the Oxford Picture House, Manchester during the time of the famous Symphony Orchestra of 42 performers afterwards at the Playhouse, Chelsea and the Premier Picture House, Widnes. At present is the lessee of the Royal Picture House, Longton. At the outbreak of war was with the fleet at Scapa ,joined the army in September 1914, commissioned in 1915, served overseas with the Lancashire Fusiliers and was wounded at the Somme.

4) J Mee: Joined the City of London Fusiliers in August 1914, eventually being transferred to the Royal Artillery as Sergeant-instructor of Signalling. Had service in France, was gassed, finishing his services in 1919 with the rank of acting Sergeant-major.

THE ARCHITECT

Mr A Glynn Sherwin was the architect responsible for the inception and for carrying out the scheme. In his capacity of architect and surveyor for Housing schemes in the vicinity he was quick to realise the importance of the crossroads site for shops and business premises in addition to the Broadway cinema. Mr Sherwin has an extensive practice with head offices in Newcastle under Lyme and has been responsible since the termination of the war in carrying through in all parts of this, and the surrounding districts, a number of large and interesting schemes including housing estate work on a large scale.

He has been responsible moreover for the alteration and modernisation of important licensed premises and is an exponent of modern design as applied to shop and business premises.

THE BUILDER

Messrs A Shenton of Longton were the firm engaged as building contractors for the Broadway cinema. They are an old established firm and the completion of this cinema is a further example of the services which they render.

The finest British manufacturers are represented in the body of the building and fine British craftsmanship is also here displayed.

THE DESIGN OF THE CINEMA

Nothing could demonstrate the success of the architectural conception better than the happy and natural manner in which the building rises to view on this corner site. It gives the impression of having grown into position and its external appearance to traffic approaching the city from the direction of Derby and the east is both dignified and welcoming.

The main structure is framed in British steelwork to the specification and design of the consultant engineer, Mr GW Costain, Neville House, Waterloo Street, Birmingham 2 and the whole of the building conforms to fire-resisting regulations and to the By-Laws of the City Surveyor and ensures the absolute safety of staff and patrons alike. The floors are of solid concrete reinforced by Hy-rib. The steel roof trusses to the main spans carry below an expanded steel ceiling and above a protected steel decking covered with ashphalte; a walking space between ceiling and roof is provided for access to lighting features and for periodic inspection.

The main staircases are reinforced artificial stone covered with Terrazzo; the staircases to the projection suite are of no-slip artificial stone. In addition there is a steel escape stair on the north side of the balcony.

Lovers of statistics will be interested to learn that a quarter of a million bricks have been used in the main walls, that the Main Balcony girder of 60 feet span and weighs 25 tons.

Fine quality brickwork of subdued and harmonious tone with a plinth of contrasting shades and terra cotta dressings are used to mark the terminal features - the broad circular pylons of the entrance front - and also to give the long Uttoxeter Road frontage by day the horizontal emphasis which is produced at night by the lines of the Neon lighting.

The richness of the entrance front, the shelter provided by the sweeping curves of the marquise, the large floodlit windows relieved by the delicately figured etching of the plate glass, the shining Staybrite Entrance doorways, the glowing signs reflected by the glaze of the Terra Cotta all combine to give an air of gaiety of warmth and hospitality which reflects the comfort of the interior and the welcome that awaits within.

THE INTERIOR TREATMENT

The auditorium has been designed cleanly and without fuss giving a calm restful atmosphere without adventitious ornament or finicky detail. We have a cinema interior which has made a clean break with tradition in order to fulfil the new requirements of the Talking Film. Inasmuch as the scheme is indebted to contemporary work, the interior may be said to be inspired by the most modern examples of continental architecture.

The main body of the auditorium is divided into Front Stalls and Back Stalls, each division having its own exits to both streets allowing the hall to be emptied rapidly and without discomfort. The Balcony access is so designed as to render the Cafe 'en suite'. Lavatory and cloakroom accommodation is conveniently disposed to serve all parts of the building.

Extreme care has been taken to afford easy raking of the balcony and to afford easy sight lines from every seat, each of which is luxuriously upholstered in contrasting pastel shades.Careful consideration has also been paid to the acoustical properties of the Auditorium. Acoustical wall boarding of cellular texture has been used extensively to this end.

A most interesting and unique feature is the series of mural paintings by a local artist, Mr H Tittensor RI who is well known for his charming Academy water colours as for his local industrial design. These panels occur at frieze level on the side walls and form a most refreshing, if not daring, alternative to the usual stock features.

THE STAGE, SCREEN AND SOUND

The Platform is of ample dimension and adequate for all purposes. The rich curtains have been carefully selected to afford under the colour changes of the elaborate electrical equipment, a setting of supreme brilliance to delight the eye in the interludes and intervals of the programme.

The lighting of the main hall is bound up with the internal decorative effect; in fact the lighting to a large degree becomes the decoration. The stage lighting is on a comprehensive scale and it is possible to provide numberless colour changes of every conceivable hue and never until recently has progress in artificial lighting made possible the fascinating effects of an ever changing sea of colour which here floods the Proscenium curtains.

The Wide Range reproducing system has been installed in this theatre and the enormous advantages to be gained with Wide Range are that it not only creates a greater intimacy between the audience and the screen artist, but that all the sound variations of speech and music are faithfully and naturally reproduced as if the artist were giving a living performance.

HEATING AND VENTILATION

The heating of the whole building is carried out from a low pressure hot water installation,the circulation of which is accelerated by means of electricity.

The Boiler is fired by an Automatic Coal Stoker. The vitiated air which is extracted by electric fans is conducted by way of ventilation grilles in the main ceiling to trunks in the roof space.

A convenient and airy projection suite has been installed with the latest equipment in which no expense has been spared.

THE MANAGER

The management has been entrusted to Mr LAV Plumpton who with this experience at the Royal,Longton has been able to study the requirements of the amusement going public of the Town & District.

Mr Plumpton is an Australian and apart from the years spent in the Great War, his career has been devoted to the entertainment business in one form or another.

A keen sportsman, it is only natural being an Australian, that he is very keen on cricket and has for the past two seasons been Captain of the Rough Close Cricket Club.

At golf he won the Birmingham and Midland Cinema Trade Golf Tournament in 1934, and was runner-up in 1936.

Mr Plumpton's appointment at the new cinema, is to use his own words "A dream come true" and patrons can rest assured that their entertainment is in safe and capable hands.

THE STAFF

The staff does not consist of merely smartly uniformed individuals. They realise it is their function to give personal satisfaction to every one who enters the Theatre and the are trained to be courteous in their manners to Patrons, polite in their answers to questions and patient at all times.

THE CAFE

A special reference should be allowed to the Cafe where a leisurely half hour for afternoon tea or for supper may well be enjoyed.

An excellent kitchen well lit and ventilated with Electrical Cooking Equipment is installed and it is intended to furnish light meals of an attractive nature.

PROGRAMME FOR THE OPENING IN DECEMBER 1936

Telephone Longton 3363

1. National Anthem.

2. Opening ceremony by the Lord Mayor (Ald JA Dale Esq JP) and Lady Mayoress of Stoke on Trent. The proceeds of th;s afternoons matinee are to be given to the Longton Hospital who will be represented by Mr T Yates Esq JP (Chairman of the Directors, Longton Hospital)

3. British Movietone News

4."JAVA SEAS" with Charles Bickford, Elizabeth Young and Leslie Fenton
(This is adventure with a vengeance!)

5. The Country Boy (Cartoon in Colour)
6. "LIMELIGHT" with Anna Neagle and the Street Singer (Arthur Tracey)
Glorious songs, spectacular dancing, great star performances.

Hours of opening: Continuous performances on Mondays,Thursdays and Saturdays from 2pm to 10.30pm. Tuesdays,Wednesdays and Fridays from 5.30pm to 10.30 pm. Children's matinees Saturdays at 11.00 am.

Prices of Admission (including Tax)
Matinees to 3.30 pm: Stalls 4d and 6d. Circle 9d (Bank Holidays excepted)

Evenings: Front Stalls 6d. Back Stalls 9d. Back Circle 1/- and Front Circle 1/3d

Car park Free to patrons: Adjoins the theatre.

Empire Day at Meir Aerodrome. The Mayor of Newcastle, Lord Mayor & Lady Mayoress of Stoke on Trent and Councillor Battison

●Amy Johnson.

Aviator flew from Meir

The Prime Minister of the Dominion of Australia and his wife arrived at Meir Aerodrome in May 1935 to fulfil a promise to open a garden party at St Gregory's R.C. Church in Longton. One of many distinguished visitors to land at Meir over the years, he came via London.

MY QUESTION "Did Amy Johnson fly from Meir Aerodrome?" has brought a reply which amounts to a definite yes.

As I suspected, the famous woman aviator and her husband Jim Mollison were both ferry pilots who flew aircraft from Meir to RAF bases in the early years of the war.

Mollie Barks, of Barlaston, tells me that her uncle, Bill Rushton, was landlord of the Station Hotel at Meir, where both Amy and Jim often stayed overnight up to 1941. In that year, sadly, Amy was drowned after crashing into the River Thames.

According to John Goodwin, of Fenton, Meir had an airfield from around 1929 when he saw Alan Cobham's flying circus perform there. Planes in those days, he writes, could crash without killing anyone.

The tragic death of a passenger at Meir aerodrome as an aircraft came in to land in a snowstorm made the newspapers in December 1935. The pilot, Dorothy Clive of Willoughbridge escaped unhurt but her cousin, Roger David Clive died at the Cottage Hospital from his injuries.

CHAPTER 15
1939
'We'll meet again, don't know where, don't know when'

The inexorable slide into the abyss during the summer of 1939 was marked by the appearance of more and more uniforms on the broad tree-lined streets of Meir. Men paraded at the aerodrome[1] now handed over to the Royal Air Force Volunteer Reserve, while units of the Territorial Army billeted at the Drill Hall in the centre of the town were a common sight. It left nobody in any doubt as to what was coming.

A bizarre flying accident during the first week in August, not too far from the King's Arms, had the locals scratching their heads, wondering if this was it. Had the balloon gone up already?

An aeroplane belonging to the North Staffs Aero Club which made a forced landing in a field at Cookshill, near Caverswall on Tuesday evening, struck and broke a high tension cable with the result that the district's electricity supplies were cut for a short time. The occupants of the plane were Mr Peter Massey, an instructor from the Aero Club, Meir and Mr Seekings, a pupil. Mr Seekings was receiving instruction in forced landings when the incident occurred. Neither pilot nor passenger was hurt and the plane suffered only slight damage, being able to return to Meir Aerodrome after a short delay.

On September 3rd, a Sunday, the country caught its breath. The tremulous voice of Neville Chamberlain announced the news and newspapers later filled in the detail. Over garden walls and outside the pub, knots of people gathered to discuss the implications which they accepted with quiet resignation. The declaration of war was later immortalised by a comedian[2] who used 'The Day War Broke Out!' as the start of his act. But just then, no one felt much like laughing.

Behind all of this, there were those with a good inkling of what might transpire, for two days earlier on Friday 1st September, a mass evacuation emptied the country's largest cities more effectively than any Pied Piper. By the first Sunday evening of the war, almost one and a half million children had been taken places of 'safety' out of London. Not all went though; in London it was a little less than 50%, while in Manchester the figure was 40% and in Sheffield 85% actually stayed put. Some relished the evacuation as an escape from the grim existence they had endured in the cities.

Thank God I was evacuated, not because I avoided danger but because it changed my way of thinking. It made me love the country. I would never live in town again. I found a refuge, quiet and peaceful, after an unhappy home life. I found another family who I really loved - and still do!

The Bishop of Lichfield declared *'the work must go on.'* Whether this was meant to convey only a spiritual urgency was soon clarified: In the cathedral the figures of Bishop Ryder and the 'Sleeping Children' by Sir Francis Chantrey of 1817 were thickly encased in sand bags whilst the magnificent stained windows were carefully removed and replaced with plain glass. *'Seven of the windows are Flemish in the Lady Chapel and are being removed by Messrs J H Bridgeman & Son, Lichfield.'*[3]

One serious worry expressed by his Grace was that *'a removal of a large numbers of men out of the influences of their army chaplains was undesirable'* and also that problems had been experienced with the vast migrations of evacuee children from our large cities.

But war is war and sacrifices had to be made. Immediately, people thought of various ways in which to help the War Effort and the era saw this island race at its most resolute. The home front was not neglected. Ways of keeping the kitchens of the nation filled got under way in Longton as Dr F R Oliver opened Longton Drubbery Allotment Association.

From now on there would be no restraining the culinary inventiveness of the more ingenious cooks, who would conjure up such delights as Woolton pie. *'Delightful & Interesting Dishes to Cook With Carrots'* would lead digestive systems into a bewildering cul de sac of instantly forgettable and inedible delicacies. With the inevitable rationing, it took real creativity to eke out the meagre supplies of 12oz of sugar, 4oz of bacon and 4oz of butter a week. There were severe penalties for failure to obey an uncompromising code of conduct and any who erred were dealt with harshly:

> *Father X was fined £20 for having a quantity of butter that had arrived in Britain from Eire and for failing to place it at the disposal of the Minister of Food.*

Many sought oblivion in the dark of the cinema; the Broadway, a favoured venue for the forces stationed in Meir, had double seats which were much in demand. In the soporific warmth, with the faintly clinical aroma of carbolic soap, it was easy to put aside what Fortune might have in store.

For those venturing further afield to Hanley, the Odeon was showing 'Wuthering Heights' with Laurence Oliver and Merle Oberon, although, even at a time like this, there was still opposition to Sunday cinemas by the Free Church Council.

Throughout this mayhem, two much beloved charities survived like dinosaurs from gentler days, helping elderly residents acquire one or two 'little extras':

> *The Henry Hill and John Aynsley Charities were distributed last week. 200 old people, many over 80 and 90 years old received a welcome addition to their slender means besides gifts of tea and sugar.*

But time was of the essence. 1939 was drawing to a close; many would die before peace would bring the promise of better tomorrows. And for Meir, too, it was the end of an era which saw it reach a maturity from which it would begin an agonising and slow descent.

In the next half century Meir became just a shadow of its former self. Neither bomb nor bullet was to change it, but the internal combustion engine in its transformation from servant to master, a Frankenstein out of control, by sheer volume would consume and destroy it. No longer a place of ease with golf links, bowling greens, tennis courts and country walks, but tattered beyond recognition and engulfed by toxic fumes. Its busy airport would become but a jumble of industrial units and suburban housing, its centre just a tangle of incomprehensible traffic lights and Meir a testament to the dominance of man's expensive metallic steed.

'Meir - it's a one horse town, and they just shot the horse!'

Notes.
1. Amy Johnson and her pilot husband Jim Mollison both flew from Meir. Amy was killed when she is believed to have drowned, after crashing during the war.
2. Robb Wilton
3. In May 1945 it was disclosed that some of the windows had been buried in crates in the Anglesey Vaults to the east side of the south door of the cathedral.

A GREAT DAY HAS DAWNED. With our hearts filled with thankfulness for victory, let us make this great resolve ! Let us continue in our striving for a land free from anxiety and want—that the sacrifices of war may not have been in vain.

GIVE THANKS BY SAVING

Issued by the National Savings Committee

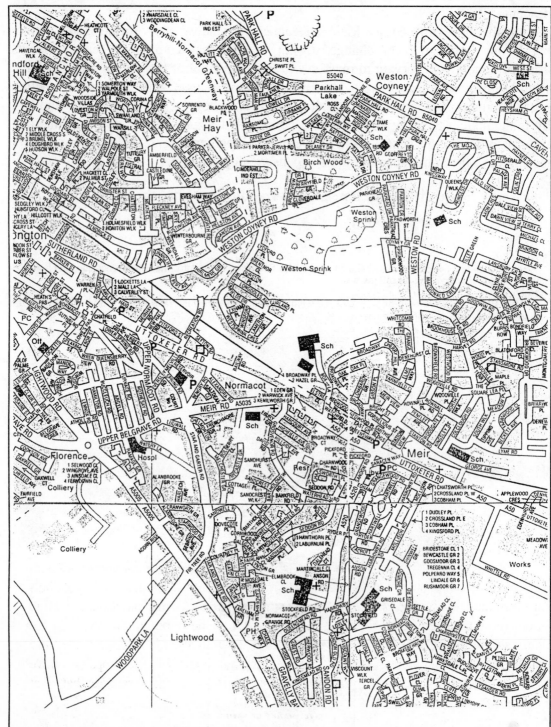

The Longton and Meir area in 1995. While the village of the Meir has been swallowed up by the City and engulfed by roads, its once 'big' twin looks little different to a century before.

Epilogue

Meir did survive all that was thrown at it during the six years of the Second World War; the remarkable aerial photograph taken during the first few days of peace gives credence to that statement. Even at this point in history Meir was still a pleasant place in which to live, with no hint of what was to come.

The King's Arms was still on the corner of Weston Road and Uttoxeter Road (the name Meir Lane had gone forever) and the military men were much in evidence at the Drill Hall and Longton High School, then in Sandon Road.

Heroes returned, like Lieutenant K Gordon, who was responsible for the capture of Lieutenant Eck, a German U Boat captain accused of firing on the lifeboats from the steamer Peleus; whose execution was postponed when the Commission needed his statement at the trial of Admiral Donitz at the Nuremburg trials.

Fifty years later, in the summer of 1995, little remains of that once proud and self-contained town. Inept town planning, together with the new A50 'improvements' have left gaping holes in Meir's fabric which leaves the whole so much the poorer. Even the Community Centre proudly opened by Councillor Doris Robinson during the 1960s has been supplanted by an architecturally superior building, high on the hill opposite Holy Trinity Church. It is to be hoped future elderly citizens of the town have the 'legs' for the march up to this windswept eyrie built on what is Meir's highest point and a contender for the town's title of 'Pneumonia Corner'.

The Trustee Savings Bank, Broadway Cinema, Swettenhams Store, the Waggon and Horses, Leese's Garage, Meir House, the Limes, the Elms, the Mount plus much of Tompkinson & Bettelley's inspired Meir Residential Estate have been demolished, while in their place there is nothing but an endless sea of seething traffic as Meir lies bleeding. The remnant of this scrag-end community will require major treatment if is it to survive.

Some buildings from the halcyon days of the 1930s do miraculously remain overlooked by the planner's so-called art: Holy Trinity, Meir Methodist, St Augustine's and Normacot Methodist churches, along with the King's Arms, old Longton High School (now renamed Sandon High School), as well as the semicircle of shops in the centre, sitting uneasily by the side of this thoroughfare. In Weston Road, much of old Meir has so far been retained; but it cannot be long before many of the shops will have to go to appease the voracious appetite of the god Car. It is a matter of sadness that what our forebears bequeathed to us has been so foolishly squandered.

This military aerial photograph was taken a few days after the atomic bomb on Japan had ended the Second World War. It is a composite from two prints which have been deftly re-photographed by Mal Beech of the Air Photo Library, University of Keele. It depicts most of Meir, parts of Normacot and the surrounding areas. Ignoring for a moment the large expanse of Meir aerodrome in the left lower quarter, begin with the small circle in the centre of the field of view, just right of centre. This is the roundabout that joined the four roads that run through Meir at its centre and later replaced by traffic lights. Turn the legend to the top; the A50 starts halfway along the bottom edge and runs up to the roundabout and then on to the upper right under 541 squadron. The middle of Meir was still quite open even 50 years ago.

From the roundabout, the Broadway cinema, the Drill Hall, the farm and Meir House are easily spotted along with the reservoirs high on the landscape. Meir Road starts under the 'right hand F' of the legend at the top and joins the A50. Returning to the crossroads, the other two remaining roads traverse the landscape. Sandon Road appears halfway up on the left. Going right it passes the council estates at Kingsmead and Queensmead Road and then Longton High School (occupied then by the Royal Military College of Science). Passing St Augustine's RC School (next door) the large estate on the opposite side of the road is the Harrowby Road estate which stretches right down the A50. Some of the roads are named after the Earl of Harrowby, a former Lord Lieutenant of Staffordshire and his son Dudley Ryder, although Ednam Place is after the sister of the Duke of Sutherland, killed in an air crash.

Sandon Road Primary School, now the Grange, is visible in Harrowby Road. The scout hut opened by the chief scout in 1941 is in Chatsworth Place. Note the oval the planners have introduced to lighten the uniformity prevalent in many housing developments. Once in the centre of Meir, crossing the roundabout, Weston Road lies directly ahead. The main Crewe to Derby railway line can been seen burrowing beneath the road and the town, running to the lower edge right of the frame. The whitened platform edges of Meir Station are a feature. In Weston Road, there is a clear distinction between the old Meir and the more recent homes. On the left and behind Weston Road are the so called 'Golf Course' houses, whose roads look like fingers, lying behind Holy Trinity church which has no vicarage. Travelling right, from the town centre, the large residences are a feature: The Elms (once the home of John Aynsley, Lord Mayor of Longton), The Limes, The Mount and Weston Coyney House (where once lived Stephen Mear) line the route. Yarnfield Close and Denehurst Close were built on this site during the last 20 years; only parts of the original stone walls remain in 1995. But Beech House, the home of James R Barlow survives as the Meir Workingmen's Club. To the right of this road, the A520, lies the Meir Square estate built by the City of Stoke on Trent in the 1920s. Notice how it has overwhelmed Woodville Terrace(1886) and Wood Farm, spreading far from this typical ribbon development.The road afterwards carries on to Weston Coyney and Leek.

Meir aerodrome shows well. Aircraft made in the Rootes shadow factory in Grindley Lane, which clips the lower left corner, were towed to the airfield and were used in the North African campaign. There are over 45 aircraft on the ground of 3 or 4 different types. On one taxiway there are 5 four-engined heavy bombers of the 'Lancaster' type. The others are a mix of single-engined high and low wing monoplanes. The effectiveness of the camouflage on the hangers leaves a little to be desired - they are plainly visible! The aerodrome, once owned by the city council and leased for 12 years to the Royal Air Force Flying School for £850 per annum, was sold for housing and development in the 1980s, but there are still many pointers to its former occupants. A comparison of this view with one taken 50 years afterwards would be revealing. Very little land now is unoccupied, with clean industries growing on Meir Park; the new name for the former airfield. It is therefore all the more difficult to understand the reasoning behind the decision taken in March 1994, to demolish hundreds of homes, businesses and shops for the 'new A50' which runs right through the middle of the old and long established communities of Meir, Normacot and Longton containing areas of high housing density.   *Air Photo Library, Keele University*

DIRECTORY OF PRIESTS AND CURATES AT CAVERSWALL AND HOLY TRINITY CHURCH, MEIR 1889 - 1939

John Gordon ADDENBROOKE	Vicar of Caverswall	1889-1902
Herbert Metcalfe FOWLER	Vicar of Caverswall	1902-1915
Thomas Heywood MASTERS	*Curate in charge, the MEIR	1889-1893
Hugh NANNEY-SMITH	*Curate at Caverswall	1892-1894
John Edward CAREY	*Curate in charge, the MEIR	1894-1897
Charles ADDENBROOKE	*Curate in charge, the MEIR	1898-1903
Edwin WHEELDON	*Curate in charge, the MEIR	1904-1905
William HERALD	Curate of Caverswall, inc the MEIR	1906-1907
Arthur A BROOKS	Curate in charge, the MEIR	1907-1912
Ralph CREED-MEREDITH	Curate in charge, Caverswall, C-in-C,Holy Trinity, the MEIR	1912-1914
Robert WALKER	Curate at Caverswall inc Holy Trinity, the MEIR	1914-1916
Theophilus CALEB	Vicar of Caverswall inc curate in charge of Holy Trinity, the MEIR	1916-1919
	and Curate in charge, Holy Trinity, the MEIR.	1919-1923
Harry Christie SHELDON	Curate in charge, Holy Trinity, the MEIR.	1923-1926
Harry Christie SHELDON	FIRST Parish priest at Holy Trinity, the MEIR	1926-1936
William BELL	Parish priest, Holy Trinity, the MEIR	1936-1946
David Alan STEVENS[1]	Curate at Holy Trinity, the MEIR	1939-1942

Although this record is complete, some additional curates did appear, very occasionally at Holy Trinity Church, the Meir, from 1889 to 1939

*Curate at Caverswall (inc curate of Holy Trinity, the Meir)

1. He became Forces Chaplain from 1942 -1946

Ecclesiastical Records of Clergy at Caverswall and Holy Trinity Church, the Meir, Staffordshire, 1889-1939

John Gordon Addenbrooke   Vicar of Caverswall
Born Walsall 20th December 1849.
Admitted pensioner under Messrs Peile, Cartmell and Wright 5th July 1876
BA 1880; MA 1885. Ordained deacon1879
Priest 1880, Lichfield

Curate of Holy Trinity, Chesterfield	1879-1880
Curate of Holy Trinity, Burton-on-Trent	1880-1882
Vicar of St Luke, Wolverhampton	1882-1889
Vicar of CaverswallL, Staffs	1889-1902
Rural Dean of Cheadle, Staffs	1901-1902
Vicar of St Mark's.Tutbury	1902-1908
Vicar of St Wenn, Bodmin, Cornwall	1908-1915
Curate of Tiverton on Avon	1918-1922

Died July 3rd 1922 at 80 Bloomfield Avenue, Bath

Herbert Metcalfe Fowler   Vicar of Caverswall
Jesus College Cambridge. BA 1887: MA 1891:
Deacon 1888:priest1889 Hereford

Curate of St James, Hereford	1888-1897
Vicar of Donington	1897-1902
Vicar of Caverswall (inc Meir)	1902-1915
Vicar of Holy Trinity, Hereford	1915-1922

Thomas Heywood Masters
Born Manchester April 9th 1865
Christ's College 1886: Inverness College and Polytechnik Hanover.
Matriculated Michalemas 1886:BA 1889: MA 1893;
Deacon 1889 (Lichfield) priest 1890

Curate of Caverswall, Staffs	1889-1893
Curate of St Mark's, Lakenham, Norfolk	1893-1895
Curate of Coddenham, Suffolk	1895-1896
Rector of N. Scarle, Lincs	1896-1902
Vicar of E. Meon, Hants	1902-1921
Served in the Great War	1914-1919
Chaplain mentioned twice in dispatches:	
Acting Chaplain-General	1918
CBE	1919
Vicar of Petersfield and Sheet.	1921-1930
Went to India as part of the Church Mission of Help	1922-1923
Hon.Canon of Portsmouth	1928-1931
Chaplain to the King	1921-1939
Provost of Portsmouth Cathedral	1930-1938
Residentiary Canon	1931-1938

Died September 1st 1939

John Edward Carey
Lichfield College 1886. deacon 1887:priest 1888 Lich.

Curate of Rushall, Staffs	1887-1893
Curate of Caverswall, Staffs	1894-1897
Rector of Otterham	1898-1904
Vicar of Treverbyn, Penwithick , St.Austell.	1904-1921

Charles Addenbrooke
Brother of John Gordon. Born at Walsall 27th March 1865
Admitted pensioner under Mr Cartmell 9th October 1885
BA 1888: MA 1893, Deacon 1888, Priest Lichfield 1890

Curate of Dawley Magna, Salop	1888-1891
Curate of St George's, Edgbaston, Birmingham	1891-1898
Curate in charge, Holy Trinity, the Meir, Longton	1898-1903
Vicar of St Chad's, Smethwick	1903-1906
Vicar of St Stephen's, Fairlie, New Zealand	1906-1909
Vicar of Okato, Taranaki, New Zealand	1909-1921
Curate of N. Wairoa, New Zealand	1921-1922
Vicar of Warkworth, New Zealand	1922-1927

Died in New Zealand in the 1940s

Edwin Wheeldon
St Bee's 1892, deacon 1893: priest Liverpool 1894

Curate of St Polycarp.	1893-1894
Curate of Ravenhead, Lancs.	1894-1896
Vicar of Biddulph, Staffs.	1896-1904
Vicar of Caverswall (in charge, Holy Trinity, the Meir)	1904-1905
Rector of Christ Church, Biddulph Moor.	1905-1920
Vicar of Horton, Leek, Staffs.	1920-

William Herald
Queen's College Cambridge BA 1889: MA 1905.
Deacon 1900: priest Southwark 1901

Curate of New Basford	1900-1902
Curate of Thornton	1902-1903
Curate of Wordsley	1903-1906
Curate of Caverswall (inc Holy Trinity, the Meir)	1906-1907
Curate of Dresden, Longton, Staffs	1907-1909
Curate of St Paul's, Wolverhampton	1910-1912
Vicar of Northenden	1912-1920

Arthur A Brooks
St Aidan 1892; deacon 1894: priest Liverpool 1895

Curate of St Thomas, Wigan	1894-1907
Curate of Holy Trinity, the Meir, Caverswall	1907-1912
Vicar of Lapley with Wheaton Aston: Diocese Lichfield	1912-

Ralph Creed-Meredith
MA 1912: deacon 1911: priest Dublin 1912

Curate of St Andrew's, Dublin	1911-1912
Curate in charge, Caverswall.(c-in-c, Holy Trinity, the Meir)	1912-1914
Curate in charge, St Barts, Armley	1914-1917
Gen. L. Diocese Lichfield	1917-1918
Curate of St Pauls, Harbourne	1919-1920

Robert Osborne Walker
Univ Cambridge B.A. 1904: M.A 1908;
Deacon 1905 priest York 1907

Curate of War Hill, Yorkshire	1905-1907
Vicar of Osbaldwick with Murton	1913-1914
Curate of Caverswall (Curate of Holy Trinity, the Meir)	1914-1916
Vicar of Edstaton	1917-1920

Theophilus Caleb
Univ of Allahabad: Chich. Theol.Coll 1905. deacon 1907 priest 1908
Diocese of St Albans

Curate of Holy Trinity, Barking Rd	1907-
and St Michaels and All Angels, Watford	1908-1911
Vicar of Royston, Herts	1911-1914
Vicar, All Saints, Stoke Newington	1914-1916
Vicar of Caverswall (c-in-c, the Meir)	1916-1919
Curate in charge, the Meir, conv.distr.	1919-1923
Vicar of Norman's Heath	1924-1926
Curate of Rossendale, Diocese Manchester	1926

Harry Christie Sheldon
S.D.C Lampeter: BA: deacon 1914 priest 1916 Lichfield Diocese

Curate of All Saints West Bromwich	1914-1918
Curate in charge, St Bartholomew and St Andrews Kings Hill, Wednesbury	1918-1923
Curate in charge, Holy Trinity, the Meir conv.distr.	1923-1926
*Vicar of Holy Trinity, Meir	1926-1936
Vicar of Silverdale, Staffs	1936-1946

*1930 address was 'Mayfield', Meir, Longton, Stoke On Trent, Staffs.

William R. Bell
University of Durham 1929; Lichfield theological College 1928;
Deacon 1931; priest 1933

Curate of St Paul's, Newcastle under Lyme	1931-1933
Curate of St Paul's, Mount Pleasant, Stoke on Trent	1933-1936
*Vicar of Holy Trinity, Meir, Staffs	1936-1946
*Chaplain, Royal Air Force Volunteer Reserve	1941-1946

Arch within Holy Trinity Church, Meir, photographed in 1992, showing position of the south transept, which was never built. Note, to the left, the chancel arch which was added in 1894. *Author's collection*